The author, third on the left, was in goal. The football match was the first scene after Bradley Wiggins rang the bell in the television show, broadcast worldwide from 21:00 UK time.

The scene, five minutes in from the beginning, shows a freeze and then movement. As the first few bars of Jerusalem are heard from a lone singer the author can be seen saving the ball and throwing it back out onto the pitch.

These scenes are also on the Official BBC *London 2012 Olympic Games* DVD which includes the Opening Ceremony. There are more shots of the football match in the Opening Ceremony Extras: *Frank Turner and the Green and Pleasant Land;* and *Nimrod*, where the football match can be seen behind the London Symphony Orchestra's On Track project.

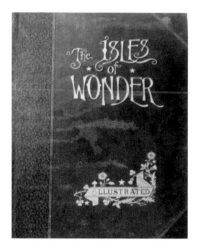

Written to honour everyone who touched our hearts in ways we did not know were possible. This is for you.

There is no very bad swearing in this book. You will have to use your imagination.

Thank you to Claire Louise Renvoize for listening and typing. Grateful thanks for their passion, guidance and perceptive comments on earlier drafts to Alex Alma, Jackie Beere, David Bowman, Theo Clarke, Jane Cole, Amanda diBenga, Ariel Graham, John Green, Mick Hutton, Patricia Hodgins, Julien Holmes, Tanya Jeffrey, Phil and Angela Gage, Aryna Kokoryna, Pat Leighton, Donna Matthews, Chris Moon, Christina Moon, Jes Moon, Kate Moore, Jack Nicholl, Beryl Phelps, Maggie Powell, David Reeve, Clare Rich, David Ross, Dalia Puertas, Louise Riddleston and Dyann and Steve Rowe.

Photographs by Russell Moon. Inside front and back cover photograph Steve Rowe. Thank you for kind permission to include additional photographs by Stephen Angell, Martin Braham, Hayley Brightman, Helen Carr, Sue Douglas, Michael Flannery, Steven Gibson, Kate Moore, Jayne Phillips, Anna Portosi, Dalia Puertas, Selvin Reid and Alejandro Enciso Ripoli.

Days of Wonders:

Inside the 2012 Opening Ceremony

A true story

Russell Moon

The Oak House Partnership

First published in Great Britain in 2012 by The Oak House Partnership

© The Oak House Partnership Limited 2012

The moral right of the author has been asserted.

The publisher would like to thank copyright holders for permission to reproduce copyright material. Every effort has been made to trace copyright holders. We apologise for any unintentional omission. If you have concerns about, or objection to, the use of any material please contact us.

1 3 5 7 9 10 8 6 4 2

First Edition. First Printing. 2012.

A CIP catalogue record for this book is available from the British Library.

ISBN: 978-0-9574731-0-2

Typeset in Palatino
Layout and design by R Moon

Printed and bound in Great Britain by TJ International Ltd, Padstow, Cornwall

Contents

Photographs

Front cover. The Cauldron, Olympic Stadium.
Inside front cover. Cricket match cast, first dress rehearsal, Olympic Stadium. (double page)
4. Football match, dress performance, Olympic Stadium.
6. Isles of Wonder book from Second to the right and straight on till morning.
2. The author, Olympic Park.
4. Danny Boyle, Artistic Director, Olympic Stadium.
6. Blokes in the pub.
7. Face Dress from Opening Ceremony, Athletes' Parade, Trafalgar Square, London.
9. 3 Mills Studios sign, 3 Mills, East London.
10. Auditions, 3 Mills Studios, East London.
14. Casting Team member, Hyde Park Reunion, London.
16. Green and Pleasants, Men's changing room, Eton Manor, Olympic Park.
18. Author's audition numbers.
19. Danny Boyle, Artistic Director, with model, 3 Mills Studios, East London.
27. Robin Guiver, Movement Assistant, in costume.
28. Ceremonies rehearsal reception.
31. The Olympic Stadium at night.
32. Green and Pleasant professional football team in costume.
36. Close up of author's costume trousers.
37. Inside the tent at the 1:1 Dagenham.
38. Dagenham East underground station sign.
45. 1:1 Dagenham with Mass Movement team member.
46. VOM 1 at 1:1 Dagenham with Green and Pleasant Land cast.
50. Green and Pleasant Land cast and cottages at 1:1 Dagenham
51. Green and Pleasant Land cast at 1:1 Dagenham
57. The author in costume with Industrials from the Pandemonium segment.
60. A rehearsal in the rain at 1:1 Dagenham
61. Brunels. 1:1 Dagenham.
64. Free ticket for the Technical Rehearsal. 25th July, Olympic Stadium.
65. The Olympic Stadium with Green and Pleasant Land set.
70. The Olympic Stadium with Green and Pleasant Land set, Tor and oak tree.
71. Working Women from the Pandemonium segment. Hyde Park Reunion, London.
75. Games Makers. Outside Stratford station and Westfield Centre.
76. Rehearsal for the Pandemonium segment. Olympic Stadium.
81. Danny Boyle, Artistic Director, signing a bib. Olympic Stadium.
82. Rehearsal for the Pandemonium segment. Olympic Stadium.
87. Shire horse and handlers. Olympic Stadium.
91. Second to the right and straight on till morning beds. Olympic Stadium.
92. NHS cast member. Eton Manor, Olympic Park.
96. Dressing room. Eton Manor, Olympic Park.

Dramatis Personae

Danny Boyle	An Irish dreamer
Russell Moon	A peculiar sort of hero
Steve Boyd	A kind American
The Blokes in the Pub	A bunch of cynics
The 'Hi-Vis' teams	Airy Spirits
The Green and Pleasants	Lovely country folk
The Mad Russian	A Fantastic
Feisty Aryna	A Plucky Ukrainian Wench
The Volunteers	The best of us
Toby Sedgwick	
and Robin Guiver	Masters of Movement
Frank Cottrell Boyce	A Storyteller
Sir Sebastian Coe	A Lord and Gentleman
The British weather	We saw the worst and the best
The British Press	They ranted … and raved
The British Public	Peculiar, contrary, warm
William Shakespeare	Our inspiration
Mercury Wings	A young Gentleman
The Nurses	Making fabulous sandwiches
The Athletes	Inspired generations
BoJo	Boris, Mayor of London
David Cameron	The Prime Minister

And a cast of thousands including Assorted Kings and Queens, Lords and Ladies, Magnificoes, Thespians, Industrials, Nurses, Dancers, Suffragettes, Mary Poppinses, Sweet Children, Scoundrels, Bankers, Hacks, Gentlemen, Officers, Soldiers, Murderers, Musicians, Gardeners, Clowns, Cutpurses, Commoners and seventy sheep, twelve horses, ten chickens, ten ducks, nine geese, three cows, three sheepdogs, two goats and no pigs.

Chapter 28 contains a full list of everyone involved in the Opening Ceremony.

Scene: London, England, 2012.

1 Isles of Wonder

27th July 2012 – 20:39. 1 minute to cue

'He found himself rolling on the warm grass of a great meadow.' *The Wind in the Willows*, Kenneth Grahame.

As we waited in the Stadium tunnel a quiet descended. This was it. The final performance.

'20:40.' Our cue. The curtains parted. I strolled out with my village football team into the dazzling lights. Across the track, up the ramp and onto our Green and Pleasant Land. Through the looking glass into another world. In a bubble of concentration, ignoring the cameras, the audience and the music; slow, steady, rural.

The flowers were real this time. Greens, reds and yellows; shimmering under the Stadium lights. I reached down and picked a daisy; the root came up with some dark lush soil. Carefully, I put the flower into the buttonhole of my smock. Drifting across the grass, past the hedges and cows. No nerves. Serene. It felt like home.

The Green and Pleasant Land was a bewitching, high definition rural idyll. Everything looked ravishing; pastel costumed villagers, a smoking cottage, geese, sheep, beehives and crops. The grass, emerald after a light rain shower. That we were in front of 65,000 people, being broadcast to an audience of a billion, only seemed to magnify the beauty and stillness of this exquisite place.

The show was a turning point; the beginning of a golden summer. Jeremy Clarkson, like everyone else, thought that the Olympics would be a disaster and that athletics was boring.

'But then, 60 million people changed their minds. There have been many fine sporting moments. And much praise has been lavished on the volunteers and service personnel who kept things running smoothly.

But for me, the highlight was Danny Boyle's magical opening ceremony. It set the mood. We could all breathe a sigh of relief. We'd climbed onto the world stage – and we hadn't cocked it up. ' (Jeremy Clarkson, *The Sun*, 11 September 2012)

2 An Announcement

4th December 2011 – 236 days to Show

'So many fail because they don't get started, they don't go. They don't overcome inertia. They don't begin.' W. Clement Stone.

For me it began with an announcement on the radio. 'We need more men – particularly if you have rhythm.' There was more. As I drove to work Sebastian Coe was being interviewed. Ten thousand people had already auditioned, but they needed more men. The deadline was January.

'This means those of you who can dance, drum, do any sport, job or hobby that involves keeping to time.'

Back then, I didn't really like Sebastian Coe much. He had always seemed cold and ruthless… and he beat Steve Ovett, my hero, in the 1980 Olympic 1500 metres final in Moscow.

It did sound tempting though. I wanted to help London make it a memorable Olympics and I'd done some salsa dancing. It was a challenge. I was getting older; this could be the last time. It was a chance that wouldn't come again in my lifetime. And I liked the emphasis on engaging young people and the aim to 'Inspire a Generation'.

That evening I went to the pub; the reaction from the blokes at the bar wasn't good. When they'd finished laughing I was met with: 'We thought you were gay. Now we know you are.'

Another had no doubts at all.

'The Olympics will be crap. No one's going to watch it.'

They made up my mind to apply. Online, a *Daily Mail* headline announced 'Dance your way to the Olympics.' Danny Boyle, one of my favourite directors, would be Artistic Director for the Opening Ceremony. I felt proud to have been born in London and loved it; its history, cultural mix, pageantry and mad energy. I wanted to help out. Up until then I'd never watched any Olympic Opening Ceremonies because I thought they were pointless and not much to do with the sport.

3 Curvy Girls and Geeky, Lanky Guys

23rd January 2012 – 186 days to Show

'What's past is prologue.'
The Tempest, Act II, Scene i. William Shakespeare.

An email pinged in with exciting news:

Dear Russell,
Thank you for completing your online registration for a chance to become a Ceremonies Volunteer Performer in the London 2012 Olympic Games Ceremonies. We are pleased to confirm your audition time as follows.
Date: Tuesday 14th February 2012. Time: 13:00
Location: Three Mills Studios, 3 Mill Lane, Bromley By Bow, London E3 3DU.

There was a YouTube video showing girls dancing at the auditions. I couldn't do any of their moves. They were young, flexible, fit; I felt old, creaky and fat. I couldn't even move my neck the way they did. Most worrying was the grim-faced panel watching the dancers. What would they think of me? I'd never been to an audition before and I was worried that I would look like an *X Factor* wannabe everyone would laugh at. The video ended with an appeal from Kim Gavin, Artistic Director.

'We want 15,000 volunteers of all sizes, shapes and abilities. There's still an opportunity. Why don't you register and come along?'

I was encouraged. According to one YouTube comment from Aeldd:

'You won't find a polished act here. These auditions are for normal people with little or no dance skills. I danced with old men in their 60's, curvy girls, geeky lanky guys and short girls with no rhythm. All were amazing and we had so much fun.'

I had three weeks, panicked and joined the gym. I hate the gym but the girl on reception convinced me that the classes could be fun. I signed up for Body Pump, Pilates, Zumba and Body Balance and stopped smoking. But, what to wear? I found some trendy Puma trainers that made my feet look smaller (too tight), a blue Adidas vest (ditto), New York Yankees three quarters length jogging bottoms (too big) and a Gino hoodie from the local gangster shop (very cool but too hot to wear for long).

The first class was Zumba with Donna. I arrived at 10:25 in my trendy new outfit. I felt like a sex offender who had been given community service in a dance class. I was the only man. Some of the girls glanced at me but none of them laughed. Donna smiled. We were straight into the first Latin beats; I was at home. The music was like the salsa I knew and the moves came easily. I was amazed that I kept up for the whole 45 minutes. Even taking off the hoodie after the first exercise seemed fine.

For the next 3 weeks I went to every class I could; Body Pump, Pilates, Body Balance. I even did some work in the gym. At the pub, the blokes were beside themselves with laughter 'Zumba, Pilates... you must be joking.' My resolve was strengthening. It felt great to be fitter and more flexible. The excitement was building.

4 Follow the Footsteps

Tuesday 14th February 2012. 13:00. Three Mills – 164 days to Show

'If I said to most of the people who auditioned "Good job, awesome, well done" it would've made me actually look and feel ridiculous. It's quite obvious most of the people that turned up to this audition were hopeless.' Simon Cowell.

When I arrived at Three Mills studios in East London the queue of hopefuls looked promising. There was everyone from proper poised dancers to much older men (even than me). All shapes, sizes and nationalities. Some had travelled the short distance from Hackney or Dagenham; others from much further away. One lady had come down from Scotland for the day. Little did we know that in the Ceremony the dresses worn by the girls carrying the names of the countries in the parade would show the faces of people who auditioned.

In the Valentine's Day sunshine everyone seemed relaxed and friendly. The floodlight towers from the Olympic Stadium peaked above the old brick mill buildings; a couple of ducks glided along the canal.

I am grasping the audition letter, my passport and driving licence. My dancer's outfit feels comfortable now, though the shoes are still too tight. As the gates open there is a swell of excitement and we show our letters to security. We're in. As we pass Studios 1 to 7 with their numbers on the huge doors I recognise a different world. There are cables everywhere, lights, bits of scenery, mysterious boxes and technicians dressed in black. A sense of purpose.

Past the porta-loos and into the Olympic Ceremonies Audition Studio. A plasma screen is playing excerpts from the Beijing Ceremony. I go to the 'M to R' line. At the check-in a girl in a high-visibility vest smiles. She scans the barcode on my letter. Ping. She looks relieved. She finds a card with my audition number on it; 200B-123. Another high-visibility girl measures my waist, inside leg and height and takes my photo.

'Go through there and follow the footsteps,' she says.

Next, a video camera. 'What your favourite place?'

'Home.' I reply.

As everyone assembles in rows of white plastic folding chairs I realise that we are all shapes, sizes and abilities. It doesn't feel competitive. Two hundred people chatting, laughing and apprehensive.

Steve welcomes us. He is a warm, kind, tall and gentle American. With him are a team in high-visibility vests, personalised with glitter initials and names. Steve asks us to find our number on the grid on the floor of the studio. Gradually the floor is filled with auditionees and we each have a 'home base' position. My home base number is 123.

We point to the north; we run to the east and then find our home base again. It's like playing Simple Simon Says in the school playground. Steve tells us 'Be enthusiastic... there are plenty of opportunities left in the Ceremonies. Don't worry, be yourself. You don't know what we're looking for.'

Then we are told it's time to learn a dance. The 'Hi-Vis' girls, as we now call them, show us the moves and we follow.

'Wake up (stretch your arms), clean your teeth, jump out of the shower, flick up your collar, put on your coat and shake.'

We move and dance to the music. The Hi-Vis girls have clipboards now. They move among us, noting down our number as we desperately follow the routine. It feels OK and I think she just wrote down my number. Does that mean I'm in or out? It all feels like a big, fun Zumba class and nobody is told they're rubbish; Simon Cowell is nowhere in sight. Some people looked hopeless but Steve says 'Good job, well done. You'll hear from us within 48 hours.'

We pour out of the studios excited, friendly and happy.

5 We'll Let You Know

Saturday 18th February 2012. 15:00. Three Mills – 160 days to Show

'To me an audition is thirty crazed people in a room waiting to be axed'. Kathie Lee Gifford.

Email: Wednesday 15th February 2012 13:30.
Subject: London 2012 Olympic Games Ceremonies – confirmation of recall audition.

Dear Russell, Congratulations!
London 2012 Ceremonies are pleased to inform you that you have been successful in your first audition for the chance to become a Ceremonies Volunteer Performer in the London 2012 Olympic Games Opening/Closing Ceremonies.
Important: We are now inviting you to attend a 'Role Specific' recall audition. Because each recall audition is dedicated to a specific role, the date that you are offered cannot be changed. This is our final set of auditions, please make every effort to attend.
Date: Saturday 18th February 2012. Time 15:00.
Your recall audition will take place at the same venue as your first audition. This letter contains a barcode that is exclusive to you; don't forget to bring this letter with you. You must bring the relevant ID (Drivers license) there will be around 200 people in each audition. No filming or photography of any kind is permitted; the total time from check-in to checkout will be 4 hours. You will be notified if you have been successful within 6 weeks.

We look forward to seeing you again and Good Luck!
Kind Regards
London 2012 Ceremonies.

At home I tell my wife that the audition was great fun and I'd love to take part in the whole adventure. I can't wait to get back to Three Mills to dance and play again but the pressure is on. This time I really want to get through.

I tell the blokes in the pub that I'm going back on Saturday and that they can still apply. There's plenty of time. On his way for a smoke one shrugged.

'There's no way you'll catch me doing any of that rubbish.'

The argument continued about whether Premiership footballers were paid too much for their own good.

As I arrive at the audition studios there's a different energy. It's mostly men. The proper poised dancers have gone. It looks more like a football crowd. We wonder why we have been recalled and what a 'role specific' audition will be like.

Through security, past the encouraging Hi-Vis girls and back onto the white folding plastic seats. We talk manly things. One guy tells us that he has been married for a few years now and it's about time he has an affair. His kids are getting him down; we all give him advice. Hopefully he won't have taken any of it.

Steve, the kind American wanders around and asks everyone 'So, why do you think we've called you back?'

His team make us feel at home. There is an air of anticipation and fun. I convince myself if I don't get through it has still been a fascinating experience. But I really want to be chosen and am desperate to get through. One girl seems out of place amongst all the men. Later she quietly disappears and doesn't come back.

My new ceremonies auditions number is 223B:34. I look across to the grid to see where number 34 is. Yes, I feel like I'm getting the hang of this audition business.

Steve is actually Steve Boyd, Head of Mass Movement Choreography. Steve has been working on mass movement at Olympic ceremonies since Atlanta in 1996. He asks us to find our home number on the grid. I was ready for that. But, this time it's serious. The dancing is harder, faster and sharper. I lose my hoodie and try to keep up. A dancer next to me is brilliant and snaps into every move, looking sharp and cool. I try to follow the man in front of me as we flick up our collars. 'Look left … and right.'

I'm trying to master new moves. As the pace quickens we step forward. The line at the front runs to the back. The man in front of me panics and dissolves into an uncoordinated mess. I forget the routine and panic too. My brain is scrambling. I'm getting closer to the front. My neck won't do the move.

The Hi-Vis girl with the clipboard is now watching the quivering wreck in front of me. Her smile is gone: he is gone too and now I'm exposed. Nobody to follow. At the front of the line, trying to hold it together. I sense the dancer beside me gracefully and brilliantly carrying it off. I've failed. As I run to the back I know my chance has almost gone. I'm desperately hanging on. Over the next hour we flick and jump, point and pose. Moving faster and faster.

'That's it... well done... sharper. Come on.'

It's starting to look better but Quivering Man in front of me still can't get the moves and I'm struggling too. Finally, there's a break and we go for water, sweating and panting. Then back to the home base. One of the Movement Assistants asks us to do some acting, still in our grid lines.

'I want you to lift up a bow and fire an arrow. Watch it as it flies into the distance. Don't forget to keep hold of your bow. Feel its weight.'

I feel at home, sense the longbow in my left hand, raise it up and fire towards the Norman forces. I am an Archer.

As I get to the front of the line again the Hi-Vis girl with clipboard seems approving as my imaginary arrow glides into the sky. I watch it land 100 yards away. Then we mime hitting a cricket ball high into the air and casting a fishing net gracefully onto the sea. I wonder what they're looking for. How can this be part of the ceremonies? But it does feel more like me. Suddenly it's all over. Steve thanks us and says we will hear within two months.

At the pub on my way home I let everyone know I'd got no chance. The dancing was too difficult and the audition found me out.

'You might as well get used to it, mate. You're too old for that sort of thing. You spent most of the time looking at the girls anyway. Or the blokes! Didn't you? Pervert.'

They descended into laughter. I felt deflated but hoped there might be some chance of getting through. The long wait began.

6 I'm In!

Tuesday 3rd April 2012. 09:15 – 85 days to Show

'Congratulations.' London 2012 Ceremonies.

Online articles began to appear from people who had been successful. I found a blog in Student Room called 'Did anyone else get an audition for the 2012 Olympic Opening Ceremony?' It ended up at a thousand pages. Hourly people were anxiously swapping information. Some had auditioned in October and had already been given roles in various segments. Others, like me, continued their wait to find out if they had a part to play or not.

The tension was mounting. After a month or so I was checking my emails every day for a message. After six weeks it was every hour. Steve did say two months, didn't he?

I was driving as the email popped in. I glimpsed the letters 'Congrat' on the phone. I nearly crashed the car and stopped at a lay-by. I scrolled backwards and forwards, trying to take everything in.

Email. Date: 3rd April 2012 09:15
From: London 2012 Ceremonies
Subject: Congratulations.

Dear Russell,
Congratulations! London 2012 Ceremonies are pleased to inform you that you have been successful in your audition to become a Ceremonies Volunteer Performer in the London 2012 Olympic Opening Ceremony. We hope that you are able to accept this once in a lifetime opportunity to be part of a Global event that expresses and celebrates the passion and creativity of the United Kingdom in front of the entire World! You have been selected to perform in the Olympic Opening Ceremony as part of the 43-Group B cast group.
Below is a brief overview of the cast group that you have been selected for together with general information regarding rehearsals and what will be required from you.

Cast Group	Olympic Opening Ceremony Segment 43 Group B
Role Outline	Character acting role in key thematic sequence
Rehearsal Site Facilities	There will be rehearsals at 3 venues in East London including 3 Mills, Dagenham and the Stadium. An overview of your rehearsal schedule is attached. Security will be strictly maintained at all venues and only accredited performers will be allowed on site.
Travel	We will allocate oyster cards to cover transport costs from Central London to the individual rehearsal venues. These will be valid from Zones 1-6. Unfortunately no other travel costs can be covered.

Rehearsals: Participation as a Ceremonies Volunteer Performer is a significant undertaking and you will need to commit yourself for the period of time required for rehearsals and the ceremonies themselves. Therefore, before accepting this offer we would like to remind you that from April 2012 there will be up to two to three rehearsal sessions per week, lasting up to four hours. These will take place on either weekday evenings or at weekends, and there will be a number of all-day rehearsals in the three weeks leading up to the Ceremony. Rehearsals will take place across 3 different sites within East London.

3 Mills

Dagenham – our outdoor 1:1 space where we replicate the scale of the Stadium. This is a fantastic resource and indispensible in order to deliver four world class ceremonies.

Important: Please note that in the event that you do not attend the required number of rehearsals, you will become part of the reserve cast and we cannot guarantee that you will perform in one of the Ceremonies. It is essential that you attend ALL of the compulsory rehearsal dates in the final weeks approaching the Ceremonies. If you miss more than 2 rehearsals throughout the whole period you will then be automatically moved to the reserve list. All time and date details are subject to change by London 2012 Ceremonies.

	Date	Time	Venue	Details
1	Sun 13 May	09.00 to 14.00	3 Mills	Orientation and rehearsal
2	Thur 17 May	17.00 to 21.30	3 Mills	
3	Sat 19 May	14.00 to 19.00	3 Mills	
4	Sun 27 May	15.00 to 20.00	Dagenham	
5	Sat 2 June	15.00 to 20.00	Dagenham	
6	Sun 10 June	10.00 to 15.00	Dagenham	
7	Sun 17 June	10.00 to 15.00	Dagenham	
8	Sat 23 June	17.30 to 22.00	Stadium	Orientation and rehearsal
9	Sat 30 June	13.30 to 22.00	Stadium	
10	Sun 1 July	09.00 to 13.00	Stadium	
11	Fri 6 July	17.30 to 22.00	Stadium	
12	Sat 7 July	09.00 to 17.30	Stadium	
13	Sat 14 July	09.00 to 17.30	Stadium	Compulsory
14	Wed 18 July	TBA	Stadium	Compulsory
15	Fri 20 July	TBA	Stadium	Compulsory
16	Sat 21 July	TBA	Stadium	Dress Rehearsal 1 Compulsory
17	Mon 23 July	TBA	Stadium	Dress Rehearsal 2 Compulsory
18	Wed 25 July	TBA	Stadium	Dress Rehearsal 3 Compulsory
19	Fri 27 July	TBA	Stadium	SHOW DAY

The deadline for acceptance of this offer is 5 April 2012. If you have also been offered a role as a London 2012 Games Maker you will need to choose which role you accept, as it is not possible to accept both roles.

Once again – Congratulations! We look forward to receiving your response and hope to welcome you as a London 2012 Ceremonies Volunteer Performer in the near future. Please remember everything we do is confidential – including all the information in this email. Please don't speak to the media about your participation in the ceremonies. Be part of the secret!

Kind Regards
London 2012 Ceremonies.

Wow! I was going to be in the *Opening* Ceremony. I wondered what 'Segment 43: Group B' was and what they would ask me to do in a 'character acting role'. There were 19 rehearsals; it was a big commitment. Luckily most of the rehearsals were at the weekend with an intensive period within the last week or so and twelve visits to the actual Stadium. I could only miss a maximum of two rehearsals and had to attend all the compulsory rehearsal dates. I couldn't wait to get home to discuss it with my wife. We agreed that I should go for it.

I signed and returned the Volunteer Performer Agreement and started to take in the enormity of it all. I had to be part of the Secret... so couldn't tell anyone about it.

At the pub the talk was about coming to the end of a dismal Ipswich Town season. I said I got through the auditions.

'Well done, mate. Now you'll be able to spend more time lusting over all those dancers!'

I explained there were loads of rehearsals, that everything we did was confidential and then quickly changed the subject.

I read more about Olympic Opening Ceremonies. The YouTube clip of Beijing looked incredible. I wondered if we could possibly do anything as good – and what my part might be.

7 What the Hell is That?

Sunday 13th May 2012. 09:00. Three Mills – 115 days to Show

'Visceral (adjective) Relating to deep inward feelings rather than intellect'. Cambridge Dictionary.

Every day at work the anticipation was building. I found out more about who was producing the Opening Ceremony. And it was clear that our British pessimism about our hopes of pulling off something brilliant was coming to the fore.

I learnt more about Danny Boyle and realised that he had directed some of my favourite films. The darkly humorous *Shallow Grave*, the quirky, druggy *Trainspotting* and Oscar winning *Slumdog Millionaire* with its overwhelming backdrop of Indian life. I watched the film halfway through but couldn't stand any more. It was the way he depicted the mistreatment of the street kids in India. I stopped watching when acid was put into the eyes of one of the child beggars to blind him. I hadn't seen '127 Hours' but knew that it was about a man stuck in a ravine who cut his own arm off to escape. This was going to be interesting.

Thank goodness they hadn't chosen Simon Cowell to do the auditions. But no, this was a different experience. I already felt a part of something very human and special.

My life had settled back into normality. I was working in Cambridge at a sixth form college, teaching Economics four days a week. The pressure was on to get the students ready for their exams and the Olympics was pushed into the background. There seemed to be more talk about the Jubilee than the Olympics and we were all waiting for the summer weather to finally arrive.

In the pub all the talk was about the Premiership title, which was coming down to the last game of the season. Nobody was interested in the Olympics. As Norwich supporters, my son and I were obsessing about whether Norwich would stay up.

'Looks as though the Scum might survive,' an Ipswich supporter in the pub conceded. I was also developing a website for my pop-up club in Ipswich, The Blue Moon Jazz

Club. I had stopped going to the gym; another January resolution fallen by the wayside.

A month later, an email arrived from London 2012 Ceremonies. This was serious:

Email: Friday 4th May 2012. 20:10
Subject: First Rehearsal Instructions – Please Read
43 GROUP B

Dear Russell
We are looking forward to seeing you at your rehearsal next week. Here is some key information for your first rehearsal. Any questions please email your Cast Coordinator. Please bring this letter with you, as the barcode is exclusive to you and will enable us to scan you in quickly.
Your rehearsal is at: Date: Sunday 13 May Time: 0900
It is essential you arrive punctually for your rehearsal – there is a huge amount to achieve!
Location: Three Mills Studios, 3 Mill Lane, Bromley by Bow, London E3 3DU. This is your first rehearsal and will include registration and Distribution of Key Information: Distribution of your Ceremonies accreditation and Oyster card. Attached to this email are the conditions of use for both your Ceremonies accreditation and Oyster cards. You will be required to sign this before either of these items is issued. Accreditation and Oyster cards will only be issued on presentation of the I.D that you used for registration.
No I.D – no entry to the rehearsal.
We can only admit those who have submitted their Performer agreement form and have satisfied accreditation requirements. (All Photo I.D and Visas must be valid until 8 November 2012)
Creative Cast Orientation and your first rehearsal!
There will be a creative cast orientation prior to your first rehearsal, to give you some more information about your role and segment. And then rehearsals begin! Have fun!
Important information.
Rehearsal Schedule: Please check the updated rehearsal schedule attached.
Attendance: Remember if you miss more than two non-mandatory rehearsals we will place you on a reserve list. We already have a healthy reserve list of people who are just waiting to get the chance to be part of the Ceremony – so do make every effort to attend and keep your place.
Confidentiality!
Regarding confidentiality, as you are aware, everything we do in the Ceremonies is confidential. In signing your Performer Agreement you are agreeing to keep all details that you already know – or may learn in the future – confidential. You can tell people that you are taking part in the Olympic Opening Ceremony – but you are not allowed to give any details

about what you are doing. This includes all forms of print, broadcast media, forums, social media channels (e.g., Facebook and Twitter) and/or Blogs.

Due to security, you may not indicate your location at anytime using GeoLocation services (e.g., Facebook, Foursquare and Google Latitude). Likewise no cameras are allowed in rehearsals – which includes camera phones, video etc. If you are approached by the media you should contact your Cast Coordinator; but please be aware any breaches in confidentiality will result in your not being able to take part in the Ceremony. Thank you in advance for ensuring this is adhered to.

Branding: Rehearsals will be filmed by the Ceremonies team; we would ask you do not wear anything too overtly branded.

What to wear? You should wear appropriate clothing but do NOT need to prepare anything or bring any equipment with you (unless previously requested). Please only bring what you need with you and there are no changing facilities available.

Food & Beverage: Bottled water, tea and coffee will be provided at rehearsals. There are no catering facilities on site at Three Mills, however there is a Tesco located by Bromley-by-Bow station. Please note you will not have time during rehearsal breaks to attend Tesco and all food & beverages should be purchased on route to/from rehearsals.

We look forward to seeing you very soon on this next exciting step of the journey!!!!

Kind regards,
London 2012 Ceremonies

On the 10th May the flame for the London 2012 Torch Relay and Olympic Games was lit from the sun's rays during a ceremony in Olympia, Greece. On the TV news the commentator gave us some history: 'The flame represents purity because it comes directly from the sun and was placed in an urn and taken to the Stadium where the ancient Olympic Games were held. It is a call to the athletes to come to London.'

We were back at Three Mills for the first rehearsal, proudly wearing our new photographic accreditation. On mine was 'OOC Cast'. The black lanyard had 'London 2012 Ceremonies' in gold letters. I felt very privileged. I looked more awful than usual in the photo. We were all '43 Group B' – none of us knew what it meant. The girls in the (even more decorated) Hi-Vis jackets were buzzing around checking that everybody had arrived. A large television stood in front of us. We wore green bibs with 'MED' on them. I had 'man flu' and had just taken a big dose of paracetamol to keep me from sweating too much. The drugs would work for four hours.

Steve asked us first arrivals to go to the back of the Studio to meet someone who would tell us more about what we were going to do. It was Danny Boyle!

He is standing by a model.

'Hello. Gather round and have a look at this.'

I thought, 'What the hell is that?'

On the table in front of him was a model of the Stadium with anglepoise office lamps and… were they cotton wool clouds? Surely not. It looked like something a bunch of able 10-year-old school children had made on a wet day near the end of term… from scraps of paper, plastic farm animals and stuff they had found in a skip.

Danny looked like he'd been up all night and hadn't checked the mirror before he came out. His wispy hair was dishevelled. The glasses needed a clean and his scruffy dark jacket was two sizes too big. But he was warm and engaging. He gathered us in with his enthusiasm and energising vision. He was that rare person; one of those teachers that everybody loves but you couldn't quite work out why. The blokes in the pub would have liked him. He probably drinks Guinness and smokes roll-ups out of an old tin.

In his warm Lancastrian accent he explained what we were going to do.

'You are the beginning of our show. It's a meadow; a real meadow, with real grass and real animals. There will be real sheep, real cows, horses and geese. We can't have pigs because everyone might get swine flu. It's our green and pleasant land.'

I was thinking either he must be crazy or he was having us on because he didn't want the real show to be leaked out. Surely, there wouldn't be live animals. But he was serious and we were drawn in.

'I want the audience to come into the Stadium and to think they're in the wrong place and to say: We've bought tickets for the Opening Ceremony of the Olympics, what's this?'

He went on to explain that we would be part of the pre-show as the audience arrived and that our segment would go on until just past the beginning of the official broadcast, which would begin at 9pm.

The 'MED' on our light green bibs meant 'meadow' and our charming rural segment would provide a contrast to the faster paced action of the rest of the show.

'It's about generating emotion, telling a story, taking people on a narrative.'

Charmingly, he seemed very proud of the bell hanging at one end of the Stadium.

'The sound of bells is the sound of England.'

He explained that the bell had been made at the Whitechapel Foundry, and was the largest harmonically tuned bell in the world. It weighed twenty-three tonnes and would be a legacy of the Ceremony. It was inscribed with a line from a speech by Caliban in Shakespeare's *The Tempest:* 'Be not afeard, the isle is full of noises'.

I was hooked, honoured that Danny Boyle was treating me as a confidante and sharing his vision in this intimate, vulnerable way.

Later I discovered that Danny Boyle was raised in a working class Irish Catholic family by his English father (of Irish descent) and his Irish mother (from Ballinasloe in County Galway). He was an Altar Boy for eight years and was headed for the priesthood when the local priest persuaded him not to go to a seminary. He is quoted as saying:

'Whether he was saving me from the priesthood or the priesthood from me, I don't know. But quite soon after, I started doing drama. And there's a real connection, I think. All these directors – Martin Scorcese, John Woo, M. Night Shyamalan – they were all meant to be priests. There's something very theatrical about it. It's basically the same job – poncing around, telling people what to think.'

As our group started to move away I looked more carefully at the funny little model. There were the bell, trees, cottages, Glastonbury Tor, the horses and sheep. This was the world that we would be living and breathing, bringing it to life over the next two and a half months.

Some impulse made me offer my hand and we shook. I mumbled a few words. He seemed distant. Perhaps he was hearing the sound of the bells. As I walked back I thought 'Oh no, I've just given Danny Boyle my man-flu.'

When we were assembled together in the white plastic chairs Danny was back, standing by the TV. He revealed that the script for the show had been written and that a great team had been pulled together to bring it to reality.

'There will be children from the six Boroughs, nurses and staff from the NHS.'

It would not be a narrative-free zone. There would be little stories. It would not be reduced to the lowest common denominator. It would use language, hard to capture in a Stadium show. Great writing was a huge part of our culture and Shakespeare was an inspiration. It was about us as people. If some don't 'get it' that was fine. It would be quirky, but that's what we are like. And, he emphasised, he wanted it to be visceral.

I wondered what visceral meant. Images of the man cutting off his arm in *127 Hours* sprang to mind along with Ewan McGregor diving into the filthy toilet to get his suppository in *Trainspotting* and the acid being put into the eye of the child in *Slumdog Millionaire*.

Later I looked up visceral on Vocabulary.com.

'When something's visceral, you feel it in your guts. A visceral feeling is intuitive – there might not be a rational explanation, but you feel that you know what's best, like your visceral reaction against egg salad. Your hatred of mice may not be rational, but it is visceral, and every time you see one, you feel like you're going to faint.'

Visceral can also mean 'relating to the viscera', with viscera being your organs. This word was key to the way the show would communicate to people. Somehow Danny Boyle was able to channel everyone's emotions and feelings into the final performance. He was there to capture and communicate and we would feel it in our guts.

Danny showed us a mock-up of a short film to be shown at the beginning of the ceremony. It took the audience from the source of the Thames, on a journey along the river and into the Stadium. He revealed that we would be performing before the film, for the first part of the show. The BBC would be showing extracts from our pre-show performance from twelve minutes past eight (20:12 – nice) until nine o'clock when the live feed went out to the rest of the world. There would be around 60,000 in the Stadium and a billion watching on TV around the world.

He then introduced us to Toby Sedgwick, the Movement Director for the show.

'This is Toby. Do you know *War Horse*? Well, Toby did the movement for that.'

Toby welcomed us and explained that we were going to spend our first three rehearsals at Three Mills, together developing the movement for our section, Green and Pleasant Land. Toby introduced us to the Assistant Movement Directors in their decorated Hi-Vis jackets. We all found our home base number on the grid and warmed up. As we danced and jumped around I was beginning to understand how privileged I was to be working with this remarkable group of people.

For the next few hours we moved round in groups, the Assistant Directors taking us through drama-school-type role-plays. We played Follow the Leader along an imagined route through the countryside, jumping across rivers, tiptoeing around cows and walking under low bridges. With another Assistant Movement Director we role-played walking into the wrong room and finding ourselves in the wrong place. It was all about reacting, playing and team building. Meanwhile, some of the Hi-Vis team were watching, making notes and gathering into animated huddles.

In one of the breaks two girls with pink Mass Cast Coordinators Hi-Vis jackets and clipboards asked if anyone played football or cricket. I said I was a footballer, having played in the Scouts in the 1960s, at college, in local leagues and being an FA coach as a young teacher. My name was highlighted on the list and a mark was put on my 'MED' bib. Before we went home I met with a group of footballers and Robin, the Assistant Director who was going to direct the football sequence. We had a kick-around. I immediately felt comfortable. Not 'drama school' stuff, but playing football with a bunch of lads.

As the drugs wore off on the way home I felt shattered, sweaty and exuberant. 'What a day.' This is going to be brilliant. I loved it and couldn't wait to get back.

London 2012   London 2012

Scan Your
Badge Here

8 I'm Out!

Thursday 17th May 2012. 17:30. Three Mills – 71 days to Show

'I know what it feels like to be an outsider.' Judith Light.

Following the first rehearsal my flu took over and I spent three days in bed. Off work and knackered. When I arrived at the evening rehearsal having driven two hours from Ipswich I was pale and still sweating but determined not to miss any rehearsals. I wondered if Danny would be there, or whether he was in bed with the flu I had given him.

At Three Mills reception the smiling girl couldn't find my name or number on the list. What had I done? Was I out? My heart sank as everyone else was assembling on the white folding plastic chairs ready for the next rehearsal. The warm-up had started and still I was outside. No bib, no number. Desolate. An outsider. I said that I was in the football section but a fierce casting girl stood firm.

'No, you're not.'

My shoes felt too tight. I was sweating in the hoodie; left out. While the girls were looking for my name I wandered through into the Studio to the warm-up and stood at the side. I started to do the movements on my own. I noticed Robin.

'They couldn't find my bib. I may not be in the football.'

Some of the Assistant Directors joined me. We warmed up together. They didn't want me to be on my own. I found their kindness very touching. Then Robin asked, 'Why don't you come and join us?'

I was back in.

When one of the Casting team came over Robin confirmed, 'He's with me'.

For the next three hours we played five-aside football, gradually getting used to working in a tiny space and not breaking each other's legs. We were all sizes, shapes, and skill levels, but we were having fun. English, Irish, Spanish, French, Russian, Ukrainian and Swiss. And, when we paused for breaks, Robin gradually coached us into working together, suggesting movements, discussing ideas and getting us to play more like village footballers from the previous century.

To make our movement more dreamlike and rural we had a slow motion race, the winner being the person who came last. We weren't getting ready to play in a premiership football match. We were becoming inhabitants of the Green and Pleasant Land.

One crazy Russian bodybuilder kept jumping into tackles and kicking the ball across the room, into the other rehearsal teams. Robin explained that we were playing a village football match in the Green and Pleasant Land in the 1890s. The aim wasn't to win but to perform like our rural ancestors.

The Russian just wanted to get the ball and score goals. When he did score, off came his shirt and he ran across the space chest exposed, spinning his bib round his head. I was surprised he didn't do flick-flacks and handsprings. In broken English he apologised and started to calm down.

A Brazilian joined us. He spoke little English but was a brilliant footballer; too brilliant. We couldn't get the ball off him and he was doing Johan Cruyff turns. Three Spanish guys were getting us to play more like Barcelona, though 'Tiki-Taka' hadn't been invented in Victorian England.

Toby Sedgwick drifted across with one of his Movement Assistants. After watching us play they went into deep discussion with Robin during a break.

When Robin returned he asked us to gather round. He had some notes from Toby. Could we slow it down even more, make it more rural and pleasant and put in some freezes. Gradually we worked out how to play and then suddenly 'freeze'. Together we worked out a routine: One. Two. Three. FREEZE. One. Two. Three. MOVE.

The drugs were starting to wear off and I felt terrible. I didn't want to let anyone know in case they thought it was because I was too old to play. Everyone else was in their 20s and early 30s. I was 54. They might think I would be better off sitting with the picnickers or, worse, at home.

Then a minor miracle happened. Nobody really wanted to go in goal. I saw my chance to have a break from running around. The Russian got the ball, slammed it towards the goal and I saved it brilliantly. Robin was impressed.

'Wow, you're a goalkeeper.'

I felt wonderful; diving onto the hard floor was easier than running around and sweating more. Over the next hour they couldn't get the ball past me. I'd found my role. The ball stuck to my hands (the sweat helped) and my reactions were quicker than I thought they could be. I still had it. Just!

As the rehearsal drew to a close Toby asked all the groups in the Studio to act out their sequences together. The room was full of movement as Cricketers, Footballers, Picnickers and Audience performed at the same time.

'See you all on Saturday,' concluded Toby.

'Well done.'

As I drove away the Stadium lights formed a dazzling crown in the night sky. They looked beautiful amongst the decaying warehouses and dark streets of East London.

The next day the arrival of the Olympic flame in Cornwall featured on the news. David Beckham brought the flame down the steps of the plane. I wondered how they carried the flame across and through airport security and thought that perhaps it should have come by land and sea. But another element was on its way towards the Stadium for 'Show Day' (as we now called it). The flame's journey would take it on a 70-day relay. It would be seen in every corner of the UK, by millions.

9 The Cave of Wonders

Saturday 19th May 2012. 14:00. Three Mills – 69 days to Show

'Open Sesame.' *Ali Baba and the Forty Theives.*

Back at Three Mills reception two days later my man flu had gone but the computer had lost my name. 'Not again'. My pass got me through security but a new temporary number on my bib put me away from the footballers and in with the 'meadow crowd'. Perhaps my goalkeeping wasn't as good as I thought it was and they had noticed that I was a sweating red mess. Maybe they were worried I might have a heart attack and didn't want a death on their hands.

I warmed up at the back with the 'misfits'. Then one of the Casting girls found me.

'We've found your tag. You're in with the football team. Sorry, let me pin your proper tag on your bib.'

The relief felt wonderful. The little tag proudly stated:

247 – Football Audience and Villagers

Entrance: VOM 1 20:50

Exit: Small Tree K6 VOM 1

I huddled in as we gathered around Robin as he went through the notes for the day. He and Toby had decided that the freezes needed to be sharper and longer. They needed to be more dynamic with a sharp, energetic stop and quick start; like pressing pause on a TV remote control. We had to do them absolutely together. There needed to be more of them as they were the main dramatic devices in our sequence. Each member of the audience in the Stadium needed to clearly see every freeze.

He also explained that two teams were playing the match; a 'professional team' against a group of 'amateurs from the village'. We couldn't let the ball go out of our small area and although we had to look like we were playing a football match we couldn't really tackle or kick the ball too hard.

Robin had some old photographs of footballers from the 1890s. He talked about the way they stood, how they might have moved and how they would have interacted with each other, particularly when they celebrated goals. So probably no hugging and kissing, then. I felt connected back to my ancestors and their rural ways.

We were now into improvisation and developing the performance as a team with our Assistant Director. There was no script; just the freezes and becoming more like our characters. We decided that Robin would blow a whistle when he wanted a stop-frame. Now the sequence was: Whistle. First Pass. Second Pass. Third Pass. Freeze. Person with the ball shouts: 'One. Two. Three. Four. Five'. On 'five' we moved.

We became sharper, more dynamic and more frozen. Most people were looking good. It was becoming like a ballet. The concentration required was enormous. As a goalkeeper I was on my toes ready to collect the ball and move it on quickly, as well as 'freeze' and help count us back into action again.

The Mad Russian was still crashing about too much and the brilliant Brazilian wasn't rural enough, but we were beginning to gel. The movement became more fluid and we began to enjoy ourselves. After 20 years break it was great to be playing football again and to be part of a team. I loved it.

Then, in a break, a smiling girl in a new kind of bib approached us.

'Would some of you footballers like to come with me?'

She was from 'Costumes'. She led us through empty studios at Three Mills and opened a huge steel door. We were into 'Ali Baba's Cave'; a huge hangar-like room. Sheets partitioned off the rest of the space but we could just see sections of huge cast-iron NHS beds and all kinds of weird props and costumes.

'Was that Cruella De Ville's head from *The Hundred and One Dalmatians*?'

Surely not.

At the desk an assertive man in a highly decorated 'Costumes' bib asked to see our cast numbers. I proudly showed him mine: '247'. As we waited to be taken through, we behaved like overexcited schoolboys (we were the football team after all). He told us to stop peeking over the top of the sheets to see what was there. Treasures lay within. This was really exciting.

Eight of us were escorted into a small room with racks of numbered costumes. Around the room were photographs and drawings of footballers and cricketers from the 1890s. We each had a member of the costume team who checked our number, re-measured us and asked us to try on our outfit. Each costumier had a little pouch with thread, scissors and tape measure.

'Take your clothes off, but keep your pants on,' ordered my girl.

I giggled and held my stomach in as my New York Yankees' trousers dropped to the floor.

Overseeing all this was the costume designer Suttirat Anne Larlarb. She watched quietly as her team got to work. I later learned she designed for *Slumdog Millionaire*, *127 Hours* and *Frankenstein* at the National Theatre. Her serene and patient grace was in contrast to our stupid schoolboy excitement.

My costume was for a 'Villager'. The rough peasant trousers had a button down flap at the front and leather lace tie up at the back. They were handmade from weathered embroidered green rustic linen. On the label was the Olympic logo.

My English Country Villager's smock was striped cream, down to my knees, and finished off with a heavy weathered leather belt. Later on, for the dress rehearsals and Ceremony, I wore hired-in original leather boots and I had two original leather dustman waistcoats to put down for goal posts.

The Professional footballers had red and white or blue and white-hooped shirts, breeches and real late 19th century football boots with cork studs and leather toecaps. I hadn't realised how much difference these beautiful costumes would make. They made us feel and look like the real thing. The detail and workmanship were humbling; I was being treated like a real character actor. Later I found out that the costumes had been made in the strictest secrecy. Seamstresses even had to move away from windows to make sure nobody could see the costumes being sown together.

The Cricket umpire had the most dazzling costume. He wore a white dress shirt, pale stripy cravat, dark waistcoat, pleated linen trousers and antique shoes. All finished off with a magnificent original black top hat.

We returned our costumes and notes were made on changes required. As we filed back through the 'Cave of Wonders' to our rehearsal area we were astounded by the quality of the work that was being put in behind the scenes.

'Did you see the massive head of the Queen of Hearts?'

It was getting 'curiouser and curiouser' and we had glimpsed wonderland. But now we couldn't put on weight.

Back in our rehearsal area we were introduced to a new group of people: the rest of the villagers – our football match crowd. They had been rehearsing reacting as a crowd and had developed family relationships. For the first time we were being watched as we played. It was difficult to keep the energy slow and rural and not to play up to the audience.

The Mad Russian became very animated. His shirt came off again after he had crunched into a huge tackle sending footballers and the ball in all directions. When we huddled together some of the members of the crowd had ideas on how we could improve things.

'The freezes look at bit ragged,' pointed out one.

'Hold on a minute,' I thought. 'Who do you think you are?'

But, Robin listened carefully to everyone's ideas and set about getting this much larger group of people to work as a team. It was difficult enough for us footballers to forget our egos. Now there were others wanting to have their say and be part of the action.

As the whole Green and Pleasant group warmed down, we were reminded that the next rehearsal was in Dagenham where we would meet more cast members and practise working on a much bigger scale.

10 A Car Park Somewhere in Dagenham

Sunday 27th May 2012. 15:00. 1:1 Dagenham – 61 days to Show

'Let's do the Time Warp Again.' *The Rocky Horror Picture Show.*

The next four rehearsals were at a top-secret location; a disused car park at the Ford Plant, code name the '1:1'. Sustainability was a key theme of the Olympics and we were told that we should use public transport. If we came by car we wouldn't be let in unless we had at least two passengers. I was driving from Ipswich and knew Dagenham well as I work in the Borough with some of the secondary schools.

I love Dagenham for its grit, energy and diversity. It is a deprived area of East London with high immigration, great schools, marvellous teachers and a close-knit community. The schools get remarkable results and the students always inspire me with their lively, funny energy and ambition to do better.

To fill my car with passengers I went to Dagenham East underground station to pick up a couple of random cast members. As people streamed past the ticket office towards the shuttle buses, I asked, 'Does anyone want a lift?' The women gave me suspicious looks and hurried past. Then two guys came over and jumped in my car. They were in the 'Thanks Tim' segment; whatever that meant. They looked like the dancer next to me at the first audition; slim, tall, lithe and confident, with cool outfits and Doctor Dre headphones.

As we drove towards the rehearsal they spoke of their tough auditions and demanding 1960s to 1990s dance rehearsals in the rainy car park. They had a different energy and I could see why I wasn't chosen as a dancer. Thank God for the Green and Pleasant Land. Then one of them asked me where I worked and we discovered he worked in one of the schools I visited. A couple of days later I was in his classroom on a visit, discussing our Olympic adventure.

When we arrived at reception at '1:1', I was given an Oyster card and a new toy; a mobile phone sized radio receiver on a lanyard with a set of cream headphones. These were our 'in-ear monitors' or IEMs.

'Don't lose these, they cost a fortune. And bring your headphones back next time', implored the smiling volunteer.

I hung the receiver round my neck and looked for familiar faces. We later found out that these monitors, specially developed for the Ceremonies, were crucial in managing the cast of 10,000.

Inside a huge striped blue and yellow circus tent there were the now familiar rows of white folding plastic seats. On the right-hand side hundreds of blue-bibbed 'TIM' Cast Members radiated energy. I was reminded of when I took a school visit to a turkey farm. The noise was deafening. Groups were practising their moves while the assembling Green and Pleasants quietly gathered together. The TIMs left in a blizzard of noise. We could hear their dance captains shouting encouragement. I didn't think they would need a warm-up; they were hyped already.

We had arrived for a start time of three o'clock but our Directors were nowhere to be seen. There was an announcement that we wouldn't be starting until about four o'clock. Some of us had discovered that we could hear the 'TIM' rehearsal music and announcements on channel 1 of our in-ear monitors. I felt exhausted just listening in to their 60s and 70s music and the shouts of 'Come on, give it more energy' from their Dance Captains.

As we relaxed and chatted in the circus tent I found out more about other members of the now 300-strong Green and Pleasant section cast. I watched the video screen flashing up messages; 'Keep the secret, no photographs, tweeting or blogging'. Things seemed less organised and a bit more chaotic than at Three Mills. Nobody seemed to be in charge. We went off to collect a food parcel and water.

In the backstage area near a hamburger stand we saw Danny Boyle wandering past with Executive Producers Catherine Ugwu and Stephen Daldry. Later I discovered that Catherine Ugwu had been involved in huge events including the Ceremonies for the 2010 Vancouver Winter Olympics, the 2002 Commonwealth Games in Manchester and the Opening Ceremony for the Asian Games in Doha, Qatar in 2006. Stephen Daldry is a theatre director and produced *Billy Elliot – The Musical* in London winning 10 Tony Awards. He had also made four films including *Extremely Loud and Incredibly Close*.

Our Directors arrived at about 4:15.

'Hello lovely G and Ps, sorry to keep you waiting. We hope you've been making friends.'

American Steve had lost his voice and Nikki, our Mass Movement Choreographer, explained that we were going out into one of two huge spaces that were the same dimensions as the Olympic Stadium – to 1:1 scale. The props and staging team were still building our set. We would see a mock-up of the 'Field of Play' (the field area inside the Stadium) and, for the first time, some of our Green and Pleasant Land.

'Take plenty of water because it's hot and we don't want you to get dehydrated. We will communicate with you through the in-ear monitors. Go to channel 5. There are lots of you so you can't all leave together. Be careful because there are wires and cables everywhere. Could the first five rows go out through the exit on your right-hand side.'

We were learning that the Mass Movement Team were crucial in moving this ever-growing horde of cast members. I was reminded of *Dad's Army* when Corporal Jones ordered the platoon into Captain Mainwarings office, who was crushed back into the corner; but, this wasn't a platoon – it was starting to become an Army.

As we wandered out into the sunshine and past the ranks of Portaloos, the area looked like a cross between a building site, a car park and the early stages of the construction of a music festival. In the distance goods trains rumbled past, delivering parts to the Ford Plant. Above the security fence we could see buses careering down the A13 towards the Dartford Bridge. Metal safety barriers, green and red tape and traffic cones marked the routes across the tarmac. We carefully stepped past a jerry-built wooden scaffolding tower. Steel trolleys held weird looking bits of old rusting machinery from a 19th century scrapyard. We stopped as two men drove past in a tractor with a long row of trailers behind it.

'Watch out or we'll run you over.'

The people in the St John's Ambulances looked on, readying their first aid kits. I thought of the scene in the Disney cartoon *The Jungle Book* where the vultures were watching the football match hoping that someone would get injured so they could run on and take someone off on a stretcher. The Mad Russian looked excited as he took everything in.

Two rural cottages with thatched roofs stood in the middle of the set. Men in hard hats were still working on rustic fences and old walls. On the tarmac I recognised the numbered grid. As the huge group of Green and Pleasants started to assemble behind the cottages we could see a Dance Captain standing on a small stage flanked by her assistants in blue high-visibility jackets. On my in-ear monitor I heard 'OK, G and Ps, we're going to do a warm-up; cue the music,' and we heard the opening bars of 'Time Warp' in our monitors.

'It's just a jump to the left
And then a step to the right
With your hands on your hips
You bring your knees in tight
But it's the pelvic thrust that really drives you insane,
Let's do the Time Warp again!'

I could see why we hadn't been chosen as dancers but this was fun, jigging away in the May sunshine.

A Movement Director explained that we were now going to find our Home County where we would be performing. She read out the locations of the various groups including Cricketers, Picnickers, Women's Passage and Beekeepers. I saw Robin, our Director, heading off and followed him to Kent. Round the fences, over some wooden bridges, past the cottages to a space back nearer the circus tent. We gathered around Robin.

'Here is our football pitch but some of this area will be for a maypole with children dancing round it. You can see the fence; the other side of that there will be geese and sheep. The whole stage will be raised and next to us will be a steep slope down onto the "M25" which is the track going right round the Field of Play.'

A goods train clattered past and drowned out everything.

'Over there will be the orchestra, down on the 'M25' so we must keep the ball under control. We mustn't let it go over the fences or near the animals, children and musicians.'

The Mad Russian was watching (with a 'far away' look in his eyes) as a group of women floated past. Was he listening?

Robin produced a football and we had a kick around. The Maypole Mothers arrived with a Props Man. They began to work out how much space they needed as they pulled ribbons out from the maypole.

'There will be children here, you'd better move up.'

The football pitch got smaller as I moved the water bottles we were using as goal posts. The heavy old-fashioned brown leather football kept going over the fences. I felt I had to save every shot or the ball would career into the Maypolers. We couldn't keep it under control; it kept disappearing under fences and crashing into other areas. It wasn't going well. After a break we gathered around Robin again.

'OK, we're now going to look at our Entrance from the VOM. The village team and villagers will come from VOM 1 at 20:50. And the professional footballers will come from VOM 6 at 20:45.'

The VOM's are the tunnel entrances into the Olympic Stadium. VOM being an abbreviation of vomitory, the name for entrances to Roman amphitheatres.

Robin took the professional footballers to the south. When he returned we began to work out our route to VOM 1, at the north end of the Stadium. We picked our way round fences, through gates, past a cottage, across the 'M25' and over to a scaffolding arch. We were in VOM 1; our tunnel from the outside of the Stadium onto the track. We then picked our way through and back to our 'Home County'.

Robin said, 'We're now going to do a whole run through of the first fifty minutes of the Pre-show. Go over to your VOM and wait for instructions on your in-ear monitor.'

Back in VOM 1, about forty 'Meadow People' were standing around waiting for starter's orders. Toby Sedgwick, the Movement Director, came over the headphones.

'Hello everyone, I'm up in the tower. Could you give me a wave if you can hear me. That's good. This is the position of the Royal Box. We're going to go for a run through of your entrances from 20:12. Keep your movement slow and don't forget you're walking across your world. These are your fields and meadows, your cottages and you're with your friends from the village. Find your own way through and we will see how it goes.' He sounded relaxed, calm, reassuring.

'I'll now hand you over to my assistant who is going to tell you more.'

It was Nikki: 'I'm going to count down the time from 20:12. When you hear your time, start to move out from the VOM. We'll start in ten minutes.'

A group of 'Ramblers' were huddled together. I heard them say they were going on at 20:15. Then a group of 'Scythers', and the 'Women's Passage'. The 'Scythers' had found a prop box with long handled old fashioned farming scythes and the 'Women's Passage' had found umbrellas which they were twirling in formation.

As village footballers we worked out who we would wander in with so that we didn't emerge as one big group. We didn't have any props. Looking at the movement of the other groups we felt like poor relations. They seemed to know what they were doing; this was getting serious. We were now going to perform our walk in front of a brilliant award-winning movement director. I wondered who else might be watching in the tower. I decided to go on with the Mad Russian. Was this a good idea?

Over the monitor I heard 'OK, guys. Here we go… 20:12.'

No one from our VOM moved. Then, in the distance we saw John, the first on stage, walking across juggling a cricket ball on his own. Was this really going to be the beginning of the Greatest Show on Earth?

'20:13.' Still nobody moved from our VOM.

'20:14.' The 'Ramblers' moved forward ready to go on.

'20:15.' The Ramblers wandered over the 'M25' and towards the cottages.

'20:16.' The 'Scythers' started to practise their weird walk and jump.

At 20:30 the 'Women's Passage' glided towards the cottages with imaginary gusts of wind pulling them along by their umbrellas.

By 20:40 most of the groups seemed to be moving around on the tarmac and we were left waiting for our entrance time. The show didn't look like much at all. I wondered what Toby was thinking up in the tower. If this was going to be the 'pre-show' would the audience in the Olympic Stadium think they were getting value for money? Probably not. No, definitely not. In the distance even the cricket match looked a bit drab. A goods train clattered past. It seemed more dramatic and dynamic than watching our Green and Pleasant meanderings. I confided to one of the other villagers: 'This doesn't look good.'

He whispered back, 'Looks a bit crap, doesn't it?'

'20:49.' As football villagers, we started to form into little groups.

'20:50.' We began to move out from the VOM, across the 'M25', slowly wandering towards the football pitch. I found myself moving more like a villager; discussing this year's crops and pointing out the imaginary sheep and cows. We walked past 'Picnickers', people harrowing the tarmac and others standing around the cottage. As we arrived, the professional footballers were already there, having a kick-about. We greeted each other and the match started. Our village crowd were more animated and our freezes sharper. Behind me the Maypole Mothers arrived and started to move around with the ribbons. We managed to keep the ball away from the fences and the imaginary Orchestra, children and animals. Well, most of the time, anyway.

As I was watching the football ready to save the ball I could hear the 'countdown' in my IEM continuing towards nine o'clock.

'21:00… OK guys, you can stop there.'

Then, Toby.

'Thank you everyone, that's our first run-through. We might have something there.'

Did I pick up an uncertainty in the tone of his voice? Still relaxed, but maybe unsure? Was it really good enough? Was it going to work? Would the world be impressed? I had my doubts. Perhaps he did too.

As we took a break Danny appeared, smiling as we filed past towards the Portaloos, sandwiches and smoking areas. He was enthusiastic, positive, and grateful. And so were we. With the encouragement from Danny and Toby and the Hi-Vis teams, we were coming together as a cast. Most of all we were beginning to encourage each other. We were making friends, swapping stories and having a laugh. For me it was wonderful to be part of the football team although we weren't playing much football this time.

As I drove away, back towards home, doubts were setting in. It was still fun but my legs were aching from being out all day on the tarmac and what I had seen didn't seem to be enough. There were only two months to go, the performance looked awful and the Dagenham car park was horrible.

11 Our Little Tree

Saturday 2nd June 2012. 15:00. 1:1 Dagenham – 55 days to Show

'I never knew how soothing trees are.' D.H. Lawrence.

May 31st was my 55th birthday. I went with my wife, son and his girlfriend to the 606 Club in Chelsea to watch a brilliant new jazz singer, Alexander Stewart. The Queen's Diamond Jubilee Bank Holiday weekend began on Saturday 2nd June. I was making preparations for a 'Jubilee Jazz' Party at our jazz club in Ipswich, The Blue Moon, on Monday 4th June. Steve Pert, a 'Rat Pack' singer was supported by a top band; we were sold out.

Back at the car park at Dagenham on Saturday 2nd June it was cold, windy and wet. The dancers I had picked up at the station also seemed a bit weary of their work on their 'TIM' section and, like me, were not looking forward to a day in the car park. At reception along with our packed lunches and radios, we picked up plastic ponchos to keep us dry.

On the tarmac, in the rain and the wind, it was time for us to practise the Strike. When we finished playing football we would walk over to another 'County' and take away one of the props for a huge change in scenery that would be a centrepiece of the beginning of the show. It was going to be the biggest set change in history.

I walked over a rickety wooden bridge into the centre of the rehearsal area. The Props Team was busy moving trees and trying to get them to stand up. A Hi-Vis man had a huge sheet with everyone's cast number and prop to strike. He was welcoming: 'Hello Russell, you're 247. Let's find your tree. You're in the orchard.'

We found tree K6. It was an apple tree on a rusted steel stand, six feet high with sharp branches and a thick trunk. Some of the other trees were twenty feet high, being held up by men in hard hats.

The Mad Russian arrived. He was also on tree K6. Feisty Aryna, a plucky and funny Ukrainian girl, was there to help us too. Aryna came over from one of the maypoles. She had more brains than me and the Mad Russian put together. She didn't look happy being stuck in a team with a pair of village idiots.

One of the 'Mass Movement' girls came over: 'You're going to carry this off and over to VOM 1. See if you can pick it up.'

The Mad Russian grabbed it and lifted it above his head.

'No problem,' he pronounced. 'I'll carry it on my own.'

The 'Mass Movement' girl was standing firm: 'You've got to carry it together. It won't be safe to do it on your own.'

'I'll be OK,' replied the Mad Russian.

'No you won't...' said Mass Movement girl. 'You're doing this as a team.'

We came to a compromise. The Mad Russian would carry the trunk. I would walk behind holding the branches and Feisty Aryna would walk in front finding the way.

'Off you go then,' instructed Mass Movement girl.

'See if you can find a route and get yourselves and the tree to VOM 1.'

Mad Russian grabbed the trunk. I struggled along behind holding the branches as they dug into me. Feisty Aryna led us over the rickety bridge and past the cottages.

The Props Team had set out a maze of hedges to negotiate. The astro-turf was slippery in the rain. Meanwhile, other Green and Pleasants were carrying fences, maypoles, walls and beehives. It was chaos. Eventually we managed to get to VOM 1 and put the tree down. As we arrived one of the twenty-foot trees marched towards us (on a bed of long wooden planks) carried by some of the footballers. They careered through shouting, 'Mind out, big tree coming through.'

Nikki, our Mass Movement Choreographer, said 'Well done everybody, that's your first Strike. Could you take everything back and we'll try it again.'

Bloody hell, not again!

Back at the orchard the Hi-Vis man with the huge check-sheet asked us how we got on.

'No problem,' replied the Mad Russian.

I said that I was afraid I'd scratch my face. Hi-Vis man answered, 'Your face is your fortune. We don't want you to get hurt,' and made some notes. Feisty Aryna laughed and started to think about an easier route, though the rickety wooden bridge was a given.

For the next two hours we practised taking away the set. People were breaking their nails, we were crashing into each other, the fences were giving people splinters and the walls of a pigsty wouldn't budge. Props men scampered around worried the props they had spent ages making were being destroyed. The astro-turf became more slippery in the rain and began to curl up.

Little did I know that from these chaotic, amateurish beginnings would develop one of the most breathtaking and iconic scenes in TV history. I just wanted to stop the tree from poking my eye out.

Back with the football team, Robin had good news. The notes from our previous week's performance from Toby were very positive. And our time had been extended! We would now be making our entrance at 20:40, ten minutes earlier. Even better, we would continue to play until around 21:05, after the show was broadcast live to the world from 21:00. We were delighted and everyone cheered.

'We're going to be on worldwide TV!'

The only snag was that we would have to play football for twenty-five minutes, instead of ten.

In another practise countdown later that day some of us had forgotten that we were going on earlier. The Mad Russian was nowhere to be seen at 20:39 but then appeared from behind some scenery boxes. After remembering that we were 'villagers in our own land' we serenely wandered towards our football match. This time the professionals arrived at the same time and we greeted each other like 19th century footballers ready to play a match.

'Good afternoon, Sir.'

Our characters were developing.

As a goalkeeper it was easier to dive on the astro turf. But it was more slippery and we had to play for twenty five minutes. Robin was putting in more freezes. The concentration was intensifying. I was exhausted. Wet, glowing and elated I saved another goal.

As we filed out past the scaffolding tower the Hi-Vis girls gave each of us a present for attending the rehearsal during the Jubilee weekend; an Olympic T-shirt with 'Ceremonies' proudly emblazoned across the chest.

12 Helicopters

Sunday 10th June 2012. 10:00. 1:1 Dagenham – 47 days to Show

'If you can trust yourself when all men doubt you'.
'If', Rudyard Kipling.

The Jubilee had been a bit of a disaster. The pageant of boats along the Thames was washed out and the media reaction was brutal. According to the *Daily Mail* online the BBC coverage of the Queen's Thames Pageant was condemned as 'inane' and 'celebrity-driven drivel'. (*Mail Online* 3rd June)

Stephen Fry tweeted that it was 'mind-numbingly tedious'.

Viewers commented the BBC show's presenters should have 'shut up' and shown the boats rather than cutting to interviews and features.

Jan Moir gave her take on what she witnessed on a historic day: 'Turn the royal trumpets to the parp and piffle setting. Muffle the funeral drums. For on a molten grey stretch of the Thames, with a global television audience of millions watching, something died yesterday. It was the BBC's reputation as a peerless television broadcaster of royal events. It just could not survive under an onslaught of inanity, idiocy and full cream sycophancy.' (*Mail Online* 3rd June)

Austin Mitchell, Labour MP tweeted: 'One hated Thames Armada. No Navy left so hoards of tatty boats. Queen freezing, BBC5 Live and TV commentary pathetic. A disgrace.'

The concert at Buckingham Palace was awful. The Duke of Edinburgh, bless him, caught a kidney infection and nearly died.

Richard from Ilminster commented: 'I don't know where to begin on this one because it was all so depressing.' (*Mail Online*)

Now that the Jubilee was over the media turned their beady eyes towards us. The pressure was really on and the mood in the country wasn't good. Everyone seemed to enjoy the two Bank Holiday days off; particularly the blokes in the pub. One of them wasn't happy.

'That Jubilee was a load of shite. Are you looking forward to the Olympics?'

I smiled and replied, 'Hmm. We'll have to see won't we?'

I didn't want to lie and say I thought it would be good. I rang my son for his twenty-fourth birthday. He encouraged me to keep going.

'You'll never get a chance like this again.'

Back at the Dagenham car park the set was developing. More hedges had arrived, smoke was coming from a cottage chimney and the proper maypoles were in place. As we practised our football the children arrived. The Maypole Mothers marched them out to the four maypoles and we gave them a big cheer.

'They're soo sweet,' remarked one of the villagers. And they were. Cute, fresh faced and tiny, beaming as we watched them march into position. They picked up their ribbons and began to dance round the maypole behind me. I hoped W.C. Fields wasn't right about never working with children or animals.

The pressure to save the ball was even stronger. I quietly asked one of the Maypole Mothers, 'Could you put the bigger, fatter ones behind the goal? If the ball hits one of the little girls, it's going to kill them.'

Then we really would have a story on our hands. Everyone played more carefully and we managed to keep the ball on the pitch.

Around the 'M25' drummers started to appear, beating out a rhythm as they marched into position. We stopped and watched as they drowned out the noise from the buses and the trains. Were my eyes deceiving me or were they really drumming on old steel buckets and plastic dustbins? When they finished there was spontaneous applause from everyone.

'That's what a thousand drummers sounds like,' said American Steve on our in-ear monitors. It was thrilling to connect with another group of cast members.

A helicopter clattered overhead as we tried to hear the countdowns for our freezes.

'Who do you think that is?' I asked, pointing into the sky.

'It's the press, they're everywhere. They were at the station trying to get people to talk to them and they really, really want to know what's going on. Security has been stopping the

photographers from peeking over the fences along the A13.'
Bastards!

Two days later, on 12th June Danny Boyle held a press conference at Three Mills Studio and showed the media the 'Blue Peter' model of the Stadium and the Green and Pleasant Land. That evening it headlined the news. The next day the newspapers were full of it. There was our sweet and innocent Green and Pleasant Land, laid open to the public for everyone to see.

The Times editorial was positive: 'Prepare for an Olympic opening ceremony that will beam to a billion viewers around the world a collage of British life they'll instantly recognise – No! Not queues at Heathrow passport control and opportunistic entrepreneurs hawking 50p umbrellas for a fiver outside rainy Underground stations.'

'The Olympic Stadium in Stratford will become a meadow on which cows will graze, horses will plod and chickens and sheep will amble; where cricketers play on a village green, as families picnic nearby; a place where the church clock stands at ten to three, and there is honey still for tea.' (*The Times*, June 13th 2012)

Simon Barnes in his commentary under the headline 'Hottest ticket has always left me cold' was less positive:

'I've been to six Summer Games and every Opening Ceremony has been dreadful... But still, we've got to have one so it might as well be good. And stylish. And witty and ironical. I will adore the Opening Ceremony, always supposing it's adorable.' (*The Times*, June 13th 2012)

I agreed with him. I've never really watched a great deal of the Opening Ceremonies and, although I love great music, theatre, dance and cinema, the ceremonies have always left me cold too.

The *Independent* quoted Danny Boyle: 'Before I started this, I had only a woolly ideal of the Olympic Dream. It's been battered about a bit now but the volunteers most beautifully express this Olympic Ideal. They give up their time and try to present something that is the best of all of us. They always say it is the biggest thing that any country does apart from mobilise for war and yet this is a celebration of peace.' (*The Independent*, 13th June 2012)

Charlotte Higgins commented in *The Guardian*: 'With luck Boyle will have clung on to the spikiness and the wit that characterises his work alongside his gift for the spectacular visual moment. Danny Boyle said: I hope that it will reveal how peculiar and contrary we are – and how there's also I hope a warmth about us. If he manages that he will have pulled off the job.' (*The Guardian* 13th June 2012)

The rest of the press were less positive.

The Sun commented: 'Some have likened the Countryside scene to the set of kids TV show *Teletubbies*.

With a cartoon showing Teletubby cows and the Duke of Edinburgh looking on saying 'Is this punishment for missing the ruddy fly-past.' (*The Sun*, 13th June 2012)

The Daily Express ran the headline: 'The Teletubby Olympics. £27m opening extravaganza is all a bit Laa-Laa.' (*The Daily Express*, 13 June 2012)

The Mirror had a question: 'Our Fields of Dreams?' with directions on how to make a model like Danny Boyle's. Ingredients included, a children's farmyard set, a plastic carpet from the local greengrocers, tin foil for the water, some Subbuteo players and cardboard toilet rolls to make Glastonbury Tor. (The Mirror, 13th June 2012)

In the *Daily Mail* Richard Littlejohn was the most damning and the funniest. Under the headline 'Bulldozer ballet, a sex mad smurf … Its Uncle Rich's Olympic jamboree' he had a photograph of his own model representing an alternative vision of our Green and Pleasant Land including:

- A symbolic launch of twenty-one surface-to-air stinger missiles from the roof of Stratford Town Hall.
- Athletes of Many Nations passing a full-scale model of the illegal Dale Farm Gypsy encampment complete with scrap yard and burning tyres.
- Happy-go-lucky members of the travelling community staging an exhibition of tarmacking and tractor stealing.
- A giant rubbish incinerator and a field full of cheering Eastern European fruit pickers.
- The flame made from a giant funeral pyre of cattle and sheep carcases to commemorate the great 'foot and mouth epidemic' of 2001.

- A re-enactment of the pitch battle between members of the 'Berkley Hunt' and the Islington Branch of the 'Hunts Saboteurs Collective'.
- A display of synchronised fly tipping.
- A sculpture built using reclaimed shopping trolleys and abandoned fridges pulled out of the local rivers.
- And a new high-speed train careering through the middle of the Stadium to the tune of 'There'll always be an England'. (*Mail Online* 14th June 2012)

Although I don't particularly like the *Daily Mail* and Richard Littlejohn, at least he was interested. It was now a topic of conversation in pubs up and down the land.

There were hundreds of comments online completely supporting the Littlejohn view that the opening ceremony would be a disaster. Mickey Mouse commented: 'After the Olympics Opening Ceremony this country will be the laughing stock of the world.'

Bruce from New Zealand was not happy: 'Reminds me why I left.'

So the Jubilee had apparently been a disaster and most of the newspapers and people commenting online thought the Opening Ceremony would be an embarrassment, at best.

When I went to the pub one of the blokes was immersed in his paper.

'Are you going to be a Teletubby?'

He had seen the articles.

'How did you know?'

I laughed and quietly ordered a drink. At least they didn't know how badly it was going at Dagenham.

I later found that almost everyone in the cast, especially the men, were facing this kind of negativity and hiding away their personal fears that it might not be successful. One of the female cast observed: 'It's worse for the men. Their mates make fun of them.'

But we kept going, determined to see it through. And anyway, that's what mates do. The more they like you, the harsher they are. As someone once told me, England is the only country where men introduce their friend with: 'This is my mate. He's an idiot.'

13 Pandemonium

Sunday 17th June 2012. 12:00. 1:1 Dagenham – 40 days to Show

'Pandaemonium: The coming of the Machine', Humphrey Jennings.

Back in the circus tent at Dagenham, the mood had hardened. I felt angry that the press weren't giving us a chance and that they were giving Danny Boyle a hard time; 'Get your hands off him and pick on someone your own size'. Leave Danny Boyle alone.

As someone who had been a headteacher in a school where we were trying to change things for the better, I knew how sapping it could be if the doubters and cynics had a chance to let the poison in. But when we emerged onto the Dagenham car park for our final time, Danny was there, waving and encouraging everyone. Toby, the Movement Assistants, the Hi-Vis teams and the volunteers were enthusiastic too. The siege mentality lifted my spirits.

As we began our warm-up dance a helicopter hovered overhead. They were there again. Everybody seemed to be trying harder to look good, but to be honest none of us were dancers really. I hoped that the cameraman in the helicopter didn't think this was going to be one of the dance routines in the show. Hopefully, if he did he would laugh so much that he'd fall out the door and splat on the tarmac in front of us.

While we were waiting in our VOM to practise the Strike again a discussion began about Danny's press conference. One of the girls, who worked as a reporter, thought that Danny had been very cute. By releasing the details of the opening section of the Ceremony, he had fed the press what they wanted, lowered expectations, increased interest and started a national debate about how Britain should be represented to the world.

Over the next month photographs would be leaked, but they only ever showed our Green and Pleasant Land section, including some of us in costume. By doing this he had strengthened the idea in the public mind that they would be just watching sheep and geese running around in a rural idyll. He knew that what would be revealed would come as a huge shock to everyone on the night. A bit like Tommy Cooper, pretending that he didn't know what he was doing and then confounding the audience with a brilliant trick.

After lunch we heard more about our first visit to the Stadium the following weekend; an uplifting prospect. Security was tight so we would have to bring our passes. It was a nine-hour rehearsal, so we would need to be ready with clothing for any kind of weather.

We were then joined by the Industrials, the cast for the Pandemonium segment that followed our Green and Pleasant Land section. They began to assemble, menacing in rough dark boiler suits with heavy hobnail boots. There seemed to be thousands of them. Toby announced that this would be our last chance to practise the Strike before going to the Stadium and that the Industrials would watch and then come on to do their own scene.

As we waited in the wind and rain, the Industrials marched in and surrounded us. Someone on our in-ear monitor explained, 'As you walk off with your props, the Industrials will be marching on. This is the first full rehearsal for Pandemonium. We're going to count you in, G and Ps. You're going to Strike. As you go off, you'll find the Industrials invading the stage. Let's all look after each other.'

As the Mad Russian, Feisty Aryna and I stood by the tree we heard the command 'Strike' in our IEM. Up came the tree and we marched over the bridge. Music pounded in our ears. Then the first of the Industrials marched across in front of us. We were trapped as they invaded.

The rain made the tree slippery. I was worried that the Mad Russian was going to use it as a battering ram. We were going to repel the Germans as they attacked Stalingrad. I saw the door to the cottage and thought we could hole up there and fight them off. They marched towards us: blue uniformed hoards, grim-faced and frightening. What had Toby said to them? They weren't lovely Green and Pleasants and seemed to have been chosen for their size and strength. They started to roll up the astro-turf, tear down the cottage and bring on bits of heavy machinery; rusty old cogs, corroded wheels and metal levers. A Hi-Vis girl saw us being trapped, 'Let this tree through. They need to come off before you come on.'

The Industrials paused, relentless, marching on the spot. Finally we made our way through and off the stage. The Industrials were tearing up our delicate Green and Pleasant Land.

'OK', concluded Steve. 'We'll pause there. Thank you G and Ps. You can go home now. You've now seen some of the next section. We've got some more work to do with the Industrials.'

We wandered out of the gates at Dagenham for the last time, thank goodness. I looked back and saw four dark figures trying to march in time, soaked in the rain, lugging a huge carpet roll of sodden astro-turf. I felt a strange affection for my lovely little tree.

14 A Flurry of Emails

Sunday 17th June 2012 – 40 days to Show

'Family is what grounds you.' Angelina Jolie.

With only six weeks to go the media and public anticipation of the games was building. Behind-the-scenes organisation for the Ceremony and the Olympics was becoming tighter. We were about to begin the first of twelve visits to Stratford, the Olympic Park and the Stadium. Now I was really excited.

Email: Sunday 17th June 2012
Subject: 43 Stadium Rehearsal Information and Updated Schedule

Dear Cast Member,
We have finally reached that moment where we take the show to the Stadium! The following information is very important. The Stadium security is very tight and we cannot admit anyone who does not have their ceremonies ID, and then the additional ceremonies accreditation after July 16th. Also attached is your revised rehearsal schedule with the changes made to the schedule to accommodate the extra time that is needed to get into the Stadium.
What time do you need to arrive?
Date: Saturday June 23. Time: 17:30 – 22:00
Accreditation
Your ceremonies ID and accreditation (after July 16th) will allow you access to Olympic Park only for your scheduled rehearsal times.
If you do not bring Ceremonies ID and accreditation you will not be able to enter the Olympic Park. There are no exceptions to this and you will be sent to retrieve it possibly missing your rehearsal. If you have lost your accreditation – you MUST notify your cast coordinator at least 48hrs before the rehearsal starts.
PSA
A PSA is a Personal Search Area located at your Stadium entrance. When you have shown your appropriate accreditation you will enter the search area. This area is similar to search areas at the airport. Any bags you have will be x-rayed. You will pass through a metal detector. You may be subject to additional random searches. Do not bring any food with you.

Although I had bought tickets for football at Wembley and weightlifting at the ExCel, I really wanted to buy tickets for the Opening Ceremony for my wife and son. Unfortunately the cheapest tickets at £20.12 were very popular and long gone. The only ones left were £1,600 and £2,012; a bit out of my budget. Anyway, I wasn't so sure that it was going to be a great success.

My wife had been incredibly supportive, helping me to get ready for the rehearsals, drying out my clothes afterwards and putting up with me lying in bed exhausted most of the next day as I complained about my bumps, bruises and scratches. Perhaps I was turning into a Drama Queen but she quietly put up with it whilst keeping down a job and doing the majority of the chores.

So it was brilliant news when the Executive Producer emailed to say I could have two Dress Rehearsal tickets; a typically considerate gesture. And wonderful to know that my wife and son would be able to visit the Stadium and watch the final dress rehearsal.

Email: Thursday 21st June 2012
Subject: Olympic Dress Rehearsal Tickets

Dear All,
It's hard to believe that we are only 36 days to the Olympic Opening Ceremony. With your talent and dedication we are well on the way to delivering the finest Ceremonies in history.
As a small token of our appreciation we are pleased to offer you two (2) free tickets to the Olympic Opening Ceremony dress rehearsal on 25 July. As you will be performing in or otherwise working at this rehearsal you are free to give these tickets to friends and family.
Gates will open at 5pm and spectators will be required to leave at around 10:15pm, in time for public transport.

Many thanks to all.

Late on the Friday, just before our first rehearsal in the Stadium, a reminder email gave last minute information about security and accreditation. It included a tough message about photos and video:

... photos/video: There has been an unprecedented amount of people reported and observed taking photos and video during the last couple of rehearsals (bib numbers are being tracked). We must remind you that you have all signed Performer Agreements that stipulate that you are not allowed to take any photos or video (even on a phone) when you are on Ceremonies/Stadium grounds. You may only use your phone as a communication device when you are on a 'break' outside the FOP and seating bowl. Anyone using a phone outside this time may jeopardize their participation in the show. This is the last thing that we would want for you. We will be chatting with those of you that have been ignoring staff requests to put your phone away. We really appreciate your massive commitment and we are super excited to see you in the Stadium this weekend.

On the Saturday three men in G4S uniforms appeared, while we were in the Stadium seats on a break. They went away into the bowels of the Stadium with a startled and worried looking Green and Pleasant. The G4S supervisor was talking very seriously into his walkie-talkie. The cast member didn't come back. Rumours circulated that she had been caught taking pictures and had been thrown out. Later some of the G4S people walked past us, through the seating, searching and chattering on their walkie-talkies.

In fact we later found out that the lovely Green and Pleasant had lost her bag and the G4S team were trying to find it for her. Not easy in a Stadium of that size. False alarm, but we were on alert and careful not to take pictures, though we wanted to – very badly. Not to share them at that moment, but to be able to look back at them after everything was over.

15 The Stadium

Sunday 23rd June 2012. 17:30. Stadium – 34 days to Show

'If you build it, they will come.' *Field of Dreams* (misquote).

The weather forecast wasn't good and my trainers were still slightly damp from the previous week. At the station I bought my ticket, 'Stratford.' I said proudly.

Another email had arrived earlier in the week announcing that my accreditation was ready to be collected from a warehouse in Canning Town, the former docks area north of the Thames. My appointment was at 10:00, before the first Stadium rehearsal. This was for my A5-size Official Olympic accreditation and London 2012 lanyard. Unfortunately my photograph was bigger and looked even worse. Even the woman on the computer laughed: 'That's one of the worst photographs I've seen yet... and I've been working here for three months.'

On the Docklands Light Railway train rattling back from Canning Town towards Stratford, I sat next to a young dancer. He was wearing his shiny, new Olympic accreditation. He had the coolest pair of training shoes I have ever seen; white Adidas with six-inch Mercury messenger wings on the heels. We chatted about our shoes (mine were relatively cool for an old bloke), our passes and our excitement at the prospect of performing. Commuters on the train smiled as we burbled away in the morning sunshine. I met him again as I was emerging from the Stadium after the Opening Ceremony performance. As I was striding out, waving at the dancers lining up to go in, I heard a shout: 'Mr Moon!'

I ran over and we did 'high-fives' while the girls in 'Mirror CD' dresses cheered.

Back at Westfield Shopping Centre, in Stratford, between the station and the Stadium, Saturday shoppers were drinking their lunchtime lattes and examining their purchases, designer shopping bags strewn across the tables. Excited groups of East-End teenagers were riding the escalators, checking each other out. But I had the coolest accessory; a 'London 2012' lanyard in purple and red and an A5 Official Olympic photo pass with the magic words 'OOC Cast' below my awful photo. I checked the 35-page Accreditation Pocket Guide. My pass gave me access to the 'OOC' – Olympic Opening Ceremony, and magically, the 'Field of Play'.

At Olympic Park security I began to meet up with other Green and Pleasants. The barcode reader bleeped green. I was through. A group of us promenaded across the wide boulevard, past the Aquatic Centre and towards the Stadium.

'Wow,' someone remarked. 'We'll be in there soon.'

Through into the Inner Security area where we collected our lunches and radio transmitters, and off up into the Stadium. Section 43 this way. We were inside.

And there it was. Danny's Blue Peter model had become reality. To our left hung the bell.

'Ah look,' said a pointing footballer, 'there's the Bell End.'

On the other side was the magnificent Glastonbury Tor. And hanging above it, dangling in mid-air, was the huge oak tree, its roots dribbling down like some gnarled sea monster. In front of us the colossal black stage with its crazy white graffiti of criss-cross lines.

'OK guys, take a seat, there's plenty of them. Props are just getting everything ready and then we'll be with you. Welcome to the Stadium. Take in the view.'

The Stadium felt intimate. I could have stayed there forever. We swapped stories, happy and contented there in the seats… under cover, dry and out of the wind. We went off and found the coffee urns, ran up the aisles and picnicked on Pringles. There were fruit and oat bars. We swapped sandwiches: vegetarian, meat and fish. Some of the footballers sang and we all laughed. Below, on the Green and Pleasant Land, a cottage trundled into place. Hi-Vis teams were setting out our hedges, trees, bridges and walls. Danny Boyle wandered through as a tractor ran round the 'M25' carrying scenery and men in hard hats getting a lift. The football team chanted, 'Danny, Danny Boyle, Danny, Danny Boyle' and 'Danny, Danny, give us a wave'.

He did and we cheered. High above us riggers clambered on ropes, fixing lights. Just in front of us, on the track, electricians were wiring up speakers in amongst the muddle of black metal boxes and cables. We spotted our entrance.

'There it is, VOM 1. Look, there's the football pitch and the Maypole.'

Although Dagenham was a tough experience, it had prepared us well for the scale of the set in the Stadium. We were eager to get on and be the first people ever to play sport there.

It is difficult to express how privileged I felt to be part of this staggering enterprise. We were being treated as equals as part of one of the most talented and creative teams that had ever been assembled in our country. Yet there was no pressure. Everyone was going about their business. Friendly and relaxed, organised and happy. Even the volunteers serving the tea knew that they had an important part to play. And they had the best view in the house. They were in on the secret too and probably knew more than most.

A man in black with a utility belt was grabbing a coffee.

'What are you doing in all this?' I asked.

'I'm fitting the electrics in the Broadcast Centre. It's a disaster mate. It's not gonna work. It's bloody chaos in there. Nobody's got an idea what's going on. They don't know their arse from their elbow. There's bleedin' cables everywhere. I'm supposed to have finished a week ago and we're falling all over each other.'

The coffee girl smiled at me as he tramped off down the stairs. Further along the two other men with utility belts were chatting.

'How's it going?' I asked, as a group in NHS bibs wandered past.

'Good. We've been fitting the pixels.'

'What are they?' I asked.

'You'll see, later on. All 630,000 of them.'

They gave each other a knowing look. Another secret yet to be revealed.

Robin, our Assistant Director appeared as I arrived back with the football team.

'OK guys, we're going to go across to the Football Pitch and have a look at our area. Put your ponchos on and be careful. There's stuff everywhere.'

We filed down through the gate and onto the Field of Play for the first time. A tractor with a long trailer trundled past, carrying more hedges and trees. Up a ramp, past the hill covered in wild flowers and onto the stage. We were ten feet above the pitch surface on the huge curved stage more than a 100 yards long and 50 yards wide. Over some rickety wooden bridges, past the cottage, around some pallets covered in railings, running our hands along a field of corn.

'Keep your hands off!' the gardener shouted as she continued planting the corn, one stalk at a time.

The football pitch seemed small. It curved down towards a steep slope planted with wild flowers that led to the track surrounding the stage. I could now see why we had to keep the ball on the pitch. Looking towards the Bell End was a forty-foot high water wheel. To my right, behind a fence, was a ten-foot slope. Robin pointed towards a semi-circle of folding white chairs down on the grass next to the track.

'That's where the orchestra will be.'

Behind us was one of the maypoles. The Maypole Mothers were slipping around, unwrapping the ribbons. Our football pitch was bounded by real hedges. The rural wooden fence now had wires to keep the ball in our area. An announcer was practising: 'Mesdames et Messieurs... Ladies and Gentlemen.' Floodlights flashed on.

Robin explained 'OK, we're just going to get used to being on the stage. The grass isn't here yet so be careful because it is very slippery.'

I put two water bottles down as a goal and we began to kick the ball around... gently at first. Most of us weren't wearing capes because they restricted our movement too much and made us look like idiots. After half an hour I was soaked through to my pants but didn't care. We were playing football, back to what we like doing best. And, in the Olympic Stadium. Out of the corner of my eye I could see the Picnickers settling down in the rain. The Courting Couple wandered past.

'Whey hey!' someone shouted. 'How far have you got with her?'

He grinned and she looked embarrassed. Probably not the first time they had been teased, and not the last. After the break we wandered down to VOM 1, ready to practise our entrance. In the tunnel we spotted sections of a suburban house, some old machines and a huge boat made out of newspaper. Somebody told me that the machines were weaving looms. The attention to detail was remarkable. The loom looked like it was made out of rusted cast iron with worn leather belts and huge cogs. I tapped part of the frame and was amazed that it wasn't made of metal at all; it was wood, painted to look like rusted iron. Inside, I could see motors and wheels.

The house looked real from the outside but from the back we could see it was made from a wooden frame covered in canvas. There was a large rip along one corner, which would need to be repaired. Each prop was a work of art. At the entrance to the VOM a director with headphones and a head-mike said, 'Five minutes to run through.'

As someone in the control booth counted through the minutes, beginning at 20:12, we prepared for our entrance from the huge tunnel.

'20:39.' The village footballers were in place with our VOM Director waiting for the cue.

'20:40.' We wandered out. Up the long ramp, onto the stage, past the fields and onto the football pitch. The Stadium lights came on for the first time. Magical.

16 Five Loaves and Two Fish

Friday 29th June 2012 – 28 days to Show

'We never imagined the power of the volunteers.' Frank Cottrell Boyce.

During the whole Olympic process, from beginning to end, I never heard one volunteer say they thought they were underpaid. They were paid nothing. For most, including me, it cost them money to take part. As my mum said to me 'They must be giving people.'

They were. I remember a Premier League footballer talking about the dressing room and saying, 'There are radiators and there are drains.'

All the volunteers I met including the Games Makers and London Ambassadors were radiators. Generous of spirit, kind and wonderful to be with.

Frank Cottrell Boyce, who wrote the opening ceremony with Danny Boyle, described his feelings in an *Observer* article published the Sunday after the Opening Ceremony.

He described his elation at the magic created and relief that he was no longer constipated with secrets. He had worked with the creative team including Danny Boyle, Suttirat Anne Larlarb, the costume designer and Adam Gascoyne, the special effects wizard. He described how the creative team gradually saw things coming together as time accelerated and the pressure mounted. He went on to say: 'Besides, something else was happening now: the volunteers. Back in our studio, we had imagined flying bikes and rocketing chimneys. We never imagined the power of the volunteers. They were creative, courageous, convivial, generous. The press was full of stories of the greed and incompetence of our leaders, but our studio was full of people doing things brilliantly for nothing – for the hell of it, for London, for their country, for each other.'

On a night of incredible rain, Danny got up and said, 'I can't bear to ask you this but Rick needs to record a massive shout. Can some of you stay behind?'

Hundreds stayed behind. When the press was trying to get some hint of what the ceremony would be like, they didn't breathe a word. Tens of thousands saw the technical rehearsals.

Danny could have asked for camera phones to be banned from the Stadium or for people to sign confidentiality agreements. Instead he asked people nicely to save the surprise. 'The volunteers are the best of them.' He said 'This country belongs to them.'

Frank Cottrell Boyce said that Danny had built some kind of Utopia, a society based on goodwill. And he was right.

Sometimes the contrast between the spirit of the volunteers and others was stark. The poor G4S staff seemed lost and badly led. Many I spoke to had only recently been unemployed. They seemed uncertain and fearful that if they put a foot wrong, they would be out of work again.

When Nick Buckles, the Chief Executive of G4S appeared in front of a Parliamentary Committee in mid-July, the contrast between his apparent grasping materialism and concern with his appearance was in deep contrast to our boss, Danny Boyle. When he told the Committee that he planned to keep the £57 million management fee, even though he had failed to provide enough staff for security for the Olympics, Keith Vaz MP replied 'I find that astonishing.'

I wish he had come down to play football with us; we would have got the Mad Russian to take him out.

When the troops arrived for security at the Stadium everything went up another level. They looked wonderful in their uniforms. We all thanked them for coming. The banter took off and we decided which one we fancied most. The Army, Navy and Air Force personnel were strong, funny, highly capable and shared the black sense of humour we had all developed. They seemed to love it. It struck me that they were disciplined, hard-working, knew their roles very clearly and had strong managers. We were the same.

As I walked across the bridge towards the Stadium for one rehearsal I saw the Barclays tower glinting down at Canary Wharf. Bob Diamond, the Chief Executive of Barclays, had resigned and then apparently 'misled Parliament' over regulators' concerns about the behaviour of the bank. He was off the same production line as the others. He seemed to measure his success in terms of money. But we were doing this without pay. Somehow this liberated us all to create something special together.

One final thought before we go back to the story. When I was at school our R.E. teacher was away for a week playing football. A kindly vicar came in to cover. He was inspiring and explained he would take a different look at the Gospels. He began with the parable of the 'Five Loaves and Two Fish'. He read the story to us and asked, 'So, what do you think happened there, was it a miracle? Do you think it was magic? Did He use his powers to make more bread and more fish to feed everyone?'

He then gave us an alternative explanation. 'What if by sharing his own food Jesus set an example to others, who shared the food they had brought with them as well? And there was more than enough to feed everyone.'

Somehow the generosity of spirit of Danny and his team set an example to us all. It was contagious. We shared whatever we had in a spirit of collective goodwill. Perhaps Danny should have been a priest after all. I was glad he chose to be a director instead.

Email: 29th June 2012
Subject: Weekend update

Hi Group 43 G&Ps!
Here is your weekend update. New stuff first; current important info and answers to some common queries at the end.
Schedule (no changes):
Saturday 13:30-22:00 (The plan is to get started pretty quickly, so please be on time and checked in)
Sunday 09:00-13:00
Food:
There are a number of big groups in the Stadium this weekend, so here's an outline of the current plan to provide meals and snacks:
Saturday Meal on arrival; snack distribution mid-rehearsal (around 19:30)
Sunday Meal on arrival
Good news!

Next week, the Friday, July 6th evening rehearsal has been cancelled! We'll be sure to announce this at rehearsal this week and send you a reminder next week.

Weather:

Don't forget your reusable rain poncho issued last week. You know we'll need it at some point.

Eyeglasses:

Dear all, As the sections of the show that you are starring in are in Period Costume we need to pay similar attention to detail to your Spectacles, if you need to wear them. The easiest and most cost effective solution is not to wear them if you feel you are safe. If you have contact lenses, could you wear them? Finally, we need the details/photo of your Spectacles if they could pass as period and your prescription so, if we have to, we could look at providing a pair. As you can imagine this will involve a great cost, so we are only at the enquiry stage at the moment. Please email your scanned or written prescription with your full name, group number, and bib number.

Many Thanks, Costume Team x

17 Bending Chimneys

Saturday 30th June 2012. 13:30. Stadium – 27 days to Show

Another Part of the Heath, Storm still. Enter Lear and Fool.
Lear: 'Blow, winds and crack your cheeks! Rage! Blow! You cataracts and hurricanoes, spout. Till you have drench'd our steeples, drown'd the cocks!'
King Lear. Act III, Scene ii. William Shakespeare.

The weather forecast was not good. Rain and 20 miles per hour winds. Maybe some sunshine, if we're lucky. On the train I read about marches by East London residents opposing plans to site surface to air missiles on the roofs of their tower blocks. There was a picture of Rapier missiles on Black Heath Common. The article explained that an 'air exclusion zone' had been put in place with fighters and missiles ready to shoot anything down that posed a threat. That would put a stop to the press helicopters!

At shiny and affluent Westfield Shopping Centre, Stratford, there had been a stabbing the previous afternoon. Large sections of the shopping centre were cordoned off and forensic detectives in white boilersuits were numbering spots of blood. Very sadly, Liam Woodards had died from his wounds.

A Twitter user, Sinner@KenishaParamore, wrote: 'Somebody got stabbed to death in Westfield. That's what happens when you bring good things to East London. #hatelondon #iwanttomove'.

Four men were in police custody and eleven charged with violent disorder. Brilliant. You bring a brand new shopping centre to one of the most deprived parts of London and a turf war begins. I wondered what would happen when the whole place was full of tourists. Would the local lads think the wealthy visitors were easy meat, with their bags stuffed with designer products? And would there be a repeat of the 2011 Riots? As I walked past the Police tape, I couldn't help wondering whether the £9 billion spent on the Olympics could instead have been used to help solve Britain's growing inner city problems.

Inside the Stadium the Green and Pleasant Land looked beautiful, even in the rain. The black stage was now covered with grass. There were wheat fields. Smoke wafted from the chimney of the cottage. Technicians were everywhere, putting the finishing touches to the huge set.

At the coffee stand there were people that I'd never seen before in all kinds of new bibs: NHS; Working Men and Women; Brunels; and Drummers, chatting and finding new friends. There were thousands of us.

I walked over to the orchard in the centre of the stage to find my little tree, surrounded by a 2ft high circle covered in grass. Two wooden bridges gave access on each side. Little did I know that underneath the raised circle was the central Olympic Ring, ready to be forged and rise up to meet the other four rings in one of the most iconic moments in Olympic history. And underneath my feet lay the biggest secret of all; Thomas Heatherwick's magnificent cauldron that would hold the Olympic flame.

In the orchard stood our little tree with its label: 'Small tree K6'. It had now grown apples and was secured to the stage by quick-removal bolts. A member of the props team showed us how to twist the tree out of the stage and lift it free. Some of the sharper branches had been removed. The apples looked red and juicy. They were exactly the size and weight of real apples and I couldn't work out how they had been made. So realistic. The Mad Russian and I tested our juggling skills with spare apples from a wicker basket. Feisty Aryna must have thought that she was looking after six-year-olds.

Back at the football pitch Robin our Director had some good news. We had a new routine to add to our performance. After about ten minutes of play a footballer would pick up the ball and run with it. Through the gate, down the steps and on to the track. We would throw the ball to each other as we ran past the Royal Box, the press and cameras. Then past the 'Posh Pit' (the posh mosh pit) and the bell, up the slope on the other side of the Stadium, on to the Green and Pleasant Land, through the fields and back to our meadow.

This became the most exciting part of our performance. We planned a few of the changeovers, but it was meant to be chaotic and free form, as we fought for the ball and careered around the track. We would be joined by other Green and Pleasants, waiting to run in from the other entrances.

As we played football we waited for the moment to begin playing rugby. Two whistles from Robin was the signal to pick up the ball; then everyone rushed in. A scrum surrounded the ball. Someone broke free, careered across the meadow and threw the ball over the gate. We ran down the steps, shouting as a group of Maypole Children were walking up the steps on to the stage. We couldn't stop; it was too slippery. Children scattered, eyes wide with excitement. On to the track, grabbing the ball, throwing it into the air and running around in chaotic abandon.

The football audience came alive as they hunted for the ball. Other villagers rushed out of the other entrances, chasing after us. A cloud floated past, held on long strings by six handlers and we hurtled past them around the track. Then a scrum, as we massed together, heads down, looking for the ball. I shouted, 'Ball gone.'

One of the village crowd screamed, 'This is so exciting. I've never played rugby before.'

She picked herself up and scrambled off. Then up the ramp, through the fields, over the fences, past a river and back to our meadow. I was exhausted but it was brilliant. We continued our football match. And then time for me to meander over to the orchard, ready for the Strike. In our in-ear monitors we heard Toby say, 'That looks really nice. We'll keep that in. Well done footballers.'

After a break there was a run-through, from the first entrance at 20:12. We would then rehearse the Pandemonium and NHS segments. Back at VOM 1 there were NHS beds everywhere. In our headphones the countdown began. We watched as the stage filled with Green and Pleasants. I went on and played football and then rugby. Then I wandered off to the orchard at the centre of the stage, ready for the Strike. As we waited by the tree in the centre of the stage I heard 'OK, G and Ps, get ready to notice the Brunels and the drummers... Right, here they come!'

We saw some Brunels walking through our Green and Pleasant Land and others running round the track. 'Bread of Heaven' came over the speakers and then 'Jerusalem'. Brunels walked on to the Tor.

'OK G and Ps, face towards the Tor.'

Then a speech… 'Be not afeared…'

'OK, now start to notice the drummers.'

Around the galleries drummers appeared. Music bellowed from the speakers. There was a roar. The oak tree began to rise from the Tor and Industrial Warriors cascaded from the resulting hole down the slopes.

'OK, G and Ps. And… STRIKE.'

We twisted our little tree, picked it up and began to march off. Another roar. A beat boomed through the speakers and from the drummers as hundreds more Industrials swarmed from the Stadium tunnels. We struggled over the bridge and got stuck in a queue as Industrials marched onto the stage and began to rip up the grass; our lovely new grass. The rain teemed down.

We found a way out, down a slope and into the tunnel as the music thundered around us. We dropped the tree and ran back into the Stadium. Up the steps and into the seats. The drummers pounded out the beat and Brunels stalked around. The army of Industrials ripped our Green and Pleasant Land to shreds and carried it off. First the grass, then hedges, beehives, bridges and fences. Cornfields vanished before our eyes. The cottage broke in half and was wheeled away. Suddenly a chimney started to appear. Beam engines rose from the stage.

'Where did they come from?'

I was dumbstruck. Everyone in the Stadium was now watching as the music pounded on. Seven chimneys rose into the sky, one bending in the wind. Astro-turf rolls were piled onto tractors. The chaos continued. Then, finally, quiet. Still. Steve Boyd said, 'OK, Industrials, show them what you've made.' They turned, en masse, and pointed into the empty sky. Green and Pleasants, the Hi-Vis teams, and crew applauded spontaneously. I was extremely moved.

'OK guys that took twenty-five minutes. Our target is seventeen. We'll reset the stage and do it again.'

Oh my God! In the centre of the stage technicians struggled as two of the chimneys wouldn't go back down as they had bent in the wind and rain. Four Industrials trudged towards a tractor to find their roll of astro-turf.

'Take a break while we practise the NHS section and then we'll do your section again.'

I was wet through again and wandered back to find a coffee and my packed lunch. We huddled together as we watched the NHS segment begin. Beds were pushed up the ramps and onto the stage.

'What the hell is this?' asked someone.

The NHS cast wheeled the beds into various shapes, rearranged them and then pushed them off. I couldn't work out how this was going to be part of the show. It looked awful.

As we wandered off for a break, I spotted a queue of cast members lining up to get Danny Boyle's signature. He was patiently signing security passes, *Slumdog Millionaire* CDs and numbered bibs. When it came to my turn I gabbled to Danny 'Don't change it. Stick to your vision. It's going to be brilliant. Thank you.'

He smiled and looked up to the sky. Two hours later the stage was reset with the Green and Pleasant Land and we were ready again. The Stadium lights came on in the gathering darkness. It was getting colder, wetter and windier. We took off our tree, ran up the stairs and watched again as the Industrials struggled with their amazing Pandemonium section. On the train home I sat exhausted, wet, cold and hungry, grateful that the rehearsal the following day was cancelled. I spent most of the next day in bed, trying to get warm.

18 A Message from Danny

Sunday 3rd July 2012 – 24 days to Show

'Don't let it get to you.' Danny Boyle.

I had finished my work at the Cambridge sixth form college and was getting back to normal, ready for the final two weeks when we would be in the Stadium every other day. A text message said that the rehearsals on the 6th and 7th July had been cancelled. Then an email came through with a message from Danny Boyle...

Email: Tuesday 3rd July 2012
Subject: A message from Danny Boyle

Dear Volunteer,
As we move into the last week of rehearsals I want to thank you for your hard work, patience and dedication – seriously, you're an inspiration to all of us on the Ceremonies team and a huge credit to the whole idea of the Olympics. These last few weeks are critical for us all so please stay focused, continue working as hard as you have been and I know if we do so we will put on a Ceremony that will make a few jaws drop!
I know many of you have been dismayed by the media scrutiny on the show; helicopters, newspaper leaks, etc. Some of you have asked why we agreed to the two media briefings we have done when 'open season' continues on trying to reveal every aspect of our work to the public ahead of 27 July. We thought they would be a good way to satisfy the media's curiosity about our show but, in the case of certain papers, it hasn't quite quenched their desire to be the first to reveal every detail possible.
I am sorry that, despite our best efforts, we appear to be unable to stop these stories appearing in the press and realise that this may make it hard for each of you to safeguard our show. Don't let it get to you. Stay virtuous! I believe we all share the desire to protect the show so our audience, in the Stadium, at home and in the media can discover the surprises for themselves on the night and piece together the puzzle with their friends and family. Again thank you from all of us for everything you are doing to deliver a fantastic show on 27 July.

Danny Boyle.

I felt honoured to receive a message from him and sorry that the media was making it so difficult for us to keep the secret. Some newspapers seemed to be doing everything that they could to ruin the surprise including printing the music set list. The cynicism was corrosive and hard to resist.

Back in Ipswich, on Thursday 5th July, the Olympic torch came to town. I was amazed as thousands of people lined the route. There were bands playing and families having an evening out as pensioners chatted and watched on. Union Jacks were waving. There was a real sense of anticipation as the flame came closer. Someone shouted, 'Here it comes'. I was surprised at how brightly it glowed in the early evening light. The runner jogged past. The flame moved up the hill, through the park and into the distance, continuing its journey to the Stadium.

On the Friday a rather odd email listed all the category 1 stuff prohibited from the Olympic Park, including, banners handcuffs and tents. Were they expecting something?

Email: Friday 6th July 2012
Subject: 'Lock Down.'
From Sunday 01st July 2012 the Olympic Park will move into a security phase called 'Lock Down'
This involves the Park security operation adopting the policies and procedures that will be operational during the Olympic Games.
Category 1 Prohibited Items:
Ammunition
Any item that may give cause for concern that the person may wish to use to demonstrate within the venue, such as ropes, handcuffs, tents, protest related placards or banners and spray paint or is intended to be used to commit an act of violence or sabotage towards person(s) or property or delay the event schedule.
Explosive devices and explosive materials.
Firearms or any device suspected to be a firearm including component parts.
Flares, fireworks, pyrotechnics, smoke canisters, signalling devices which emit smoke, dye or flames.
Hazardous substances including suspicious powders, pastes, chemicals, irritants, toxic substances and gas canisters.
Incendiary devices.
Offensive weapons or implements i.e. anything made or adapted for use for causing injury to a person. 'Made offensive weapons' include bayonets, flick knives and extendable batons or belt buckles and loose blades fashioned into a weapon.

Personal protection sprays such as CS, Pepper or other irritant sprays.

Controlled drugs and substances which have the appearance of being a controlled drug.

Items which have the appearance of an illegal or prohibited item e.g. replica firearms or hoax Improvised Explosive Devices whether capable of causing actual harm or not.

On the same day a more routine email gave us details of the long rehearsals and dress rehearsals as the whole show was put together. There were going to be some long days and plenty of sitting about, which I love. It also said we would not be able to watch the show.

Email: Friday 6th July 2012
Subject: 43 Weekend Update for July 6-7

Hello G & P,
21 days to go!
SCHEDULE (no changes):
Friday   Cancelled
Saturday   Cancelled
SECURITY: As you saw last weekend, the military has taken over security. Please see the attached 'Stadium Prohibited Items' for guidance on what not to bring. If you really want to know the finer details, the attached 'STA Lock Down Prohibited Items' will be good bedtime reading. Please note that these security restrictions have been put in place by LOCOG and security services. Ceremonies does not have the ability to waive any security requirements.
-- Other stuff you've been asking about this week –
The primary questions this week have been in regards to what happens at long rehearsals, dress rehearsals and show day. Here are some of the answers compiled by the Cast team.
What happens at rehearsals that are really long? So far we have been rehearsing your segment individually. Next we will start putting the Ceremony together – so we will rehearse the transitions from what happens before you and after you. Also we will be rehearsing how you leave your holding area and get onto the Field of Play. With a cast of 10,000, what happens backstage is very important and we need to get it right.
Dress Rehearsals (a.k.a. Technical Rehearsals): We will soon be able to give you better refined times for when you need to get to the Stadium for all Dress Rehearsals and the actual show day. As you may have seen in the press, the final Dress Rehearsal will be in front of an audience. Please be aware that we will not be doing a full Dress Rehearsal for our audience. We are, in fact, asking the public who attend the Dress Rehearsal to leave at 10:15pm in order to guarantee they can get to public transport in time.

During Dress Rehearsals, you will wear costume and make up. You will also start rehearsing your walk from your holding area to the Stadium according to what happens before and after you. At Dress Rehearsals which have an audience, you will also have to get into the Stadium before the doors open to the public. For these many reasons, we have asked you to come to the Stadium very early. Be prepared, because you will spend several hours waiting (you might want to bring a book or magazine). As you probably already understand such a complex show – made up from many different and complicated segments – is a huge machine. We are all part of this machine, and we have to act and move at exactly the right time for the machine to work as a whole. As all Dress Rehearsals are conducted as per show day, after your performance you will be led back to your holding area to change out of your costume and then leave the Olympic Park. Unfortunately, there will not be an opportunity to watch the show. As soon as your performance is done you will be asked to leave.

The Olympic Opening Ceremony – Friday 27th July 2012: The hard work, the sweat, the laughs, the frowns – we promise it's all worth it, and it ends with the World's Biggest Show: an 80,000 person live audience and 3 billion people watching around the globe. Like the Dress Rehearsals, unfortunately after you have completed your role it is not possible to view the rest of the ceremony. At the conclusion of your performance you will return to your holding area to change and then exit. This way you can get safely away on public transport before 80,000 members of the audience, dozens of coaches, and 10,000 athletes all leave at the same time. In this way it is like all other shows; as a participant you do not get to watch. We recognise this is a hard thing, but experience has shown us over many ceremonies that this is the best way to ensure that the cast has enough time to get off site safely and home. It is a night to set the video recorder and watch it later with a glass of something special.

We look forward to seeing you NEXT Saturday, July 14th at 9:30am.

On July 11th I went to Guildford to see my brother Jes, his wife Amanda and my nephews George and Albert and neice, Polly. Amanda had arranged for me to talk to Polly's year 5 primary school classes. My mum came along as well. I couldn't tell them much because the secret had to be kept. But they were excited. I showed them some of the Beijing ceremony and asked if they thought London would be as good. I said it was going to be a real surprise and that we should be very proud that London was holding the Olympics for the whole world to enjoy. They liked seeing my silly audition dance (brush your teeth, jump out of the shower) and they laughed at the awful photograph on my official pass.

19 Blood on the Floor

Saturday 14th July 2012. 09:30. Stadium – 13 days to Show

'We all make the games.' McDonald's.

I felt slightly bereft having not been to rehearsals and seeing my new friends for almost two weeks. But it was good to rest and get back to normal before the final push. In the pub one builder confessed that he was fed up with getting soaked: 'I've been tiling outside and this rain has got into my bones.'

It seemed that summer was never going to arrive. There were floods, saturated ground and cancelled festivals. Country shows were called off. The newspapers concluded that it was likely to be 'The worst British summer for 100 years'. The Jet Stream had come south. Our weather was coming from the North Atlantic; wet, cold, dull. Relentless downpours were making life miserable.

As the early morning train rattled towards Stratford, the weather forecast was again miserable. Rain, cold, dull. Again.

At Stratford things had moved on. Signs pointing to the Olympic Park were everywhere. Huge sponsor billboards wrapped the buildings. A new entrance had been opened under the station. McDonald's had put up posters everywhere under the tagline 'We all make the Games'. They included photographs of:

The Blubbering Wreck (Man in tears)

The Sulky Pants (Man on his own, arms crossed still sitting in his seat, when everybody had gone)

The Hello How Can I help?-Ers (Smiling Games Makers)

The Showing The Way-Er (Games Maker with big foam hand).

Up at the entrance to Westfield two athletes in Russian costumes strolled past. Groups of Games Makers in their new uniforms were striding towards the Stadium for their Venue Specific training. A Japanese television crew was interviewing two athletes. A girl in a Union Jack jacket was texting.

Up at security outside the Olympic Park the troops were in their smart Army, Navy and Air Force uniforms. I had read that the aircraft carrier HMS Ocean was now moored in the centre of London. Typhoon jets were on standby. Rapier Missiles were ready. At the airport style security, I had to leave my bottles of drink behind. Inside the Olympic Park, as I walked over the wide bridge towards the Stadium, it felt like coming back home.

As we waited in the Stadium-seating bowl, two magnificent shire horses loped up the ramp and onto one of the fields. We let out a collective 'Ahh.' With their broad foreheads, large eyes, thick necks and white-feathered legs they took us back to a bygone age. Somehow their slowness and gentle strength calmed us all. Their grooms led them across a field, a plough dragging behind. They ripped up the grass, the staging and everything else. Oops!

Later, when they came back, the stage had been repaired and they were pulling a country hay cart. In the Opening Ceremony, white and black shire horses drew two cartwheeled, vintage London General Omnibuses that brought in Brunels at the beginning of the 'Pandemonium' sequence. Danny Boyle came over our in-ear monitor.

'Hello everyone. I'm up in the control room, near the Royal Box. Give me a wave if you can hear me.'

Danny confessed he'd had a bad week.

'There's been blood on the floor. We're getting pressure to cut the show because people are worried it's going to go on too long.'

He explained that the Athletes' Parade was the key element in the show. It was difficult to work out how long this would take, with a record number of teams and athletes at the Olympics. There were also transport issues. And, for the lighting to be seen to full effect, the show couldn't begin until dark, at 21:00.

We found out later that if the show finished too late, there would be problems with trains and security. People at home watching on television might have to stay up until past midnight. This story got into the press. Another disaster loomed. In fact, on Show Night, the trains ran until 02:30 in the morning and the audience stayed in the Stadium until well past midnight. In the UK 20 million people were still watching the show at midnight, the biggest audience in history for that time of night.

Danny continued, saying that he wasn't going to cut any sections out of the show because everyone had put in so much work and we were volunteers. He did say that we would shave a few minutes off each section and 'We will each have to take a hit for the team.'

We would have done anything for Danny. He sounded quite battered and I felt sorry that he was being pressured to compromise his remarkable vision.

Later that week, *The Sun* came out with an article entitled 'Olympic Meddle – Olympic Ceremony cut by 30mins over security'. The article stated that 'The extravaganza was chopped by half an hour because of fears of delays at G4S checkpoints and a travel shambles.'

The article went on to say that several scenes had been shortened and one involving daredevil 'flaming stunt bikes' had been axed altogether.

'Disappointed performers had been told about the cuts – and warned a scene in which costume nurses dance around old fashioned NHS beds may be cut completely.'

Considering how badly the NHS section was going, and how awful it looked in rehearsal, I wondered if Danny might have been relieved to have an excuse to cut it. But, of course, he didn't. We heard it was the section he was most proud of.

The Sun article rubbed salt into the wounds by saying that 'The latest blow follows bungles in which athletes' buses got lost on the way to the athletes' village from Heathrow and huge traffic jams were caused by Olympic Lane VIP routes in the capital.'

It reported that security staff were preventing people bringing in Walkers crisps and Ginsters pasties because they were not made by Olympic sponsors. As well as this the taxi drivers were staging a protest. Amongst the 246 comments on 'The Sun' website about the article, 'urban_fox52' commented: 'Yes, we have now confirmed that we are the anus of the planet.'

In the Stadium we spent the rest of the day running through the first three sections of the show: The Green and Pleasant

Land; Pandemonium; and the NHS section, called 'Second to the Right, and Straight on Till Morning'. My cue came over the in-ear monitor.

'20:40.' I wandered out and took on the gentle lope of the shire horses. There was no hurry because the Green and Pleasant section of the show wasn't going to be cut. It was mostly before 21:00, so there was no real time pressure.

As the rain poured down we watched the Industrial men and women struggle with increasingly heavy waterlogged real turf. It looked more and more like 'The Somme'. I found out later that, because of these problems, the props team had sourced special lighter turf with shorter roots that wouldn't soak up so much rain. The VOM resembled a Crimean War field hospital, with the NHS cast pushing out their heavy iron-framed Victorian hospital beds.

As I left the Stadium in the early evening the NHS beds were scattered across the stage, abandoned. I walked out past tired-looking Industrials and exhausted nurses. I wondered whether it would ever come together. The Stadium lights blazed as the rehearsals continued into the night.

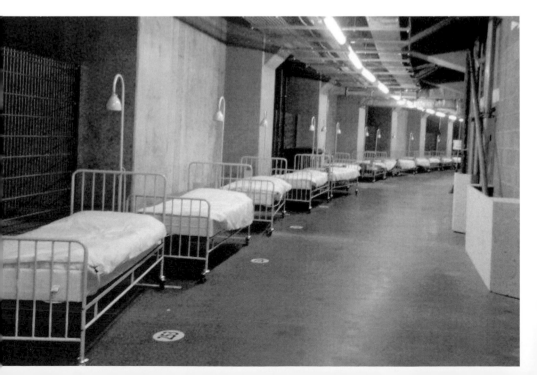

20 The Changing Rooms

Wednesday 18th July 2012. 11:30. Stadium – 9 days to Show

Miles Davis: 'What did you think?'
Critic: 'I thought you played brilliantly.'
Miles Davis: 'No, the suit man, the suit.'

Email: Tuesday 17th July 2012
Subject: Update for 18 July
10 days to go!
Please read below because there are some BIG changes in store tomorrow:
Do not go to the Stadium – Your holding area has changed:
Your cast group is being held at Eton Manor starting tomorrow. Cast will NOT be held in the seating bowl. Eton Manor is a purpose built Paralympics venue so it is available for Ceremonies use during the Olympics.
Reminders:
Do always bring your little ceremonies pass and your big LOCOG accreditation. Do always bring your headphones (if you have extra ceremonies ones, or accidentally taken home your unit, please bring it back). Do dress appropriately (closed toe shoes) And don't forget your poncho.
No photographs, no video, no tweeting etc... we are so close – please don't spoil the surprise. People taking photos are jeopardising their place.
You are in a creative segment, which precedes the Athletes' Parade, so by the time you return to your holding area and get changed the Ceremony will be drawing to its conclusion. Experience shows it is best to leave the park before the audience and athletes in order to get onto Public Transport in good time.
Many thanks
Cast Coordinator – Volunteer Performers

On the train down to Stratford I sat with three 'Games Makers' in their purple and orange uniforms. They were chatting excitedly about their roles. One had started to work with the Australian Women's Basketball team, supporting them as they prepared for the games. Another was working at the Velodrome, inside the track. The third was going to arrange interviews in the 'Press Room' after athletes had competed their events. It was uplifting to see how positive, energised and professional they were, proudly wearing their uniforms.

The weather forecast was bad again. Rain and wind. I checked the email from our Cast Coordinators and wondered what the 'Eton Manor Holding Area' was. How could it be a 27-minute walk from the Stratford Gate?

As I walked over the bridge past the Aquatics Centre I saw a sign saying 'Eton Manor – 30 minute walk'. How big is this park? The route took me past the Stadium, along London Way and by the Copper Box. As the sun came out for a few moments the wild flowers in the park looked lush and beautiful. Then over a bridge, across the river, past the Basketball arena and the Velodrome, over the A12, with official Olympic BMWs cruising underneath in the Olympic Lane, and up to Eton Manor. Little did I realise that we would be taking this 30-minute walk to and from the Stadium many times over the next couple of weeks.

Eton Manor was a series of sports centre-like buildings and marquees. I met up with some footballers and we walked into our new home. Inside, NHS cast members were changing into their blue nurses' uniforms. In the men's changing room were our Costumes Team.

'Hello. Find your costume and try it on.'

Around the room there were racks of clothes. I found a hanger, '247', my cast number. There were my trousers and smock, two long Victorian leather waistcoats, a leather belt and some boots. Everywhere men of all shapes and sizes were in various stages of nakedness.

A queue was forming at the Costume Team table. Over the speaker the announcer was a bit tetchy: 'Would the men please keep out of the women's changing rooms.'

Big cheer. The Hi-Vis girls made notes on last minute alterations and did swaps on boots and shoes. One villager beamed as he tried on a magnificent pair of thigh high leather boots.

'What can I do for you, sweetheart?' asked the smiling Costume Team leader.

'Could you put a button on the collar of my smock because it's a bit too open. And have you got any more of those boots?'

'I'll have a look,' she offered.

From a large cardboard box she produced a pair of antique soft leather pointed toe boots.

'Try these on' she suggested, 'nobody else wants them. They're different sizes.'

They fitted perfectly. Oh, yes!

'Those are really expensive,' she explained 'we've hired them in and they're genuine. Kenneth Branagh probably wore them last.'

They felt supple and soft. I posed around for a bit. One of the footballers asked, 'Where did you get those boots from?'

I replied, 'Go and ask the girls. Quickly. They might have some left.'

Over the dressing room speakers came an announcement: 'Welcome to Eton Manor. Make sure you wear your passes at all times. Don't lose your headphones. Try out your costumes to see if any final alterations are needed. You'll be called up to the Stadium in groups. There will be a full dress rehearsal on Friday.'

Back up at the Stadium we practised our entrance, the freezes, the rugby and then on to the Strike. In the orchard my tree had grown more apples as the props team put the finishing touches to the set. The Mad Russian and I were seeing how far we could throw an apple into the air without dropping it. I think Feisty Aryna had disowned us. We chatted about the after-show party some of the G and P cast had organised for all the Green and Pleasants at Bumpkins restaurant in Westfield.

When we had taken off the tree for the strike, the Industrials ripped the stage apart again. Up came the chimneys and the beam engines. Again, one of the chimneys wouldn't rise properly. Another of the chimneys was bending in the wind and wouldn't go back down. The rain continued to pour. Then the NHS cast tried their section, which still wasn't working out.

The stage was reset and we all tried again. The changeovers were improving but we were getting tired. The first dress rehearsal was on Saturday and the first audience was coming to watch on Monday. It looked like we wouldn't be ready. There seemed to be no way the Industrials could get their huge stage change down to 14 minutes – or that the NHS section would ever work at all.

21 Laughing Stock

Friday 20th July 2012. 12:30. Stadium – 7 days to Show

'Now I'm beginning to understand all this mystery, and to appreciate your most generous intentions.' *The Marriage of Figaro*, Beaumarchais.

With a week to go, the Olympic Opening Ceremony became one of the top stories in the media. *The Mail Online* had photographs of the Green and Pleasant Land set, cricketers practising and performers in Green and Pleasant Land costumes walking towards the Stadium. Some of the timings for the show were also revealed. But there were no photographs of any other part of the ceremony. I suspected that the press team fed the photographs to them. The secret was being kept. The British public had absolutely no idea of what would be revealed from under the amazing stage.

Most of the 675 comments on *The Mail Online* article were completely negative.

'I am dreading this major embarrassment, we don't want this, this is embarrassing, it's not as if other countries don't have chickens and horses.' (Janet, UK. *Mail Online* 18th July 2012)

Big Mac from Middlesbrough wasn't pleased either: 'We are going to be an absolute laughing stock around the world; after a magnificent opening at the Chinese Olympics we're going to play cricket and round up sheep!!!... God help us'. (*Mail Online* 18th July 2012)

The next day the Mail Online followed up with another article entitled: 'A cast of 10,000. A budget of £27m. An audience of billions. With the Opening Ceremony a week away... will we WOW the world?'

The Mail commented that Andrew Lloyd Webber and Sir Cameron McIntosh had been passed over in favour of 'Lefty Darlings' Danny Boyle and Stephen Daldry. The finish would be after midnight because the start had been delayed from the usual 19:30. This would mean that the athletes wouldn't get back to their village until 00:30 at the earliest. Animal Welfare groups were up in arms. Animal Aid had called the show a 'highly stressful and probably terrifying experience for the animals'.

Anna, from Armenia posted one of very few positive comments (bless her): 'I'm sure it's going to be spectacular, you Brits have no equals when it comes to staging a jaw dropping show, waiting forward to the Opening Ceremony ☺'.

When I arrived at the changing rooms at Eton at 12:30 one of the footballers told me that we probably wouldn't be taken down to the Stadium until about 17:00, so we had ages to wait. Inside the dressing room there was an announcement.

'Would everybody who needs hair and make-up please get it done as early as possible because there are lots of you to do and not many of us to do it.'

One of the cricketers was having his hair slicked back. The hair girl was applying a moustache and whiskers. When he had finished I didn't recognise him. The new hair was exactly matched and looked completely real. He told me that each moustache was handmade and cost about £60. The attention to detail was remarkable. When he was in full costume he looked magnificent.

The nurses didn't have enough mirrors and so some came into the men's dressing room to curl their 1940s hairstyles. Their uniforms were quite heavy and hot so they wandered around wearing petticoats and bras. We were making 'nurse sandwiches' for photographs; two nurses with a footballer as the filling. A nice place to be. So this is what show business is like.

Outside the changing rooms it was a surreal dream. A bare-chested Industrial walked past covered from head to waist in black coal dust. Some dancers in tiger print jumpsuits mixed with girls in 80's Acid House party costumes. Cyclists looked like the sperm from the Woody Allen film *Sleepers*. An announcement came over the speaker.

'Would the women please keep out of the men's changing rooms.'

Huge cheer. One of the nurses wanted to stay: 'I want to be in your dressing room to be near some male energy.'

I couldn't see the attraction. Mostly, it was half-dressed pasty fat blokes talking about football.

I carefully put on my costume, making sure that the IEM transmitter was hidden and that I wouldn't fall on it when I dived in goal. A member of the make-up team taped our headphones so that they couldn't be seen. At around 17:00 the Green and Pleasants were called out onto the lawn. We were led in VOM groups through the park to the Stadium. We looked magnificent in our pastel coloured costumes and some of the Industrials cheered as we floated past. In the distance was the Stadium. We bubbled with excitement.

In the tunnel the village footballers and audience gathered around Robin. He was in his costume for the first time; a brown bowler hat with silk ribbon, long brown jacket, granddad shirt, waistcoat and heavy brown boots. He explained that we were going to run through everything to 'real time', exactly as it would be on the night so our entrance would be at 20:40. We had a couple of hours to wait. We had to be at the Stadium early so the audience would not see us arrive on show night. He encouraged us to keep doing what we had practised.

'Don't walk faster when you go on. Keep it slow and remember – it's your countryside and your land.'

We discussed minor last-minute changes, as two stilt walkers glided by. Robin then left us to go to the other side of the Stadium where he would meet the professional footballers who would join us on the football pitch at 20:40. I noticed that the Mad Russian wasn't there and wondered if he was late. Where was he? I was missing him. While we waited in the tunnel we started to explore what was around us.

'Oh my God, look over there. The flags for the parade.'

We posed for photographs with the flags and I noticed a mark on one of them. Oops. Was that us? We walked away quickly. Beside the flags we found huge boxes containing signs with all the countries names. On the wall there was a list entitled 'London 2012 Parade of Athletes', with all the countries in number order…

Code March	English	Athletes
LAO 103	Lao People's Democratic Republic	12
LAT 104	Latvia	43
LIB 105	Lebanon	17
LES 106	Lesotho	14

I wandered off to find a toilet and noticed a long corridor curving round under the Stadium. Dancers were lying on the floor loosening up. Further along I reached the middle of the Stadium. More nurses' beds were lined up ready to go on stage. In my in-ear monitor I heard '20:10. Two minutes to first entrance.' I rushed back along the corridor. In VOM 1 everyone was assembled, ready to go on.

At 20:40 we started to move out. We were making the conversation up as we went along and took it in turns to talk about the weirdest things while looking like villagers walking through our own land. I started to tell my 'villager son' that I was worried about his girlfriend. She was from the next village and there had been rumours that she was sleeping with other men, for money.

'For money?' he asked.

'Yes, I'm only telling you what everybody else knows.'

He said that he loved her and that he was going to marry her whatever I thought. I explained that his mother was very upset and didn't want him to marry someone from such a bad family. These conversations got more and more disgusting until my wife reminded me that some people in the audience would be able to lip-read. We toned it down a bit after that.

When we arrived at our meadow the professional footballers looked magnificent in their hooped white and red and claret and blue tops. Some of them now had mutton chops and moustaches. All had their hair slicked down, with centre partings.

And then the match began. The ball moved around beautifully. I was focused, on my toes, ready to save the ball. The intensity was exhausting and exhilarating. The freezes were sharp and co-ordinated. The village crowd cheered as the ball pinged around. In the background I could hear music from the Stadium speakers. Some of the lights were on. Then the whistle blew twice – the rugby match.

The ball was picked up and everybody gathered round it. Then someone made a break. We had worked out a move where as soon as we were onto the track, I would grab the person with the ball, wrestle it from them and run forward before passing it to an Irishman, who would be tackled and dropped to the floor. As we careered round the Stadium the ball was kicked high into the air. We surged towards an exit. Another group of villagers attacked us. We turned and ran up the slope on the other side of the Stadium onto the fields, through gates, over hedges, across a bridge, over a stream and back into our meadow. It was joyful and intoxicating.

Then back to more football. I heard 'Jerusalem' over the Stadium speakers and began to move to the orchard. I wandered past the maypole, along a line of hedges, past the scarecrow, the beekeepers and the cottage where villagers were making bread. I waved to the courting couple as they sauntered past and then onto the bridge to the orchard. In my headphones I heard, 'Here come the Brunels, start to notice them'.

Brunels in their top hats and black tail coats marched across the fields. Others walked on to the Tor at the other end of the Stadium.

'Everyone in Strike positions.'

Then we heard Kenneth Branagh begin his speech: 'Be not afeard, the isle is full of noises.'

In our headphones we heard 'Get ready to notice the drummers... cue drummers.'

I watched as drummers poured into the Stadium. Music pounded from the speakers.

'And Strike.'

The Mad Russian still wasn't there. Where was he? Feisty Aryna tucked up her skirts and grabbed the tree. Off we went, me in front with the trunk and Aryna struggling with the branches. Marching along as the drums crashed and the music pounded.

'Quicker, quicker' shouted Aryna 'keep going.'

Out past the cottage, down the slope and off. We dropped the tree and cheered. That was the quickest we'd ever got off the stage, though Aryna had blood coming from a cut on her leg.

'I hope you haven't got blood on the poor little tree,' I remarked.

I was covered in sweat, rain and mud. Exhausted, intoxicated, buzzing. Some of us ran back into the Stadium, up the steps and watched as the Industrials performed. This time the lights were on. The music was louder. Strobes flashed, chimneys rose, everything was movement and chaos. It looked astonishing. And it was much quicker. As we made our way back towards the changing rooms through the park, the whole Stadium pulsated and pounded behind us.

Back in the changing rooms one of the costume girls was waiting: 'OK, sweetheart, make sure you put your costume back exactly as it should be ready for tomorrow. Would you like a cake?'

And then the 30-minute walk back past the Stadium to Westfield and a beer. The bar was buzzing with performers, games makers, athletes and technicians. But no Mad Russian.

As I arrived home at around 01:00 I felt proud and elated. I knew it was going to work, apart from the NHS section. I couldn't wait to do it all again tomorrow.

22 Sebastian Coe

Saturday 21st July 2012. 14:00. Stadium – 6 days to Show

'If you can talk with crowds and keep your virtue,
Or walk with kings – nor lose the common touch'
'If', Rudyard Kipling.

When I arrived at Eton Manor at 14:00 people were gathered in groups on the grass outside; chatting, having picnics and swapping stories. Everyone seemed chilled and relaxed. It had a festival feel. Some cast members had brought music. We knew that we had plenty of time before we were called down to the Stadium, so we had time to chat and relax.

As I wandered around I noticed some cast members huddled in a group near one of the entrances. A nurse knew what was going on.

'It's Sebastian Coe.'

Over by his official car some burly men in dark suits watched on. He was signing autographs. I presented him with my official Olympic pass to sign.

'I'm not allowed to sign those,' he said. 'Go and get your other one and I'll sign it for you.'

I went through into the changing room and grabbed my credit card-sized Ceremonies pass that Danny Boyle had signed. I thought that by the time I got back he would be gone, as he was Head of LOCOG, the London Organising Committee of the Olympic Games and had plenty to do. But he was still there. I queued up again and he signed. Everyone was thanking him for the opportunity to be part of the Olympic Games and he was thanking everyone for the effort and time we had put in.

About an hour later, when I wandered back past the same entrance I was amazed to see that he was still there, patiently signing passes, bibs and anything else that people presented to him. His patience and kindness was impressive. He was gracious and inspiring. More and more cast members were surrounding him. Perhaps he would be there all night.

By 17:00 almost everyone was changed and in costume. Some sat quietly, focusing ready for the performance. One of the footballers was sleeping off a heavy night. Others chatted or wandered around meeting the other performers; NHS, Green and Pleasants, Industrials, Dancers, Cyclists. We swapped stories, checked out the costumes and found out more about the other sections in the show. I asked if anyone had seen the Mad Russian, but nobody knew where he was. Had he been thrown out? Was he ill? We didn't know.

Then it was call time. The Green and Pleasants marched off towards the Stadium. Cast members from the other sections cheered and encouraged us on our way; 350 of us floating in all our pastel glory on the half-hour walk to the Stadium.

This time the whole rehearsal flowed. The show was coming together. Still a few details to change, but I now knew for certain it was going to work. The producers also knew that things were finally falling into place and decided that we didn't need to arrive at the changing rooms at Eton Manor until 15:30. The Monday performance would be in front of members of the London Olympic Organising Committee and the Games Makers, who had been given free tickets. So Monday would be the first time in front of an audience.

Security had become even tighter. Without the A5 Olympic accreditation there would be no entry. No exceptions. If I lost my pass I wasn't going to get in. It was the most precious thing I had.

Email 22nd July
Subject: Update for Monday. Schedule change.

Brilliant job yesterday! We have a big week ahead.
Monday, July 23 – Full Dress Rehearsal
- With Audience (our LOCOG friends and non-Ceremonies Games Makers!)
- Full costume and makeup
o No jewellery (wedding bands/religious items OK)
o Contacts if you have them; glasses if you need them for safety
o Skin shade or tan ear buds... no white, no colours
o Basic rule: you're in period costume so additions should fit in or not call attention to themselves.
Schedule Change!
New later arrival time (applies to all future days):

15:00 at Security (as you have seen, lines are getting longer); 15:30 check-in at Eton Manor

Security/Accreditation:

- LOCOG Accreditation enforcement in full effect. No LOCOG accreditation, no entry. There is nothing we can do to override this. If you have forgotten your accreditation, please return home to get it. There will be no 'lists' at the front gate and your Ceremonies ID will not get you in. You must have OOC on your LOCOG accreditation or Upgrade Card (if applicable), to get into Olympic Park.

- BIBs: No need to bring your bib. It's yours to cherish forever and ever.

Photos: Please refrain from posing and taking photographs. We know it is exciting, and you look amazing in costume, but please don't let it impact the safety of cast movements.

- No Bowl: Sitting in the seating bowl after your performance is not permitted. We have an audience now. It is imperative to return to Eton Manor, change, and get on transport before it shuts down.

- Tickets: No, there are no additional dress rehearsal tickets. No need to ask.

- Fun: Have a great time. We love your energy and performance!

See you tomorrow.

23 Be Not Afeared

Monday 23rd July 2012. 15:30. Stadium – 4 days to Show

'The sacred radiance of the sun.'
King Lear. Act 1, Scene i. William Shakespeare.

Finally the sun had arrived! It was forecast to be 24 degrees with no wind. A beautiful day. On the train an email pinged in from Danny Boyle. He reminded us not to look at the cameras, to look after our costumes and that this was the first time we would introduce the public to what we had created together.

Email: Monday 23rd July 2012 – morning.
Subject: A note from Danny

Dear Volunteers,
Good luck tonight and Wednesday and remember amongst the many surprises the single biggest surprise will be how professional you are. Couple of thoughts to help you achieve this:
Look after your costumes! They are your passport to Friday night. Hang them up in the holding area; care for them and you will look even more fabulous than they do.
Don't look at the cameras and they will look at you. Look at the cameras and the editor will avoid you. Obviously this doesn't apply to the curtain call when you can finally gaze back into one billion adoring eyes!
In Green and Pleasant, Pandemonium and Second Star on the Right (Swing out Sisters!) please don't wear anything anachronistic; jewellery, visible piercings, spectacles etc and try to disguise your IEMs as much as possible please.
Finally remember these are dress rehearsals for us all to discover what it is like to perform in front of an audience, to improve our show as well as to entertain, and begin to introduce the public to what we have created together. Oh, and wouldn't you know it, it's going to be hot, so drink lots of water and look out for each other.

Thank you
Danny

As we arrived in our costumes at the Stadium tunnel at around 18:00, things had changed. Huge black curtains hung at the entrance from the VOM into the Stadium. It was over two hours before we went on stage. In the tunnel were the industrial revolution weaving looms and the two sections of the suburban house. There were technicians and props people everywhere.

I wandered along the corridor around under the Stadium. Dancers from the Akhram Khan company were stretching and warming up, intense and focused. Further along, the orchestra were practising in their dress suits and bow ties with blue, yellow and red Converse trainers. Further along there was a room full of the 'Beautiful Girls'. They would be carrying the countries' names in the Athletes' Parade. Over 200 of them relaxing, chatting and doing their hair and make-up. A fierce woman at the door wouldn't let anyone in or any of them out. I dared one of the handsome Zoot Suited dancers in a fedora hat to blag his way in. He failed too. We found a food station and grabbed some sandwiches.

Further along I stopped at another tunnel.

'Just wait there for a moment,' asked a stagehand.

'The geese are about to go on.'

A narrow corridor had been made from wooden boards. Their handlers shouted, 'Here they come.' The geese cackled past, waddling along towards the ramp onto the stage.

'Just wait a bit longer, the cows are next.'

Cowherds led the cows past us onto the Green and Pleasant Land. As I walked back towards VOM 1 I felt like I was in Danny Boyle's surreal dream. I wanted to stay there forever. We all did. Some Pearly Kings and Queens were chatting loudly in their spangly black and pearl costumes and feather hats. One started to sing a bawdy East End song and we all roared with laughter. '... And a pair of Jack the Rippers, and a cup of Rosy Lee, what could be better than this, a nice old cuddle and kiss.' For a moment I was back in a 1930's East End pub with my grandfathers, having a singsong.

In the Stadium we could hear Danny Boyle asking the audience to 'keep the secret and save the surprise'. As we waited for our cue to go on I could hear the audience talking.

'Oh my God. They're bored. There isn't enough going on. They've started to chat.'

For this preview, the audience would see the show from 20:12 when the first Green and Pleasants came on until 22:15, the end of the TIM section. They wouldn't see the Athletes' Parade or the lighting of the torch, which was still being kept deadly secret. And they wouldn't see the stars of the show like the Queen, James Bond, Mr Bean, JK Rowling or Tim Berners-Lee. As I arrived back at the Stadium after the performance the audience was pouring out, making their way towards Stratford station.

'What did you think of it?' I asked a family as they queued at the gates on the way out.

'We can't tell you. It's a secret.'

'I was in it,' I said, and showed them my Cast Member pass. One held me by the arm and looked into my eyes, 'It was amazing. It was the most incredible live show I have ever seen. In fact, it was one of the most incredible things I have ever seen full stop.'

A man in a business suit was walking away towards the station with his wife and three daughters.

'What did you think?' I asked as we queued for the trains.

'I thought it was boring,' he answered, 'I was not impressed.'

One of his daughters scowled,

'Dad, you're an idiot. That was fantastic.'

His wife looked at me and shook her head.

'We can't take him anywhere. Everyone thought it was absolutely wonderful.'

As they headed toward the train he was being brow-beaten, standing firm in the onslaught. As we queued for the trains I spoke to two Americans.

'Good job' one said. 'It was spectacular, funny and very British. You and your sense of humour. It was genius. I want to tell everyone back home all about it but I can't.'

I then asked what they thought of the NHS segment, expecting their bubble of enthusiasm to burst.

'I loved it. Absolutely loved it. So much happened. It was beautiful when the children went to sleep with their bedtime story. The lights in the duvets made it like a fairytale. Then the Mary Poppinses flew in right over my head and we all cheered. It was hard to follow the industrial revolution but it was quite magical in a different way.'

So Danny was right to keep it in… of course he was. On the train a group of burly East End men looked stunned as they tucked into their cans of beer.

'Did you see it?' I asked one.

'Yes mate,' he replied. 'I was in the first section,' I said 'but I haven't seen the rest of it. What was it like to be in the audience?'

I expected them to say they didn't like it. One of them answered, 'It made me proud to be British,' and he clenched his fist to his chest. His mate couldn't wait to give his opinion.

'There were bits of it that I didn't understand, but it was amazing. It was slow at first but when it got going it was awesome. We can be proud to be Londoners. I'm going to tell all my mates to watch it. Danny Boyle is a bloody genius.'

When I got home I couldn't sleep as image after image flashed into my head. The next day I was exhausted. *The Daily Mail* ran an article about the rehearsal…

'Don't spoil the surprise! 60,000 fans watch Olympic opening ceremony rehearsal – but are sworn to secrecy by organisers. Hashtag #savethesurprise starts trending as people rush to give it rave reviews without revealing any detail.

'It has become one of Britain's most closely guarded secrets. But now it is in the hands of 62,000 people lucky enough last night to watch a dress rehearsal of Danny Boyle's extravagant £27million Opening Ceremony that will spark London 2012 to life. Fans invited to the sneak preview in the Olympic Stadium in Stratford, East London, were urged personally by the Slumdog Millionaire director to "save the surprise" for the one billion around the world who will watch on Friday night.

'The event received hundreds of glowing reviews from those lucky enough to be at the rehearsal. Though no one gave details of the ceremony.' (*Mail Online* 24th July 2012)

Prashant Mistry wrote on Twitter: 'I have to #savethesurprise, but today's opening ceremony dress rehearsal was epic! You guys are in for a treat on Friday!'

In the pub on the Tuesday night one of the blokes quietly came over: 'A friend of mine went to the dress rehearsal on

Monday. He couldn't tell me anything about it but he said it was brilliant. How's it going?'

I explained that it had all come together and I hadn't seen it all, but the audience reaction was off the scale.

'We can't wait to see it. We're having a party on Friday night and we're going to watch the whole thing. It's really nice knowing someone who is in it. Makes it really personal.'

As I walked home from the pub one of my neighbours ran up to me: 'I hear you're in the opening ceremony. Everyone's talking about it. It must be so exciting to be taking part.'

I said that it was one of the most incredible experiences I'd ever had, that the audience reaction so far had been remarkable and that it had all finally come together. She explained that she was going to be in France on the Friday night but couldn't wait to see the show on French TV.

A friend of mine, who was London Ambassador, had been in the audience for the dress rehearsal. He phoned me and said he had been really blown away.

'Oh, the sound of those drums. If anyone still wants to vote Conservative after seeing that, they need to be taken outside and shot.'

His wife, who was in the audience as well, said that it was heartwarming and wonderful. They had made plans to go ten minutes before the end to avoid the crowds, but in the event didn't want to leave the Stadium and chatted for ages with other people in the crowd.

'It was marvellous and we were totally bowled over. Wow!'

24 Stop Thief

Wednesday 25th July 2012. 15:30. Stadium – 2 days to Show

'Stolen sweets are best.' *The Rival Fools*, Act 1. Colley Cibber.

My wife and son had tickets for the final dress rehearsal. We met my son at 14:00 at Starbucks in the Westfield Shopping Centre in Stratford. I brought with me forty medals engraved with 'Olympic Opening Ceremony 2012', presents for the football team and the villagers in the football audience.

As we sat chatting and looking at the athletes and Games Makers in Starbucks, I reached down to pick up my bag by my feet. It had gone! And in its place was another black rucksack. I looked inside. It was empty. Someone had stolen my bag with the medals, my lovely green numbered bib and car keys. They had done a switch from right under my feet.

We couldn't see how they had managed it. Luckily I had taken out my Olympic pass and put it around my neck a few minutes before. At least I could get into the Olympic Park. Otherwise, my Olympics would have been over.

The manager at Starbucks kindly put the bag the thief had left into a plastic bin liner. I phoned the police. I felt devastated. The medals were to be a special souvenir for my friends to be given out before the final dress rehearsal. Now they were gone.

I phoned the medal makers. They promised they would courier a new set of medals to me by the next morning, but they wouldn't be engraved.

Down at the changing rooms one of the footballers asked 'You look a bit down Russell, what's wrong?'

I explained that the medals had been stolen. I felt sad and angry. The team picked me up and got me ready for the final dress rehearsal.

The replacement medals arrived the next day. I found a local engraver and we were able to give them out to everyone in the football segment before the final show on the Friday. Another challenge, but in the end it all worked out perfectly.

On the morning of the Opening Ceremony I met a Detective Inspector from a special team working on the Olympics. He took down the details and promised they would do everything they could to catch the thief. Three weeks later I received a phone call to say that they had DNA tested the bag and matched the DNA to the thief, who was on CCTV. They were out hunting for him. As soon as he returned to one of his addresses the police would pick him up.

Down at the changing rooms everyone was relaxed and happy. The weather was even better: 30 degrees; no wind and a cloudless sky. Volunteers in Hi-Vis jackets were wandering around giving out suncream. There was a festival atmosphere on the lawns outside the changing rooms at Eton Manor.

After the final rehearsal I emerged from the Stadium, lights blazing and music thundering, and began to walk back towards the changing rooms. I was jubilant and knew that it had been an even better show. To my right, lined up into the distance, was the Athlete's Parade. For this final dress rehearsal Games Makers had been brought in to rehearse the Parade. The line seemed to go on forever. How many countries beginning with 'A' were there? Further along, as I turned a corner, the Portugal volunteers were assembling behind their flag. I spoke to a man in his 60s in his Games Maker uniform. He was from Lisbon. He said this was the proudest moment of his life. Tears welled up in his eyes.

'I'm going to march into the Stadium with my country's flag. If I died after this, I would die a happy man.'

A text pinged in from my son,

'Amazing show! Very proud x.'

I was very moved.

On the Thursday night in the pub one of the blokes found me in the garden: 'We're all going to be watching it. Go down and make the pub proud of you.'

25 It's Show Time!

Friday 27th July 2012. 15:30. 0 days to Show

'If a man will begin with certainties he shall end in doubts; but if he will content to begin with doubts, he shall end in certainties.' Francis Bacon.

Email: 26th July
Subject: The Final Update

It's Show Time!
Here is some critical, useful, and just fun information for tomorrow night and beyond.
Exiting The Olympic Park:
Tomorrow there are three big changes to the show: Athletes, fireworks and the audience staying to the end.
- It's About The Athletes: Our travel back from the Stadium may require us to cross the path of the waiting athletes. Please use the managed crossways to avoid the wrath of security.
- There is both pyro (fireworks) at the end of the athletes' parade and the end of the show. There is a 'Pyro Exclusion Zone' that comes into effect about 11:15 or so (depends on the parade). This means you should be clear of Eton Manor by 10:45pm if you are exiting via Stratford Gate. If you are late, the Pyro Exclusion Zone means you will be held in position for up to 1 hour... not something you want to happen. We highly suggest you exit via the Eton Manor Gate.
- Audience: Unlike the last two dresses, the audience will be leaving at the conclusion of the show... sometime around midnight. Keep this in mind.

That's it from us! See you tomorrow!

We were all watching the weather forecast and praying that it wouldn't rain or be windy, but the omens weren't good. It would probably rain just as the ceremony was starting. We were ready for anything. But, please don't let it rain, just this once.

That morning the announcer before the BBC *Breakfast* Show set the scene: 'The countdown clock has just hours to go. Welcome to BBC1 on a historic day for the nation and the capital. Live from London, it's *Olympic Breakfast*. The games are about to begin. The seven year wait is finally over.'

There behind the presenters was the Olympic Stadium, where I would be performing in a few hours. They would be previewing the opening ceremony and following the flame on the final leg of its journey to the Stadium. Sebastian Coe looked slightly nervous in his television interview: 'I hope we're able to say to the world, When our time came we did it right.'

At 08:12 bells were rung across the country to welcome the Olympics. An event the satirical BBC television programme *Twenty Twelve* called the 'Big Bong'.

Danny Boyle looked relaxed at his press conference that morning: 'Any kind of nervousness I feel is for them [the performers] really, because my nerves are not important. And the excitement I feel is the excitement they feel. So, yes, I am looking forward to it really. Whatever comes our way, comes our way, because it's live and one time only.'

As I got ready to head down to Stratford for the last time I put on my precious pass. It felt to me remarkable to think that I would walk from my house, on a path that led right into the centre of the Stadium on a night that would go down in history. I felt calm and relaxed, ready to enjoy every single moment of the day.

At Stratford it was buzzing with Games Makers, television crews, cameramen, reporters, and members of the audience arriving for their big day. We had the after-show party at Bumpkins and I had tickets for Women's Weightlifting at the ExCel the next day. So I had arranged to stay overnight at a hotel in Stratford.

At the hotel reception when I checked in I mentioned that I probably wouldn't be returning to my room until very late as I was performing in the Opening Ceremony. The girl on reception asked me what I was going to be doing and I explained that I would be in the first segment from 20:12 until 21:10. I asked if they could arrange for a taxi to take me to Stratford.

Half an hour later I came back down from my room. The receptionist had a surprise: 'We've arranged for a special car for you. You won't have to pay. You're our guest.' A chauffeur came over and took me out to a Mercedes limousine. I was driven back to Stratford in style.

At Eton security there was a special gift; an Opening Ceremony Programme and Certificate signed by Danny Boyle. The beautiful gold and silver covered programme included the names of all the cast members, including every one of the volunteer performers. We all looked through to find our names. There were also 2,012 photographs of cast volunteers. Thankfully, not mine though. Another lovely touch from Danny Boyle and his team.

In the changing rooms there was a sense of quiet anticipation and gentle excitement. This would also be the last time we would be together, as the end of our six-month journey neared. We presented the medals to the football teams and villagers. We also gave medals to our make-up and costume girls and Robin, who took a medal each for Danny Boyle and Toby Sedgwick.

As we readied ourselves for the last walk to the Stadium, we checked each other's costumes for the final time and made sure we had our little plastic ponchos in case it rained. We gathered outside, ready to make our way from Eton Manor to the Stadium.

Then we were off. Our route was lined by cheering Industrials, covered in soot, waving dancers and clapping nurses in their blue and white dresses. 'Break a leg' one of the Hi-Vis girls shouted. We were off over the bridge towards the park. Three hundred and fifty Green and Pleasants meandering along. The clouds grew darker overhead. Then down through the Olympic Park gardens patting the guide dog of one of our Green and Pleasant team.

The Stadium came into sight. The route was lined by Games Makers, wishing us luck, smiling and taking photographs. To our right, the lights from the BBC TV studio glowed as the clouds darkened. Then a final group photograph outside the Stadium, down the slope and into the entrance to VOM 1. Just as we got inside the clouds opened and it poured with rain.

A few minutes later the tunnel was full of NHS nurses, shaking the rain from their ponchos. Then a group of menacing looking Industrials, covered in grime, poured into the tunnel. They looked like they had just come out of a coalmine or a filthy factory.

I wandered off through the tunnel around the Stadium and got to the VIP area. A group of dancers were peeking through a gap in the door to see which VIPs they could spot. One dancer shouted 'It's Michelle Obama.'

A security man quickly pushed the door shut. Through my in-ear monitor I could hear the countdown: '20:12.'

It was time for me to get back to VOM 1, ready for the entrance. The orchestra had arrived. The curtains were across the entrance, the Stage Manager stopping anyone from peeking out. The first group of Green and Pleasants moved out; 'Let's make it a good one.' The curtains parted for them and we saw the audience for the first time. The grass across the track glowed under the lights.

'20:35.' We assembled together at the entrance and reminded each other to be slow and rural and not to speed up when we sensed the crowd or the cameras. Still no Mad Russian. Where was he?

'20:40.'

The Stage Manager opened the curtains. We were out. Not looking at the cameras, not looking at the crowd, just in our own Green and Pleasant Land. A cow mooed and put her head over a wooden fence as I walked past. I turned with my 'villager son' and said how healthy the cows were looking this year. The cowherd smiled.

The wild flowers were real and looked stunning. I picked one and put it in the buttonhole of my smock.

I could hear announcements and blasting music but blocked everything out. Next to me a wheat field looked dazzling under the lights. Beyond, crops of real broccoli and country vegetables were growing, being tended by villagers. Past the scarecrow as Frank Turner started to sing 'I Still Believe... The time is coming near'. At the football pitch we met the professional footballers. I put my waistcoat goal posts down and we began to play.

I heard '20:47' in my in-ear monitor. Frank Turner finished his song and there was a roar from the Stadium audience. We focused on the football. Then, two whistles, and we were into the rugby section. Down the steps, along the track, careering around, under a cloud. We threw the ball into the 'Posh Pit'. They cheered as they juggled it around before passing it back. Around past two entrances as other Green and Pleasants joined us. Up the slope, past the sheep, over the river and back onto our football pitch. As we arrived back the orchestra were performing 'Nimrod' by Edward Elgar; an incredibly moving piece of music. I panted for breath, getting ready to play football again.

Behind us the Maypole Children had arrived and were frolicking backwards and forwards, as the music from the orchestra soared from the speakers. The huge mill wheel began to turn. From the corner of my eye I could see the crowd passing huge blue sheets over their heads. It felt like we were on an island in a rippling sea.

'Focus, focus.'

We played on as the shipping forecast came over the speakers. I dived down to save the ball before passing it back out into the game. As the last notes of 'Nimrod' wafted into the air there was another deafening cheer from the audience.

Over the speakers I heard:

'Ladies and Gentlemen, we have one minute until we go live to the world.'

As we played on I heard 'God Save the Queen' by the Sex Pistols, 'London Calling' by The Clash and 'Pomp and Circumstance' by Elgar. Then the whole Stadium audience counted down from ten. A deafening cheer. As we went into a freeze I heard 'Ladies and Gentlemen, welcome to London and to the Games of the 30th Olympiad.'

Another cheer. A lone voice sang 'Jerusalem' and then 'Flower of Scotland' surged over the speakers. I dived on the ball and passed it out to one of the team. It was nearly time to start to move towards the orchard, ready for the Strike. Then we heard 'Danny Boy'. My cue. I moved past the maypole dancers, along the hedges, past the cottages and onto the bridge as the Brunels' coach clattered around the track to 'Bread of Heaven'. Some Brunels walked across near the orchard as the second verse of 'Jerusalem' played. In my in-ear monitor I heard: 'Start to notice the Brunels for the first time. Strike positions in one minute. Begin to look towards the Tor.'

I could see Brunels assembling at the base of the Tor. Kenneth Branagh, in his long coat and top hat, book in hand, standing half way up by the flagpoles. The audience had gone quiet.

'OK, everyone, still and ready for the speech.'

'…In England's Green and Pleasant Land.' As Jerusalem came to a close there was a round of applause from the audience. Did they know what was about to hit them? The Stadium fell silent. Then Kenneth Branagh turned and gave his speech, as 'Nimrod' played underneath his rising voice.

'Be not afeard…'

'Be not afeard; the isle is full of noises,
Sounds, and sweet airs, that give delight and hurt not.
Sometimes a thousand twangling instruments
Will hum about mine ears; and sometimes voices,
That, if I then had waked after long sleep,

Will make me sleep again: and then, in dreaming,
The clouds methought would open, and show riches
Ready to drop upon me; that, when I waked,
I cried to dream again.'

(*The Tempest,* William Shakespeare)

A tear ran down my cheek. In my monitor I heard 'Prepare to notice the drummers and prepare for the strike... turn as the drummers begin.'

The lights went down. Hundreds of drummers appeared around the Stadium. I turned to look, frightened of what I was seeing invading our pleasant land. There was a huge roar as the drummers beat out their rhythm. The oak tree lifted into the air. Out of the hole it left in the Tor poured the Industrial Warriors. It was overwhelming... visceral.

'And... Strike.'

There was another huge roar. Industrials streamed from the tunnels into the Stadium. Without the Mad Russian, Aryna and I twisted our tree from the stage and raised it above our heads. We were off. Over the wooden bridge, joining the other Green and Pleasants. Past the cottage, down the slope, over the track and gone. The music pounded on.

We dropped the tree as more Industrials marched past us into the Stadium. Nurses cheered as we exited under the tunnel and out into the night. A man in a Hi-Vis jacket was pushing us along: 'Once you've finished out and up the slope please.'

Behind us the cottage rolled off as a Caribbean band waited to go on. Two Industrials came past carrying our bridge. Three cricketers danced up the slope as we walked past rows of NHS beds, music throbbing and lights flashing from the Stadium above.

Outside the Stadium, a thousand dancers were waiting in the dark, watching the show on a huge screen. They screamed as they saw our Green and Pleasant Land being torn apart. The Olympic rings gradually moved into the centre of the stage. One of the dancers shouted 'Come on London, you run this world tonight.'

124

On the screen the rings came together in a fire of sparks and smoke. The dancers whooped as we watched the smoke rise above the Stadium. Then we heard the clatter of the helicopters. The Queen and James Bond jumped out. Their Union Jack parachutes opened and the James Bond music boomed into the night sky.

'Go Danny, we love you,' called out a dancer.

Further along, the athletes were queuing up. Greece, Afghanistan, Albania, Algeria, American Samoa… Lining their route towards the Stadium were hundreds of primary school children, cheering and waving with illuminated globes and flags. The athletes cheered and waved back. The atmosphere was incredible, as the parade snaked back towards the Athletes' Village. I called my brother who told me that Mr Bean had just stolen the show.

'Who? What's he doing in it?' I asked.

I had no idea.

Back at the changing rooms we quickly stuffed our costumes in our bags and went off to find the station at Eton Manor. Eventually we arrived back at Stratford, into Bumpkins restaurant for the after-show party.

As we walked in the Opening Ceremony was on the big screen. Jacques Rogge was giving his welcome speech. It was surreal to think that two hours before I had been on the other side of the looking glass. The show was still going on in the Stadium, being broadcast to the world. We saw the torch arrive and the stunning spectacle of the petals being lit, drawing together into the spectacular Olympic cauldron.

We ran outside to watch the fireworks burst from the Stadium. Then we watched the beginning. I was very proud that our football match (with me in goal on the left) was the first picture shown live to the world after Bradley Wiggins rang the bell. Nobody wanted to go home when the party finished at 03:00, so we found a pub that was open all night and stayed there until dawn. As we left one of the footballers said there was a photograph of us in the *New York Times*.

When I got back to the hotel at 06:30 I jumped in the shower and heard the phone ringing. I wrapped a towel round my waist and ran back into the room.

'Hello, it's BBC Radio Suffolk, are you ready to do your interview?'

I'd forgotten my promise to do a post-ceremony live interview for the breakfast programme. The producer told me

'You're live on air now.'

'Hello Russell,' said the interviewer 'how are you feeling?'

'I haven't had much sleep.' I replied.

'Well, we've watched it. We don't care how tired you are. We've got to know what it was like to take part.'

I can't remember what I said but I hope it sounded OK. He said that the responses to the Olympic Ceremony on phone and text had been overwhelming.

26 The Verdict

Saturday 28th July 2012. The next morning.

'How can anyone not get emotional?' Paula Mariani, from Barcelona.

I was going to meet my mum at 12:30 at Stratford to go together to the weightlifting at the ExCel. So I bought the Saturday newspapers and read them over breakfast. It was on every front page. I was stunned by the reaction, particularly as I hadn't seen the show myself. Sitting outside the café I was overwhelmed, sobbing in the Saturday morning sunshine.

The Times described the ceremony as 'a masterpiece'.

The Telegraph commented: 'Loud and defiant, above all gloriously tumultuously, spine-tingling British. It was 90 minutes of dazzling theatre, dance, film and music, a mash-up of our cultural history delivered at breakneck speed. Warm, witty and full of surprises it spun the head, brought a tear to the eye and made everyone lucky enough to witness it smile hard and long.'

The Sun front page had: 'WOW! The Greatest Olympic Show ever' – 'Pageantry, parody and Pistols … it was perfect' and inside, 'A great night to be British.'

The Star front-page headline was: 'Greatest Show on Earth' and commented 'If ever there was a time to prove the doubters wrong, this was it. The Olympics opening ceremony was just as spectacular as mastermind Danny Boyle said it would be – and a whole lot more.'

The Mirror front page headlined 'Maj-ical' and inside: 'Unpredictable and inventive as the British themselves it was the People's Opening Ceremony.'

Another comment was: 'Never has our nation seen its story told so passionately, poignantly and originally. And on such an epic, jaw-dropping scale.'

The Independent had the front page, 'London sets the world alight' … 'Greatest show on earth (And it's only just begun).'

Across the world the reaction was just as ecstatic. In France, the *L'Equipe* front page was: 'Déjà Magiques'.

In the pub the next day, as I quietly sat nursing a beer, one of the blokes was waiting to give me his verdict: 'That was absolutely fantastic. We watched it right to the end in the pub. We didn't see you, but we thought it was brilliant. You made us very proud'.

After the show Paula Mariani, from Barcelona, sent an email summing up her feelings to Dalia Puertas, one of the Green and Pleasants. Dalia has translated her words from Spanish to English and here are some of them.

'While our government [in Spain] is dismantling our public health system, the British are proud of theirs and thanking the NHS. That part was very emotional with Mary Poppins falling from the sky, JK Rowling reading the excerpt from *Peter Pan* ... How can anyone not get emotional? The British have contributed so much to our collective imagination.

'The Cauldron was awesome, and even more that seven youngsters, who were "nobodies", were in charge of lighting it. A great example. The torch goes from the hand of those who have won everything to those who are the future of the country.'

My mum loved it too.

27 A Letter from the Prime Minister

September 2012. Some weeks later.

'What do we do now, now that we are happy?' *Waiting for Godot*, Samuel Beckett.

The Opening Ceremony was just the beginning. Like everyone else, after I recovered, I was glued to the television as we watched inspiring athletic performances, one after another. Then came the Paralympics. We met the 'Superhumans' and found a new way of seeing people with disabilities. According to one of the women in the pub: 'The Paralympics was even better. It touched you right here, in the heart. If they can do that, we can do anything.'

Her friend had a different view: 'I didn't watch any of the Olympics. Not the beginning, the middle and certainly not the end. NCIS was on in the Opening Ceremony and I never miss an episode.'

After the Olympics I was invited to the special section of The Mall for the Athletes' Parade on 10th September. All the Olympic and Paralympics athletes paraded through London in front of a million people lining the streets. It was a truly special day, full of joy and laughter. I met up with some of the volunteers and we sat in a pub all afternoon, just happy to be together again.

On Saturday 15th September volunteers from all four ceremonies had a picnic in Hyde Park. It was wonderful to get together again to sing and dance and swap stories. As one of the people at the picnic said, as she looked across at the warm, kind and funny people gathered together 'This is what it was really about.'

I asked everyone about the Mad Russian. Where had he gone and why didn't he come to the last performances? Finally, I found someone who heard that he was just too busy and couldn't find the time off work. Perhaps we will never know, but I still have a medal waiting for him. We had connected and it was hard not to say goodbye.

On 13th September I received a letter from David Cameron, the Prime Minister: 'To see tens of thousands of people giving up their time to support London 2012 has been truly inspiring. As a ceremonies' volunteer you have made London 2012 stand out as much more than a sporting event, showing the best of British talent and creativity to the world. You and your fellow volunteers have been an essential ingredient in a remarkable summer that millions of people across the country have shared and will remember for a lifetime. You have sent an incredible message about the warmth, friendliness and can-do spirit of the United Kingdom right around the world.

'Whether this has been a new experience for you, or you have volunteered before, I hope the wonderful memories you have taken away from the Games will encourage you to continue to make a difference.'

The golden memories will live with me forever. I'm moved to continue to try to make a difference in whatever small way I can. Inspire a generation? Yes we did. More than one.

28 The Closing Credits

'Everyone makes a difference, but no one is bigger than the Olympics.' Steve Boyd.

Thousands of performers worked with hundreds of creative people behind the scenes to devise and deliver the Opening Ceremony. The official programme listed each and every one. It couldn't have been done without them. So, here they all are. Start the music and roll the credits...

Principals

Her Majesty The Queen, Jacques Rogge, President of the International Olympic Committee, Sebastian Coe, Chair, London 2012 Organising Committee, Rt Hon David Cameron MP, Prime Minister, Boris Johnson, Mayor of London, Rt Hon Jeremy Hunt MP, Secretary of State for Culture, Olympics, Media and Sport, Rt Hon Tessa Jowell MP, Shadow Minister for London and the Olympics, Rt Hon Sir Menzies Campbell MP, Liberal Democrat spokesman for London 2012, Rt Hon Don Foster MP, Liberal Democrat spokesperson for London 2012.

Artistic Team

Danny Boyle, Artistic Director, Mark Tildesley, Designer, Suttirat Anne Larlarb, Designer, Rick Smith for Underworld, Music Director, Frank Cottrell Boyce, Writer, Paulette Randall, Associate Director, Sascha Dhillon, Video Editor, Adam Gascoyne, Visual Effects Supervisor, Tracey Seaward, Producer, Toby Sedgwick, Movement Director, Temujin Gill, Choreographer, Sunanda Biswas, Co-Choreographer, Akram Kahn, Choreographer, Frank Cottrel Boyce, Writer, Kenrick H2O Sandy, Choreographer, Thomas Heatherwick, Cauldron Designer.

Principal Performers

Arctic Monkeys, Rowan Atkinson, David Beckham, Sir Tim Berners-Lee, Kenneth Branagh, Daniel Craig, Dockhead Choir, Dame Evelyn Glennie, The Kaos Signing Choir for Deaf and Hearing Children, Sir Paul McCartney, Mike Oldfield, Dizzee Rascal, Sir Simon Rattle, Elizabeth Roberts, JK Rowling, Emile Sande, Alex Trimble, Frank Turner and, of course, Her Majesty The Queen.

Performers

Prologue/Green and Pleasant Land – Frank Turner's Performers Tarrant Anderson, Emily Barker, Christopher Capewell, Simon Cripps, Anna Jenkins, Benjamin Lloyd, James Lockey, Ben Marwood, Matthew Nasir, Nigal Powell, Gillian Sandell, Joanne Silverston, Francis Turner **Movement Assistants** Polly Bennett, Laura Cubitt, Paul Fillipiak, Robin Guiver, Joyce Henderson, Paul Kasey, Eric Mallett, Diane Mitchell, Anna Morrissey, Emily Mytton **Brunels** Nicholas Beveney, Rikki Chamberlain, Richard James-Neale, Adam Jones, Dermot Keaney, Alex McNally, Jermaine Oguh, Phil Snowden, François Testory, Tam Ward **Animal Handlers** Lucy Atkinson, Daniel Brown, Mark Brown, Jill Clark, Nikki Cole, Joanne Coombes, Sophia Cordwell, Janette Duncan, Sally Dunsford, Katherine Eaglen, Ryan Evans, Gabby Farr, Roger Farr, Chris Few, Olivia Forrest, Malvyn Groves, Jenny Harris, Michael Hartland, Claire Hawthorn, Lisa Hawthorn, Samantha Jones, Holly Levinge, Sharon Rafferty, Elizabeth Rutherford, Paul Stanley, Danny Stevens, Gavin Stevens, Nara Stevens, Shane Stevens, Steve Tubbs, Christopher Tucker, Katy Tucker, Leigh Tucker, Kay Weston **Pandemonium – Drum Consultants** Paul Clarvis, Mike Dolbear, John Randall, Ralph Salmins **Drum Captains** Barnaby Archer, Oliver Blake, Daniel Bradley, Rebecca Celebuski, Jason Chowdhury, Jonathan Colgan, Oliver Cox, Fabio de Oliveira, Robert Eckland, Daniel Ellis, Richard Elsworth, David Holmes, Oliver Lowe, Nicola Marangoli, James O'Carroll, Gerard Rundell, Ramon Sherrington, Corrina Silvester, Alex Smith, Owain Williams, Justin Woodward **Suffragettes** Rachel Bingham, Madeleine Bowyer, Kaye Brown, Lucy Casson, Janine Craig, Luisa D'Ambrosio, Louise Davidson, Alison Kirrage, Tracey Lushington, Meg McNaughton-

Filipidis **Chimney Riders** Remy Archer, James Booth, Ben Brason, Graeme Clint, Chris Gage, Terry Lamb, Hasit Savani, **Ring Riders** Eric Adame, Jono Fee, Adam Laughton, David Rimmer **Stilt Walkers** Gina d'Angelo, Desiree Kongerod, Adrian South, Mark Tate.
Happy & Glorious – Stunt Performers Gary Connery, Mark Sutton **Helicopter Pilots** Sam Edding, Marc Wolff **Flag Team Leader** Squadron Leader Lambert, Royal Air Force, RAF Brize Norton **Flag Raisers** Corporal Adam, Royal Air Force, RAF Leuchars, Able Seaman Drew, Royal Navy, HMS Excellent, Able Seaman Class 2 Fasuba, Royal Navy, HMS Drake, Sergeant Reains, Army, 1 Irish Guards **Flag Bearers** Gunner Bateman, Army, Kings Troop Royal Horse Artillery, Flight Lieutenant Cadman, Royal Air Force, RAF Cranwell, Marine Edwards, Royal Navy, Commando Logistic Regiment, Colour Sergeant Hiscock, Royal Navy, 10 Training Squadron RM Poole, Corporal of the Horse Puddifoot, Army, Household Calvary Mounted Regiment, Sergeant Raval, Royal Air Force, RAF Halton, Corporal Robins, Army, 20 Transport Squadron, RLC, Lieutenant Weller, Royal Navy, DES Abbeywood.
Second to the right, and straight on till morning – Dance Captains/ Choreographic Assistants Tim Hamilton, Carolene Hinds, Sam Lane, Junior Laniyan, Yami Lovfenberg, Richard Pitt, Russell Sargeant, Alan Vincent **Assistant Dance Captains/ Choreographic Assistants** Damien Anyasi, Julian Essex-Spurrier, Jreena Green, Warren Heyes, Emiko Ishi, Rebekkah Knight, Eilidh Ross **Dancers** Afi Agyeman, Ben Ajose-Cutting, Lucy Alderman, Abdul Ali, Michelle Andrews, Yaa Appiah-Badu, Clara Bajado, Isaac Vitamin Baptiste, Hanna Bardall, Sasha Biloshitsky, Martha Carangi Bishoff, Nader Kayzar Boulila, Lexi Bradburn, Angelica Brewster, Abigail Brodie, Renata Carvalho, Loveday Chamberlain, Darren Charles, Alexandra-Louise Cheshire, Konrad Ciechanowski, Lisa Clarke, Lee Crowley, Olivia Daniell, AJ Daniels, Brenan Davies, Shannen Devlin, Sara Dos Santos, Kage Douglas, Kieran Edmonds, Shangomola Edunjobi, Victoria Ekundayo, Rachel Ensor, Adrian Falconer, Lulu Fish, Kara Fogerty, Maureen Francis, Steph Furness, Poppy Garton, Jennifer Gauss, Tarryn Gee, Kit Glennie, Phil W Green, Hattie Lauren Grover, Dominika Grzelak, Chloe Hallett, Selina Hamilton, Anna Haresnape, Cathryn-Anne Harries, Dani Harris-Walters, Samantha Haynes, Samantha Hayes, Denny Haywood, Keith Henderson, Sarah Hitch, Anthony Jackson, Hannah Jackson, Julie Jade, Peter Johnson, Jahmai Jam Fu Jones, Naa-Dei Kwashie, Simon Lee, Kamila Lewandowska, Amanda Lewis, Issie Lloyd, Daniel Aaron Louard, Devon Mackenzie-Smith, Antoine Marc, Katie Marcham, Laura Kate Marlow, Lindsay McAllister, Stella McGowan, Ross McLaren, Lee Meadows, Azara Meghie, Ella Mesma, Hayley Michelle, Simone Mistry-Palmer, Tashan Muir, Wolfgang Mandela Mwanje, Chris Neumann, Ellesha Newton, Emma Nightingale, Abena Z Noel, Joanne Odro, Lauren Okadigbo, Isabel Kayzar Olley, Olufunmilola Fumy Opeyemi, Emma O'Regan, Mark Parton, Jole PJ Pasquale, Ashley Patricks, Lee Payne, Karis Pentecost, Bethan Peters, Marianne Phillips, Tania Pieri, Yohemy Prosper, Andrea Queens, Adam Rae, Avalon Rathgeb, Alexis KA Roberts, Julien Roussel, Amy Rowbottom, Jack Saunders, Justin Saunders, Julie Schmidt Andreason, Jody Schroeder, Nathaniel Scott, Aaron Entropy Shah, Benjamin Shogbulu, Francesca Short, Victoria Shulungu, Ashley David Simon, Candice Szczepanski, Sorsha Talbot-Hunt, Benjamin Taylor-Shepherd, Aleta Thompson, Nefeli Tsiouti, Katrina Vasilieva, Julie Vibert, Gavin Vincent, Keigan Westfield, Jezz-Lee Wood, Carly Woodridge, Katie Wymark, Adelle Young **Aerialist Captain** Matt Costain, Jono Fee, Robyn Miranda Simpson **Mary Poppins Aerialists** Katherine Arnold, Helen Ball, Anna Serena Bindra, Teresa Callan, Tamlyn Victoria Clark, Vanessa Cook, Pippa Coram, Laura Cork, Clare Elliott, Hege Eriksdatter Østefjells, Kimberley Eyles, Naomi Giffen, Sophie Page Hall, Maria Hippolyte, Allie Ho Chee, Marada Manussen, Victoria McManus, Tori Moone, Collette Morrow, Valerie Murzak, Michaela O'Connor, Nikki O'Hara, Claire O'Neill, Catrin Osborne, Amy Panter, Jennifer Paterson, Dela Seward, Zoey Tedstill, Philippa Vafadari, Natalie Verhaegen, Annette Walker **Nightmare Aerialists** Cornelius Atkinson, Matt Costain, Abagail Evans, Lucy Francis, Jack Horner, Kate Sanderson, Anthony Weiss **Trampoline Consultant** David-Roy Wood **Trampolinists** Nathan Adams, Anton Anderson, Libbie Brown, Cole Burrell, Tye Crawford, Roman Woody Elliott, Samantha Katkevica, Jessie Koon, Keziah Livingston, China Mattis, Logan Maxwell, Thomas Mitchelmore, Iona Moir, Parise Simpson, Francesca Sweet, Lewis Walsh **Elevating Bed Children** Leo Ayres, Yaris Lee-Lawrence, T'Khai Phillips, Fleur Sweet **Skaters** Amanda Valentine Constantinou, Leroy Ricardo Jones **Puppetry Consultants** Mark Down, Nick Barnes **Lead Puppeteers** Andrew Dawson, Tom Espiner, Sean Myatt, Rob Tygner **Puppeteers** Derek Arnold, Caroline Bowman, Ashleigh Cheadle, Fiona Clift, Iestyn Evans, Sean Garratt, David Grewcock, Brian Herring, Matthew Hutchinson, Rachel Leonard, Irena Stratieva, Ivan Thorley, Jon Whitten

Interlude Mr Atkinson's Rival Performer, Stephen Campbell Moore.
frankie & june say... Thanks Tim – Dance Captains/ Choreographic Assistants Bradley Charles, Danielle Rhimes Lecointe, Skytilz Mantey, Bruno Perrier, Nadia Sohowan **Assistant Dance Captains/ Choreographic Assistants** Jenni Bailey-Rae, Brendan Syxx Isaac, Charlene Mini Willets **Assistant Dance Captains** Gemma Hoddy, Nathaniel Sweetboy Impraim-Jones, Kofi Mingo, Theo Oloyade, Eloise Sheldon, Duwane Taylor, Mary Weah, Serena Williams **Dancers** Danella Abraham, Stephen Aspinall, Lindon Barr, Minica Beason, Conan Belletty, Karen Bengo, Ivan Blackstock, Filippo Calvagno, Simeon Campbell, Kieran Daley-Ward, Dominic Spin Daniel, Kerri De Aguiar, Kloe Dean, Israel Donowa, Odilia Egyiawan, Magnus Einang, Shannelle Fergus, Sam Field, Sam Fleet, Melissa Freire, Jemma Geanaus, Darron Gifty, Lucy Gilbert, Jeanette Gonzalez, Natasha Gooden, Jade Hackett, Clarissa Hagan, Carrie Hanson, Todd Holdsworth, Corinne Holt, Christina Ibironke, Rachel Kay, Mila Lazar, Kayla Lomas, Jaye Marshall, Miha Matevzic, Yolanda Newsome, Angela Nurse, Kelechi Nwanokwu, Andry Oporia, Holly Penny, Karim Perrineau, Jack Pointer-Mackenzie, Chantelle Prince, Kieron Providence, Michelle Queen, Serina Raymond, Nimmer Riaz, Tia Sackey, Alex Schoendorf, Michael Simon, Tomas Simon, Letitia Simpson, Stephan Sinclair, Tashan Sinclair-Doyle, Matt Sussman, Sian Taylor, Jodie Tye, Robyn Walker, Josh Wharmby, Dwain Talent White, Emily Williams, Aaron Witter, Zehra Zem **Starmen Aerialists** Eric Adame, Remy Archer, Alex Poulter, Ted Sikström **Power Skippers** James Booth, Ben Brason, Graeme Clint, Jono Fee, Chris Gage, Jack Helme, Terry Lamb, Dan Lannigan, Adam Laughton, Hannah Lawton, David Rimmer, Samantha Rockett, Hasit Savani, Steve Williams, Hadyn Wiseman **Zorb Performers** Conor Kenny, Rachael Letsche, Ahmahd Thomas, Kylie Walker.
Abide With Me – Dancers Jose Agudo, Kristina Alleyne, Sade Alleyne, Azzurra Ardovini, Helena Arenbergerova, Inma Asensio, Eva Assayas, Eulalia Ayguade Farro, Aymeric Bichon, Patsy Browne-Hope, Amy Butler, Magdaléna Caprdová, Melodie Cecchini, Rudi Cole, Vittoria De Ferrari Sapetto, Pauline De Laet, Laura De Vos, Yentl De Werdt, Kamala Devam, Vanessa Guevara, Thomasin Gülgeç, Kenny Wing Tao Ho, Reiss Jeram, Martijn Kappers, Matthias Kass, Nicholas Keegan, Sung Hoon Kim, KJ Lawson, Elias Lazaridis, Yen-Ching Lin, Katie Love, TJ Lowe, Colas Lucot, Katie Lusby, Maya Masse, Joachim Maudet, Cherish Menzo, Rhiannon Elena Morgan, Stephen Moynihan, Andrej Petrovic, Nikoleta Rafaelisová, Nicolas Ricchini, Chanel Selleslach, Gemma Elizabeth-Sarah Shrubb, Ryu Suzuki, Devaraj Thimmaiah, Teerachai Thobumrung, Melissa Ugolini, Lenka Vagnerová, Lisa Welham, Josh Wille.
Bike a.m. – Keyboard Player James Ford **Let the Games Begin** - Flag Team Leader, Raisers and Bearers (see Happy & Glorious).
There is a Light That Never Goes Out – Drum Consultant Paul Clarvis **Drum Captains** (see Pandemonium).
And in the end... Paul McCartney's Band Rusty Anderson, Abe Laboriel Jr, Brian Ray, Paul Wickens.

Executive Team
Bill Morris, Director of Ceremonies, Education & Live Sites, Martin Green, Head of Ceremonies, Catherine Ugwu, Executive Producer, Production, Stephen Daldry, Executive Producer, Creative, Hamish Hamilton, Executive Producer, Broadcast & TV, Mark Fisher, Executive Producer.

Production Team: Creative
Aerial & Special Skills Phil Hayes, Aerial & Special Skills Consultant, Alex Poulter, Aerial & Special Skills Associate **Audio Visual & Broadcast** Justine Catterall, Head of Audio Visual, Adam Dadswell, Presentation Manager, David Watson, Digital Media Manager, Lizzie Pocock, Audio Visual Department Coordinator, Charlotte Andrews, Archive Coordinator, Lisa Brown, Digital Media Assistant, Emma Gaffney & Damien Pawle, Assistant Video Editors, Steven Harris, Video Documentation, Graham Carlow, Photographer, Matt Askem, Video Screens Director, Tracey Askem, Video Screens Production Assistant, Jane Jackson, Broadcast Liaison Manager **Bike Choreography** Bob Haro, Bike Choreographer, Paul Hughes, Bike Project Manager **Casting** Gillian Schofield, Cast Manager (Professional), Sarah Chambers, Andrew Ramsbottom and Jane Salberg, Cast Coordinators (Professional), Penny Davies, Cast Coordinator (Professional & Volunteers), Rhian Davies, Assistant Cast Coordinator (Professional), Sarah Murray, Casting Assistant (Professional), Solomon Wilkinson, Casting Assistant (Volunteers) , Nichola Bouchard & Katy Bryant, Company Managers, Sara-Ellen Williams, Cast Manager (Volunteers), Sara Berutto,

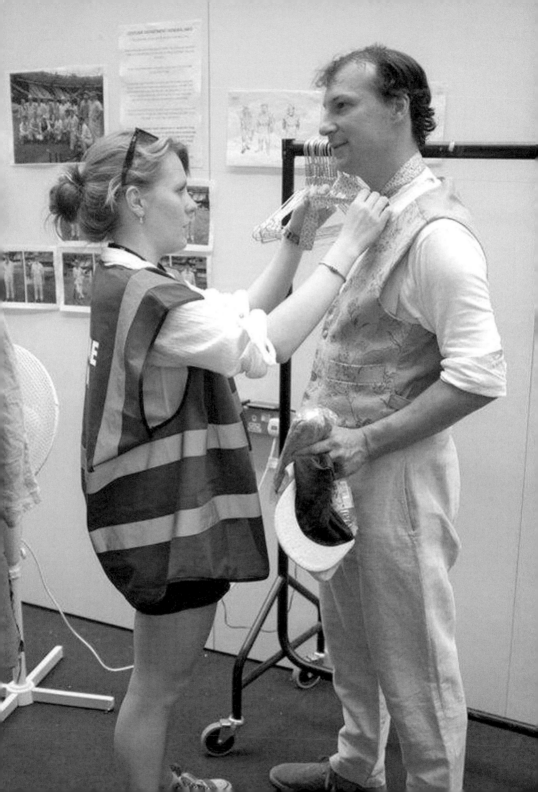

Maz Bryden, Diane Leach, Trish McClenaghan & Laura Windows, Senior Cast Coordinators (Volunteers), Barbara Lisicki, Access Manager, Michael Foley, Glenda Genovesi, Vanessa Griffiths, Helen Lam & Haitham Ridha, Cast Coordinators (Volunteers), Jenny Rogers, Cast Coordinator (Schools), Cheryl Galbraith, Martin Malone, Lesley Raymer & Kieran Shekoni, Assistant Cast Coordinators (Volunteers), Genevieve Baker, Hannah Caple, Joanna Griffith, Ellena Jones, Andrea Mangerie & Diana Prociv, Casting Assistants (Volunteers) **Costume, Hair & Make-up** Tahra Zafar, Head of Costume, Hair & Make-up, Lorraine Ebdon & Anna Lau, Costume Supervisors, Matthew George, Hair & Wigs Design Supervisor, Amber Sibley, Make-up Design Supervisor, Katie Newitt, Costume Department Coordinator, Lesley-Ann Halls, Costume Department Volunteers Coordinator, Fiona Parker, Assistant Costume Supervisor, Caroline Brett, Senior Costume Buyer, Rebecca Mills, Samantha Langridge & Charlotte McGarrie, Costume Buyers, Vanessa Bastyan, Costume Workshop Fabrication Supervisor, Angie Pledge, Costume Workshop Supervisor, Elaine Battye, Costume Workshop Senior Costumier , Becky Johnson & Thea Keenan, Costume Workshop Senior Fabricators , Cheryl Mason, Costume Breakdown Supervisor, Nicola Beales, Helena Bennett & Robin McGrorty, Costume Workshop Assistants, Maisie McCubbin, Costume Workshop Junior, Olima Rolf, Creative Division Assistant, Jamie Mendonça, Garment Stock Logistics & Driver **Lighting & Audio Design** Patrick Woodroffe, Lighting Designer, Bobby Aitken, Audio Designer, Adam Bassett, Associate Lighting Designer, Scott Willsallen, Audio Systems Designer **Design** Ala Lloyd, Design Studio Manager, Emma Child, Design Studio Coordinator, Basmah Arafeh, Rebecca Brower & Hatty Morris, Design Studio Assistants, James Collins, Art Director, Anita Dhillon, Graphic Designer, Brendan Houghton, Storyboard Artist **Mass Movement** Steve Boyd, Head of Mass Movement Choreography & Parade of Athletes, Gina Martinez, Mass Movement Choreographer (Thanks Tim), Rocky Smith, Mass Movement Choreographer (Second to the right), Nikki Woollaston, Mass Movement Choreographer (Green and Pleasant Land), Nathan Wright, Mass Movement Choreographer, Steve Boyd, Mass Movement Choreographer (Pandemonium), Paul Neaum, Manager (Parade of Athletes), Soha Frem and Bryn Walters, Mass Cast Leaders, Ben Clare, Laura-Anne Gill, Vicki Igbokwe, Jeanefer Jean-Charles, Natasha Khamjani, Katie Pearson, Barbarana Pons and Wendy Steatham, Mass Cast Coordinators, Edwina Allen, Taylor Anthony, Rachelle Conroy, Marianne Howard, Sean Mulligan, Brenda Jane Newhouse, Darragh O'Leary, Joseph Pitcher, Simone Sault, Carla Trim-Vamben, Claira Vaughan and Jayde Westaby, Mass Cast Assistants **Music** Peter Cobbin, Allan Jenkins & Kirsty Whalley, Associate Music Directors, Mike Gillespie, Music Supervisor Underworld, Martin Koch, Music Supervisor, Tom Jenkins, Associate Music Supervisor, Clare Hazeldine, Music Department Coordinator, Nick Gilpin, Audio Supervisor, Mikey J Asante, Music Editor for Kenrick Sandy **Producers** Claire Terri, Associate Producer, Joan Schneider, Production Manager (Opening Ceremony Films & Bike a.m.), Hallam Rice-Edwards, Production Coordinator, Alex Barrett & Lex Donovan, Production Assistants, Kaz Hill, Headline Talent Manager, Sarah Casey, Headline Talent Coordinator, Danielle Buckley, Headline Talent Production Assistant **Publications** Fiona Richards, Publications Manager, Jess Anstee, Publications Coordinator **Stage Management** Sam Hunter, Production Stage Manager, Guido Foa, Deputy Production Stage Manager, Carola Altissimo, Liz Copp, Debbie Cronshaw,Hilary Davis, Ben Delfont, Anthony Field, Duane Harewood, Marianne Kuehner, Claire Loftus, Jordan Noble-Davies, Sam Pepper, Helen Smith, Ian Stephenson, Jorge Tapia, Peter Wakeman & Matt Watkins, Senior Stage Managers Holly Anderson, Miriam Bertaina, Abigail Dankwa, Lee Fowler, Miguel de la Fuente Graciani, Rhiannon Harper, Gareth Hulance, Bianca Jones, Dominique Pierre-Louis, Ryan Quelch & Gemma Thomas, Stage Managers, Abigail Mills, Associate Stage Manager, Julia Whittle, Show Caller **Video Design & Visual Effects** Leo Warner, Video Creative Director, Lysander Ashton, Video Designer, Jonathon Lyle, Associate Video Designer, Zsolt Balogh, Christian Debney & Lawrence Watson, Video Animation Directors, Joseph Pierce, Video Design Editor, Tim Caplan, VFX Producer, Kaveh Montazer and Mervyn New, VFX Artists, Noga Alon Stein, VFX Coordinator, Mark Grimmer, Video Designer, Remi Harris, Project Manager, Akhila Krishnan, Assistant Video Designer, Jessika Strataki, Assistant Designer, M.I.E. Ltd, Animation (Computer Game House) , Derrick Ligas, Animator, Quentin Dachy, Animator, Nick Simmons, Programmer, Benjamin Pearcy, Programmer, James Long, Media Manager, James Roxburgh, Company Manager, Aneil Karia, Director (Live Action Shoots), Molly Einchcomb, Art Director (Live Action Shoots), Megan Kearney, Assistant to the Video Designer, Katie Jackson, Production Assistant, Marco Sandeman, Animator, Roxy Harris, Composer (60 Second Countdown), Vanessa Whyte, Director of Photography

(Countdowns), Chloe Thompson, Director of Photography (Title Cards), Jonathan Harris, Director of Photography (Title Cards), Stuart Bentley, Director of Photography (Title Cards), Pete Fowler, Artist (Street Art House), PARLEE ERZ, Artist (Street Art House), Demane, Artist (Street Art House), Pure Evil, Artist (Street Art House), Cedar Lewisohn, Artist (Street Art House), The Folio Society (Letterpress Shakespeare), Joel K. Rainsley, Gaffer (Title Cards), Andrew Woodcock, Grip (Title Cards), Emil Davidov, Camera Assistant (Title Cards), Henry Lockyer, Camera Assistant (Title Cards), Libby Spencer, Production Assistant (Title Cards), Robyn Clogg, Production Assistant (Title Cards) **Creative & Executive Administration** Tina Jaffray, Senior Administrator (Creative) , Jennifer Hutt, Executive Assistant to the Head of Ceremonies and Executive Producer, Kate Hinchliffe, Executive Assistant to the Producers, Nicky Cheung, Personal Assistant to Director of Ceremonies, Education & Live Sites, Annie Corrigan, Protocol Manager, Veronique Haddelsey, Protocol Coordinator, Alison Wade, Script Manager, Clare Ellis, Administration Assistant **Internship Placements** Lexi Boynton, Colm Dunhrosa, Jacqueline Field, Elizabeth Howe, Lexi Hyland, Anisha Patel, Janita Patel, Katie Radha Osterholzer,Claire Thorn and Daniel Vincze.

Production Team: Technical

Technical Executive Piers Shepperd, Technical Director, Andrew Morgan, Senior Administrator (Technical), Elena Dogani, Production Coordinator (Technical Contracts), Ross Nicholson, Production Assistant (Technical) **Aerial & Special Projects** James Lee, Technical Manager (Aerial & Special Projects), Glenn Bolton, Senior Production Manager (Capital Works & Special Projects), Luke Mills, Production Manager (Pyro, Flame & SFX), Edwin Samkin, Deputy Production Manager (Pyro, Flame & SFX), Sammy Samkin, Production Manager (Fireworks), Nick Porter, Deputy Production Manager (Aerialist Training), Paul English, Deputy Production Manager (Show Vehicles), Anna Cox, Assistant Manager (Special Projects), Emma Neilson, Production Coordinator, Nick Levitt, Production Manager (Torch Journey) **Audio, Comms & Broadcast** Chris Ekers, Senior Production Manager (Audio & Comms), James Breward, Deputy Production Manager (Comms, CCTV & Mass Cast IEM), Alison Dale, Deputy Production Manager (Principal Performer IEM & Wireless Mics), Trevor Beck, Audio Playback, Richard Sharratt, Audio FOH, Hannah Charlesworth, Deputy Production Manager (Backline) , Steve Watson, Audio Monitor Engineer, Steve Williams, Audio Broadcast Systems Engineer, Andy Rose, Audio Broadcast Sound Supervsior **Lighting, AV & Power** Nick Jones, Technical Manager (Lighting, AV & Power), Andy Loveday, Senior Production Manager (Lighting), Ben Pitts, Production Manager (Lighting Set LX), Dan Sloane, Production Manager (Video & LED Screens), Tim Routledge, Senior Lighting Operator, Andrew Voller, Lighting Operator, Pryderi Baskerville, Lighting Operator, Lee Threlfall, Set Lighting Production LX, Dave Bartlett, Project Manager (Pixels) , Mike Dawes, Deputy Project Manager (Pixels) **Staging & Scenic** Jeremy Lloyd, Technical Design & Staging Manager, Nigel Mousley, Senior Production Manager (Staging & Scenic), Steve Richards, Senior Production Manager (FOP), Chris Clay and Dave Williams, Production Managers (Staging & Scenic), Kieran McGivern, Deputy Production Manager (Staging & Scenic), Scott Seaton, Deputy Production Manager (FOP), Lianne Bruce, Production Coordinator (Staging & Scenic), Johanna Eaden, Production Assistant (Staging & Scenic), Tom White, CAD Manager, Andrew Bailey, Ben O'Neill and Philip Wilding, CAD Operators, Moose Curtis, Magnus Harding and Kevin Jones, Staging Crew Chiefs, Peter English, Head Carpenter, Phil Perry, Staging Crew Chief (Rehearsal Venue), Ray Bogle, Field of Play Crew Chief, Mike Grove, Stage Manager (Main Stage) , Rasti Bartek, Aran Chadwick and Glyn Trippick, Consultant Engineers, Richard Bentley and John Prentice, CAD Consultants **Technical Services** Scott Buchanan, Technical Manager (Technical Services & Special Projects), Annette Stock, Production Manager (Schedule, Crew & Contractors), Jess Noakes, Production Coordinator (Technical Services), Dave Wilkie, Production Manager (Plant & AP), Matthew Beardsley, Production Coordinator (Crew & Logistics), Terry Hubble, Production Staff Quartermaster, Laura Lloyd, Grant Peters and Kate Ramsey, Production Staff Runners **Workshops & Props** Ted Irwin, Technical Manager (Workshop & Props), Dan Shipton, Production Manager (Props), Pam Nichol, Deputy Production Manager (Props & Rehearsals), Eric Hickmott, Production Manager (Workshop), Rhiannon Newman-Brown, Production Coordinator (Workshop), Nick Bloom, Deputy Production Manager (Carpentry), Jo Cole, Deputy Production Manager (Props, Crew & Volunteer Chief), Sherri Hazzard, Deputy Workshop Manager (Props), Sally Christopher and Sean Flynn, Production Coordinator (Props), Mark Moore,, Deputy Production Manager (Metal

Fabrication), Will Sumpter, Deputy Workshop Manager (Props), Steve Dart and John McGarrigle, Props, LX, John Pratt, Workshop Coordinator & Buyer, Dave Blacker, Props Coordinator and Crew & Volunteer Chief, Tanya Bond, Props Buyer, Stephen Jeffrey, Crew & Volunteer Chief, Sarah Whiting, Workshop Volunteer Coordinator, Krissy Lee, Technical Assistant **Internship Placements** Laura Rixson and Chris Tani.

Production Team: Operations

Operations Executive Mik Auckland, Director of Operations and Health & Safety, Adrian Bourke, Senior Manager (Venues & Facilities), Joseph Frisina, Senior Operations Manager, Donna McMahon, Senior Manager (Logistics), Neil Russell, Senior Manager (Health, Safety, Welfare & Medical), Hannah Dorey, Senior Administrator, Nathan Farquharson, Logistics Coordinator, Jacinta Gee, Operations Coordinator, Luke Woodham, Venues & Facilities Coordinator, Alice Larmer, Logistics Production Assistant **Health, Safety, Welfare & Medical Show Operations & Scheduling** Conrad Schwarz, Deputy Manager (Health & Safety), Sally-Ann Dod, Health & Safety Advisor, Inductions & Contractor Liaison, Sarah Jones, Medical Services Manager, Danielle Bromley, Steve Brown and Alan Law, Health & Safety Consultants, Samantha Coles, Coordinator (Health & Safety), Dean Jewel, Show Operations & Schedule Manager, Paddy Bettington, Show Operations & Schedule Assistant, Leah Harris and Sam Mount, Schedule Production Assistants Sally Downey, Health & Safety Inductions Assistant, **Logistics** Kirsty Thomson, Operations Manager (Catering, Cleaning & Waste), Julia Bowditch and Lynsey Jackson, Coordinators (Catering, Cleaning & Waste), Rebecca Fletcher, Sandra Goetz, Gareth Lewis, Ria Maycox, Alexander Thomas, Sarah Yates, Production Assistants (Catering, Cleaning & Waste), Melissa McVeigh, Operations Manager (Accreditation), Melanie East, Tyler Ffrench and Vincenzo Ianniello, Coordinators (Accreditation), Karen Cosgree and Emily Whitaker, Production Assistants (Accreditation), Laura Marakowits, Operations Manager (Volunteers), Shelly Donaghy, Coordinator (Volunteers), Grace Birkbeck, Laura Salvatore and Pete Thomson, Production Assistants (Volunteers), Valie Voutsa, Operations Manager (Accommodation & Travel), Marie Albrecht, Assistant Manager (Accommodation & Travel) [Staff], Leticia Gonzalez-Galvez, Assistant Manager (Accommodation & Travel)[Principal Performers], Eloise Crevier and Eirini Zoi, Production Assistants (Accommodation), Georgina Huxstep, Operations Manager (Transport & Fleet), Sarah Hinchelwood, Assistant Manager (Children's Transport), Matthew Howlett, Assistant Manager (Fleet & Site Vehicles), Kate Blomfield and Asha Slade, Coordinators (Transport), Simon Galicki, Laura Gallen, Charlotte Howley, Emma Lester and Emily Webber, Production Assistants (Transport), Debbie Paul, Operations Manager (Principal Performer Logistics), Craig Lear, Green Room Manager, Anna-Maria Kreuzer, Coordinator (Principal Performer Logistics), Victoria Sandford, Kieran Smith and Ed Woodhouse, Production Assistants (Principal Performer Logistics) **Venues & Facilities** Russel Bedford, Operations Manager (Workshop & Rehearsal Venues), Pete Williams, Assistant Manager (Rehearsal Venues), William Francis, Coordinator (Workshop & Rehearsal Venues), Sonya Gandras, Coordinator (Rehearsal Venues), Billy Cheeseman, Ralph Cullum and Charlotte Jordan, Production Assistants (Venues), Robert Madeley, Site Assistant (Rehearsal Venue), Lucinda Erskine-Crum, Operations Manager (Olympic Park), Al Parkinson, Assistant Manager (Olympic Stadium), Toni Stockham, Coordinator (Olympic Stadium), David Gregory, Assistant Manager (Compound), Marcia Connell and Will Gunnett, Coordinators (Compound), Robert Schnaiberg, Assistant Manager (MDS, Storage & Freight), Sarah Adams and Olivia Pole-Evans, Site Assistants (MDS, Storage & Freight), Lottie Cresswell, Assistant Manager (Common Domain, Chui-Yee Cheung, Coordinator (Common Domain), Ryan Tate, Coordinator (Venue), Lily Sutton, Production Assistant (Venue), Holly Gregory, Compound Assistant (Stadium), Trish Murphy, Venue Manager (Eton Manor), Claire Ewings, Assistant Venue Manager (Eton Manor), Kayleigh Dean and Megan Wise, Venue Assistants (Eton Manor), Alina Murcott, Project Manager (Water Polo Arena), Maddie Cupples, Assistant Manager (Water Polo Arena), Emma-Jane Cotsell, Project Assistant (Guard of Honour) **Internship Placements** Tanisha Malkki, Dimitry Ragozin and Bryony Mitchison.

Production Team: Administration

Administration Executive Sara Donaldson, Joint Chief Operating Officer, Chris Laue, Joint Chief Operating Officer, Dion Carter, Finance & Commercial Director **Finance** Andrew Slater, Financial Controller, Veronica Bailey, Management Accountant, Kathleen Anderson, Production Accountant, Mladen Ivezic and Farishta Yousuf, Senior Purchase Ledger Administrators, Hayden Porritt,

Purchase Ledger **Human Resources** Chidimma Chukwu, Finance, Payroll & HR Clerk, Rebecca Janiszewska, Human Resources Manager, Geraldine Daly, Derek Taylor and Cherise Scotland, Human Resources Coordinators, Selina Donald, Executive Assistant to Chief Operating Officer, Christianne Gandossi, Internship Placement **Information Technology** Campbell McKilligan, Head of IT & Comms, Dilraj Sachdev, Database Manager, Allan Whatmough, Application Developer, Gyula Keresztely-Krall, Systems Administrator, Grant Cassin, Mac Specialist, Abdullah Al Mamoon, Regis Joffre,Rica Mackay, Irfan Mohammed and Khizzar Younis, Desktop Engineers, Marita Samuel, IT Department Coordinator, Mick Turvey, Service Desk Manager, **Legal** Will Hutchinson, Head of Legal (Culture, Ceremonies, Education & Live Sites), Chris Loweth, Senior Ceremonies Lawyer, Shirin Foroutan, Senior Ceremonies Legal Advisor, **Procurement & Contracts** Simon Aspland, Head of Procurement & Contracts, Natalie Foster, Robert Graham, Ilyas Rahman, Stephanie Tillman and Marlon Trotman, Procurement & Contracts Administrators Monique Pennycooke and Rachel Williams, Procurement & Contracts Coordinators **Ceremonies, Education & Live Sites** Caroline Ainley, Financial Control Accountant, Anna Blackman, Programme Manager, Mark Smith, Finance Manager, Kristina Richmond, Procurement Manager. **London 2012 Ceremonies Ltd** Scott Givens, Managing Director **Board of Directors** Scott Givens (Chair), Sara Donaldson, Martin Green, Chris Laue, Bill Morris, Catherine Ugwu, Frank McCormack (non-executive), Alan Robertson (non-executive).
London 2012 Ceremonies Committee Bill Morris (Chair), Charles Allen, Doug Arnott, Jackie Brock-Doyle, Seb Coe, Paul Deighton, Martin Green, Will Hutchinson, Catherine Ugwu, Neil Wood.

Production Credits

Acknowledgements Helle Absalonsen, Omer Ali, Tom Balkwill, Nick Barnes, Neil Blair, Barbara Broccoli, Mark Down, Richard Curtis, Richard Folkes, Kye Forte, Al Gurdon, Su-Man Hsu, Hugh Hudson, Sir Nicholas Hytner, Geoff Jukes, Lois Keidan, Joe Lawlor, Chris Livett, Jamie Longstreet, Daniel Marks, Father Alan McLean, Lucy Moffat, Christine Molloy, Paul O'Reilly, Pankhurst Family, Geoff Posner, Lord David Puttnam of Queensgate, Steve Rushbrooke, Mark Rylance, Sir Nicholas Serota, Amanda Softly, Patrick Stalder, Andy Stephens, Jane Thompson, Stephanie Tillman, Raymond Boyd, Andrew Lennie **Audience Pixel Content** Created by Crystal CG, Al Liddell, Andrew Gooch, Andrew McKinna, Cath Elliott, Chai Ke Fu, Cheng Xinrong, Chris Ratcliffe, Daniel Balzer, Ed Cookson, Ed Fyfe, Fillipo Bianchi, Giles Maunsell, Henry Flitton, Jamie Shiels, Jing Huang, Joe Winston, Jude Greenaway, Kate Dawkins, Liam Corner, Liberty Dakin, Liu Jian, Liu Yi, Mark Lindner, Martin Stacey, Neil Evan, Nicol Scott, Pete Mellor, Robert Grieves, Shi Cheng, Shi Yan, Will Case, Zhang Jianzhi, Zhang Zhihong, Zhu Keming, Zsuzsanna Voros **Audio Visual** Sim Canetty-Clarke, Mark Grimmer, Akhila Krishnan, Tobias Lloyd, Tom Moss, Max Tipple **Casting** Miles Allen, Phil Aller, Alexander Anderson, Steve Artus, Mark Atkins, Timothy Ayres, Jon Barnett, Joel Bennett, Adam Bessell, Davinder Bhatia, Julian Blackler, Jurek Blaszczak, Ruth Bradford, Tony Bradford, Adam Bradshaw Clive Brennan, Leo Brennan, Ellis Bright, John Brooks, Ben Broomfield, Jake Brown, Tracy Brown, Martin Burden, Amos Burke, Sarah Burns, Mario Carelse, Gary Carter, Vanessa Celosse, Johann Chan, Alex Coleborn, Martyn Cooper, Paulo Cotrim, Alex Crawford, Collarbone Ron Crawley, Lucy Cuppleditch, Aram Delgado, Robert Desmond, Bruce Dixon, Joel Down, Jess Duffy, Danny Dwyer, Clive East, Ryan Elcock, Jake Ellis, Joe Embrey, Jaygun Evans, Chris Fishburn, Alaina Fletcher, Jason Forde, Robbie Francis, Ian Franklin, Lloyd Gale-Ward, Jamie Girven, Colin Goodman, Steve Gower, Steve Green, Dayle Guy, Ryan Hall, Simon Hall, Scott Hamlin, Sebastian Denver Hejna, James Heyes, James Hitchcox, Tom Holmes, Richard Hoult, Michael Hoy, Sarah Hughes, Tamas Jano Paul Jeffries, Ronnie Johnson, Martin Gareth Jones, Oliver Jones, Ben Joyce, Tom Justice, Kate Kartal, Ho Ke, Dina Koulama, Elaine Lancaster, Isaac Lesser, Ian Lloyd, John MacDonald, Joe Maher, Chris Mahoney, Lily Makurah, Bob Manchester, Ben Manuel, Jack Marchant, Luke Marchant, Caroline Maxted, Steve Maxted, Peter McDermott, Alan McKenzie, Paul Mckeown, John McMillan, Paul Meacher, Jeff Meerdink, Tom Milham, Ric Moore, Tian Moses, Ross Nelson, Justin Neville-Rolfe, Terry O'Connell, James O'Neill, Norbert Onodi, Jeremy GW O'Sullivan, PJ O'Sullivan, Tom Palmer, Vince Parkes, Vladimir Parshikov, Anthony Pearson, Keelan Phillips, Sean Pointing, Jason Pooley, Matt Priest, Billy Purcell, Martin Purvis, Kit Rackham, Ada Raczynska, Morag Reavley, Yasemin Richards, Natalia Rodionova, Nathan Rowe, Daniel Rudd, James V2 Samuel, Zack Shaw, Sandra Simon, Louie Smith, Adrian Spender, John Spicer, Stan, Tika Stefano, Craig Stevens, Paul Stewart, Alan Swain, Jon Taylor, Craig Teague, Stephen Thurgood, Neil Tunnicliffe, Kelvin Waterman, Claira Watson

Parr, Andrew Waud, Mark Webb, Stefan Weidmann, Lola Karolina Welch, Mark Welch, Stephanie Wheatley, James White, Michelle Wilkinson, Gareth Wilson, Joshua Wyles **Chaperones** Marsia Charman, Mary Chilton, Meredith Coombes, Ann Cranmer, Natalie Emuss, Pauline Glanville, Sonal Jeram, Dineshkumar Jeram, Melanie Sargeant, Daniel Twine, Deborah Wright **Costume** Debbie Boyd, Sue Crawshaw, David David, Emma Hardy, Yasemin Kascioqlu, Sasha Keir, Angela Kelly and all her team, Nasir Mazhar, Margarida Santos, Neal Scanlan, Christopher Shannon, Will Skeet, Jane Smith, Michael Van der Ham, Mervyn Wallace, Marion Weise, Chris Winter **Costume, Hair and Make-up Specialist Crew** Nikki Belding, Jennifer Barnard, Elizabet Berrgren, Sylvaine Champeau, Katy Cherry, Charlie Cooper, Andrea Cracknell, Sarah Deans, Ian Denson, Emma Fairfield, Liam Farrelly, Leon Fernholdt, Pam Foster, Mandy Gold, Karen Gurney, Kit Hall, Gustav Hoegen, Gemma Hoff, Lauren Isles, Lizzie Judd, Marialena Kapotopoulou, Adam Keenan, Alexandra Kharibian, Shelley King, Sukie Kirk, Spencer Kitchen, Charlotte Lander, Josh Lee, Melanie Lenihan, Morna Macpherson, Cat McLoughlin, Kimberley Murray Kirsteen Naismith, Emily Newbold, Jo Nielsen, Tanya Noor, Jess O'Shea, Rosie Octon, Jon Revell, Mary Richardson, Milo Sabariz, Amy Sachon, Joe Scott, Emma Sheffield, Charlotte Simpson, Elaine Solomon, Helen Spink, Mariella Spoto, Kerry Spring, Guy Stevens, Jane Stoner, David Stringer, Janine Summerhayes, Wendy Topping, Sékou Traoré, Jo Tuplin, Gemma Vincent, Aurelie Vogt, Laura Watkins, Nicola Webley, Julia Wilson, Laura Wisinger, Jenna Wyatt **Design** Gerry Bunzl, Bec Chippendale, Charlie Cobb, Nick Evans, Gina Fields, Will Fricker, Tom Godfrey, George Guest, Karolina Kendall-Bush, Bronislawa Pratt, Jacqueline Pyle, Lorraine Richer, Dennis Schnegg, Martin Sutherland **Stage Management Specialist Crew** Eleanor Butcher, Grace Cameron, Stuart Campbell, Shaun Corcoran, Henrietta Curtis, Anthony Earles, Chloe French, Gemma Friel, George Hims, Scarlett Hooper, Osnat Koblenz, Tom Leggat, Dan Miller, Connor Mitchell, Zanna Orage, Georgia Paget, Christopher Mark Smith, Phillipa Sutcliffe, Sarah Sweet, PK Thummukgool **Technical Specialist Crew**, Guy Aldridge, Chris Aram, Gibson Arpino, Hamish Bamford, Mike Becket, Malcolm Birkett, Mike Bownds, Francesca Boyle, Belinda Clisham, Gary Connery, Terry Cook, David Patrick Emerson, Dan Evans, Jonathan Finch, Andy Fugle, Dario Fusco, Jason Gilbert, Ian Glassbrook, Chelsey Goord, Andrew Graves, Alex Hatton, William Hayman, Martin Hinkins, Patrick Hollingsworth, Brendan Houghton, Linford Hudson, Hannah Knox, Ingrid Mackay, Cattrina Mott, Nick Mumford, Sienna Murdoch, Rebecca Nelson, Jem Nicholson, Stephanie Pasiewicz, Chris Patton, Pip Ratcliffe, Jo Savill, Simon Sayer, Michael Scott, Elliot Sinclair, Anna Stamper, Erica Stokes, Pauline Stone, Mark Sutton, Jamie Taylor, Chris Tidmarsh, Tim Timmington, Elizabeth Vass, Joe Vassallo, Frances Waddington, Zoe Walker, Rachel Walsh, Oliver Welsh, Sharn Whitehead, Andrew Wilkinson, Jack Willis, Marc Wolff, Robert Woodley, Richard Young **Broadcast & Film Broadcast** BBC, CTV Outside Broadcast, Bill Morris, Technical Producer, Emily Cobb, Outside Broadcast, Production Manager Done & Dusted, Melanie Fletcher, Producer, Barrie Dodd, Camera, Supervisor Olympic Broadcasting Services **Isles of Wonder / Happy & Glorious** Produced by the BBC Lisa Osborne, Adam Gascoyne, Liz Allman, Tamana Bleasdale, Caterina Boselli, Nicolas Brown, Zoe Brown, James Buxton, Julie Clark, Mark Clayton, Alex Gladstone, Jodie Gray, Joanna Gueritz, David Gunkle, John Marzano, Adrian McCarthy, Michael McDonough, Mervyn New, Sam Renton, Benjamin Richards, Gemma Ryan, Deborah Saban, Will Samuelson, Astrid Sieben, David Smith, Richard Todd, Andrew Wood **Four Nations** Leonie Bell, David Brown, Roisin Browne, Francesca Canty, Derek Livesey, James Lucas, Chris Myers, Ian Russell, Cian Smyth, Kate Southwell, Gwyn Williams, Rhian Williams **Chariots of Fire / Thanks Tim** Simon Baker, David Brown, Luke Coulter, Jamie Edgell, Hugh Gourlay, Jo Harrop, Richard Hewitt, Ed Kellow, Lizzie Kelly, Daniel Landin, Olivia Lloyd, Nathan Mann, Jason Martin, Adrian McCarthy, Orla O'Connor, Sylvia Parker Amelia Price Larry Prinz, Oliver Roberts, Ewan Robertson, Gemma Ryan, Deborah Saban, Gordon Segrove, Colin Strachan, Dorothy Sullivan, Gary Weekes, Tim White **Torch Journey** Jon Bray, Ben Davis, Alex Gladstone, David Gunkle, Yvonne Ryan, Kenny Underwood, Daisy Wallace, Tommy Holman, Matt Choules, Kim Armitage, Sam Renton, Andy Woodcock, Lee Grumett.

Volunteers

Prologue Lucy Abrahams, Angela Adler, Doreen Agyei, Marian Agyeman, Vivienne Ahmad, Minhaj Ahmed, Eren Ali, Hannah Allen, David Alli-Balogun, Syed Al-Nahiyan Ishtar, Praveen Amarasinghe, Komal Amin, Clare Anderson, Faye Andrews, Vicky Annand, Bevlyn Anyaoku-Clough, Adria Aranda-Balibrea, Niellah Arboine-Todd, Dioni Arvanitaki, Lorna Asante, Sophie

Ashdown, Tania Austin Herdman, Sola Awoberu, Tessa Baartmans, Amanda Bailey, Julia Bailey, Lucy Baker, Tatiana Baratto, Sonja Barber, Cassandra Bardot, Ursula Barzey, Michael Beard, Katharina Beck, Kate Beeching, Gabi Beer, Geoff Bell, Kate Bennett, Gloria Bernard, Anne-Marie Bevan, Sana Bhadelia, Varun Bhanot, Alexander Bishenden Moon, Rosa Bishenden Moon, Lynn Blackman, Kat Blake-Pink, Katherine Blightman, Wendy Blow, Elisa Bodden, Lydia Bolwell, Emma Bond, Laura Bonifacii, Nicole Boran, Sylvie Bornat, Jessica Bosworth, Rhiannon Brace, Penny Breia, Hannah Broad, Karen Brock, Elizabeth Brooks, Larissa Brown, Camilla Brueton, Julie Bryant, Kirsty Bullen, Katy Burke, Richard Burke, Mulgrew Cameron, Annie Campbell, June Campbell, Charles Campbell-Peek, Amy Carrick, Nicola Carsons, Albert Carter-Phillips, Finn Casey, Emma Chalk, Danielle Chamberlain, Chor Hon Chan, Ann Charles, Qi Chen, Natalie Chivers, Nazish Choudhury, Severino Chuquivala-Jos, Ernests Cirulis, Lauren Coates Lewis, Bianca Cole, Annie Coleman, Anne Corbett, Penny Costa, Anne Costello, Sarah Cowan, Lois Crane, Claire Cranmer, Cristiane Crauford, Jumar Cristobal, Melisande Croft, Oliver Crooke, Gillian Dacey, Eleni Danika, Leaphia Darko, Carol Davis, Miranda Dawkins, Rhiannon Daye, Cara de Reuck, Barbara De Rios, Maryam Delavar, Zu Ning Ding, Yaxin Ding, Alexander Dmochowski, Amada Dorta Cerpa, Jane Dotzek, Rachel Drew, Thorsten Dreyer, Adrian Dutch, Kara Earl, Insiah Edgecombe, Helen Edwards, Georgia Emm, Marialaura Ena, Jason Eustice, Lilinaz Evans, Charlotte Eves, Christina Farley, Victoria Farmer, Matteo Fernandes, Madeleine Field, Liz Findlay, Ann Foley, Cabe Franklin, Arnold Frazer, Feonia French, Emma Fuller, Sonja Garsvo, Aaron Gauntlett, Fiona Gaze-Fitzgibbon, Raphael Geldsetzer, Annie Gleeson, Judith Glossop, Graciete Gomes De Pina Costa, Serena Gonsalves-Fersch, Claudia Gonzalez Burguete, Juliet Goulding, Rhian Greaves, Aprille Green, Steve Griffin, Bethany Grogan, Robert Grogan, Keith Grout, Eleanor Gussman, Jan Halloran, Lynsey Hamilton, Madeline Hammond, Kate Hands, Beatrice Harbour, Penelope Harris, Tayfun Hassan Onder, Carole Hayward, Peter Hayward, Felicity Hearn, Naomi Heathcote, Rosemary Henderson, Emily Herrett, Amy Hession, Grace Hewitt, Jan Hickman, Anna Hirst, Clare Hodgkin, Cynthia Holness, Veronica Hooles, Ellen Hooper-Doku, Jonathan Hoxby, Michelle Hsieh, Ethan Huang, Kellie Hughes, Nicola Hunter, Susan Innes, Judith Irwin, Eleanor Ivens, Wioletta Jablonska, Ian Jacobsberg, Aissatu Jalloh, Sue James, Amy Jankiewicz, Yvette Jarvis, Judy Jenkin, Eleanor Jenkins, Xiya Jia, Jo Johnson, Hebe Johnson, Luke Johnson, Cat Jones, Dylan Jones, Susan Jones, Jill Jordan, Lydia Julien, Christopher Karwacinski, Molly Kavanagh, Finnbar Keating, Teresa Kennedy, Beth Kershaw, Aida Khalil Gomez, Montserrat Kidwell, Suzanne King, Alex Kolton, Ursula Kopp, Silvia La Greca Bertacchi, Laura Lagana, Jenny Laidlaw, Kirsten Laird, Treveni Lall, James Larter, Sami Latif, Heidi Latronico-Ferris, Elaine Lau, Ana Lavekau, Hilary Lawrence, Van Le, Julia Lee, Inova Lee, Camilla Leonelli, Sok Leong, Dez Lewis, Sisi Li, Joseph Linton, Manila Lippi, Illia Lisak, Sofia Lisak, Jingjing Liu, Nicola Lloyd, Tracy Lodge, Fabia Lonnquist, Mia Lowry, Julie Lung, Ellis Lusted, Katherine Lynch, Rachel Lyons, Amy Majumdar, Sacha Mandel, King Mason, Ashby Mayes, Michael Mcauliffe, Geraldine Mcewan, Angela Mcintosh, Marie Mclernon, Thomas Mclucas, Kate Mcswiney O'Rourke, Hema Mehta, Dom Melaragni, Charlene Michael, Lina Michael-Imobioh, Madeleine Mills, Sally Mills, Pam Milsom, Chris Minton, Margaret Mitchell, Hannah Mizon, Jasvir Singh Modaher, Natalie Mooney, William Morley, Annette Morley, Mary Morrell, Natasha Morrison-Osbourne, Anusha Muhundan, Lesley Mulley, Menelik Mulugeta Claffey, Nicky Mutale, Muhammed Neeliyath, Demelza Nelson, Sam Thi Nguyen-Neugarten, Benjamin Norris, David Nunn, Jacob O'Ceallaigh, Chinedu Ofoegbu, Rofiat Ogundapo, Joyce Ogunfeyimi, Ines-Amael Olenga Disashi, Sofia Oloyede, Joey O'Neill, Stan Onyejekwe, Julie Oram, Karen Orwell, Afua Osei-Asibey, Natalie Osei-Owusu, Sabrina Oufella, Joseph Owen, Amy Page, Jyoti Patel, Sharron Patrick, Debra Payne, Jennifer Payne, Sarah Payne, Stephen Payne, Laura Pethers, Andrea Phillips, Pickard Price Pickard Price, Rebecca Pinder, Michel Pinte, Pearl Prashar, Rachel Pratt, Hannah Pyper, Wesley Quadros, Me! Raghwani, Heenal Raichura, Shanmugapriya Raju, Suzanne Read, Shayne Reason, Fiona Reid, Cheryl Richardson, Angela Riches, Ezra Rimell, Elizabeth Rook, Maria Rosiak, June Rowlands, Vicky Royall, Mayra Ruiz, Davina Russell, Shereen Russell, Lois Russell-Moyle, Zahida Saddiq, Christina Sage, Victoria Salcevich, Nathalie Salic, Jasvin Sanghera, Buledy Sangwa, Alexander Sarriegui, Denise Savill, Natalie Schofield, Peter Scott, Lorayne Seaholme, Lily Seddon-Cox, Rutu Shah, Sonia Shah, Laura Sheldon, Caterina Shepherd, Fiorenza Shepherd, Ingrid Shiel, Alex Sierra Rodriguez, Maria Sierra-Negrete, Joao Roberto Silva Barros, Mandy Simpson, Nisha Sivalingam, Anna Slater, Graham Smith, Lauren Smithers, Luella Solomon, Mim Spettigue, Philly Spurr, Leili Sreberny-Mohammadi, Justas Stanislovas, Julie Stanning, Tracy Stedman, Elizabeth

Stevenson, Azul Strong, Paula Suciu, Janet Ann Sullivan, Penelope Summers, Lucy Sutton, Daniel Swani, Carole Swift, Paul Tame, Nhyim Tandooran-Sentain, Hellen Thatcher, Anjila Thomas, Carmenleta Thomas, Helen Thomas, James Thomas, Donna Africa Thompson, Amanda Thorne, Elias Tomarkin, Angela Tomkinson, Victoria Tucker, Karen Tweddle, Silviya Valkova, Jose Antonio Vazquez Mata, Natalia Velaz Ripa, Jayro Viapree, Aaran Vijayakumaran, Caroline Viple, Charlotte Vowden, Andy Wakeford, Samantha Walker, Sarah Walker, Rebecca Wallace, Aileen Walsh, Nancy Wang, Matthew Ward, Rachel Wedderburn, Polly Wells, Lucy Whyte, Bernadine Williams, Lorraine Williams, Clare Wills, Kirsty Witherden, Chris Wolff, Chi-Chung Wong, Gulfem Wormald, Hollie Wynne, Nelia Yakupova, Jun Yang, Carlotta Yannopoulou, Sarah Yarrall, Pei Ye, Rosalind Zeffertt, Cen Zhang, James Zhang-Ly, Min Zhou, Julie Zhu **Green and Pleasant Land** Leance Abi, Maliek Abrahams-Maynard, Yaqub Abukar, Phoebe Adams, Opeyemi Adeyiga, Samuel Adu, Sundeep Aeri, Fatima Ahmed, Hibak Ahmed, Romeo Ajala, Elizabeth Akeju, Victoria Alade, John Alderman, Jolanta Alexandre, Khadijah Alhamdan, Safia Ali, Zahrah Ali, Jaya Rela Alifandi, Sonia Allen, Deshi Alleyne-Fung, Alex Alma, Ricardo Amaya, Kajan Anand, June Andersen, Valerie Anderson, Sylvia Andonopoulos, Stephen Angell, Bronwen Anthony-Downs, Alba De Luna Arce De Kelbaba, Paul Arkilander, Oruccan Arslan, David Ashley, Nicola Ashley, Zachary Aspery, Firdaous Attioui, Kieran Auguste, Christina Babatunde, Sanjit Badhan, Simone Bahr, Alex Bailey, Lisa Bailey, Sue Bailey, Zoe Baird, Blessing Bakare, Victoria Bakare, Bronwen Baker, Holly Baldwin, Ralph Ballard, Jane Barber, Katy Barker, Ashshan Barnaby, Zuriel Barnes-Maselino, Fadumina Barre, Helena Barrowclough, Neil Barton, Simon Bass, Alex Bates, Deepak Batta, Gebru Bayeh, Joshua Beckford, Samuel Beckford, Corinthia Bell, Gemma Benjamin, Mia Benjamin, Christine Benn, Julie Bennett, Lauren Bethune, Eva Bianchi Burgos, Hannah Billington, Catherine Blackwell, Natalia Blake, Natalie Blenford, Hayley Boateng, Nia Boateng, Tyra Boateng, Lailia Boaten-Rolfe, Marc Boettcher, Mateusz Boniewicz, Mariam Boota, Lucia Borrero, Moira Borrero, Sonia Borrero, Joost Bosdijk, Brian Boston, Rachael Bowker, Martin Braham, Catherine Bray, Catherine Breen, Hayley Brightman, Jamie Broadbent, Christian Bromley, Holly Brou, Lizzie Brown, Kate Brown, Brianca Browne, Omari-J'Nay Brown-Smith, Chris Buck, Jane Bugg, Ken Bullen, Ellie-Marie Bunn, Victoria Burton, Des Busteed, Gemma Butterworth, Abraham Byleveldt, Joseph Byrne, Tom Cadley, Calum Callaghan, Max Campbell, Millie Campbell, Nigel Campbell, Shian Campbell, Margaret Canty-Shepherd, Alicia Caprice, Rosalyn Caprice, Christine Carter, Matthew Carter, Lucy Casal, Linda Cearns, Kawthar Chakrouni, Shimari Chang, Muhammad Choudhury, Ann Clark, Sianna Clark, Matt Clawson, Jodie Clerck, Jason Cole, Isabella Collins, Elizabeth Colman, Stephen Concannon, Rachel Connolly, Charles Conrath, Nicola Constantinou, Suliann Conteh-Njawah, Tom Conway, Lynne Copperthwaite, Barry Costas, Helen Coupe, Deja Creary, Tony Crease, Alicia Crockford-Jeffries, Marco Cruse, Mark Cumberworth, Demelza Cundy, Paola Cuneo, Anthony Curran, Kaitlin Cutress, Przemyslaw Czuj, Matthew Dale, Audrey Daley, James Dartnall, Darren David, Jacqueline Davidson, Owen Davies, Alasdair Daw, Anita Dawit, Dina Dawit, Fiona Dawit, Shammai Dawit, Jhon De Souza Leao, Olivia -Rose Deer, Ruth Deer, Lauren Derry, Isabella Dixon, Ella Dokk-Olsen, Serena Dolan, Zakairiya Donaldson, Tamara Donn, Hugo Doswald, Elijah Doueu, Stephen Drew, Moira Duhig, Lindy Dumas, Rachel Dunkley, Jenny Dunne, John Dunne, Michelle Durant, Laura Eagland, Teresa Earle, Onella Edde, Sophie Ede, Nils Edelman, Anne Elise Efejuku, Annette Efejuku, Marie Antoinette Efejuku, Lucy Elwell, Ann Emmons, Alex Enciso Ripoll, Helen Enebeli, Billy Eskelson, Grace Evans, Rory Evans, Oluwabukola Eweoya, Audrey Eyre, Lindsay Fallows, Akin Fashola, Yu Feng, Susan Jane Ferguson, Michael Fernandez, Michael Flannery, Julian Ford, Tyane Forde, Selina Frazer, Antonio Furione, Matthew Gardner, Regat Gebreu, Sabrina George, Sue Germon, Robert Ghazi, Deborah Gibbon, Matthew Gibson, Steven Gibson, Sabina Giri, Vesela Gladicheva, Tim Goldman, Matt Goldsmith, Thomas Goodman, Kamaal Gordon, Kamari Gordon, Colin Granger, Siobhan Grealy, Melanie Greenstock, Maya Greenwell, Patrik Grega, Lisa Gwinnell, John Hague, Henry Hall, Sharon Halliday, Frances Hamilton, Rhys Hamilton, Kate Hammond, Jennifer Handovsky, Megan Handovsky-Boyd, Kailan Hanson, Daniel Harland, Nicolette Harley, Cameron Harmon, Anita Harper, Patrick Harrild, Michael Harris, Kelly Harrison, David Harvey, Kerry Harwood, Jasmine Hassan, Camille Hastings-Prosser, Sebastian Hau-Walker, Paige Hazel, Sian Henderson, Virginia Henry, Andres Hermosa, Harry Hill, Emma Hills, Isaiah Hills, Maddy Hilton, Helena Hird, Gary Hoang, Dianne Hoctor, Vince Hoctor, Jamie Hodge, Patricia Hodgins, Neil Holloway, Anthony Holme, Craig Hopkinson, Charlotte Horobin, Gareth Horton, Antonio Hrinko, Simon Hubbert, Danny

Hughes, Zakir Hussain, Chikwe Ibeakanma, Cleopatra Idemudia, Hayder-Marie Igbonachi-Obioma, Khadeejah Imran, Alice Ingham, Lewis Inglis, Kay Instrell, Irmak Islek, Hugo Iturralde Caballero, Evelina Jakaite, Christine Janssen, Pavithra Jayakumar, Louise Jefferson, Beverley Jenkins, Mark Jenner, Steven Johnston, Bethany Johnstone, Hilary Jones, Linda Jones, Kelly Joyce, Paul Jubb, Malachi Junaid, Katia Kaczynski, Aminata Kamara, Harriet Kamu, Sharad Kanwar, Sedef Karayel, Maame-De Karikari Brobbey, Adwoa Karikari-Brobbey, Eryk Karys, Louise Kearney, Dorothea Keeper, Humphrey Keeper, Ayman Kemal, David Kenneth-Elue, Selma Khelifi, Thea King, Richard King, Aryna Kokoryna, Andrea Kovacs, Samantha Kowalczyk, Shanice Kowfie, Gramos Krasniqi, Rahime Krasniqi, India Kumar, Anita Kusi, Maxine Kwok-Adams, Ken Lalobo, Winnie Lam, Zubeida Lambat, Ryan Langley, Marcos Lastra Castro, Laiba Latif, Yahya Latif, Ayshah Lawrence, Anjola Lawson, Boluwatife Lawson, Una Le Meur, Ryan Lee, Danielia Lee, Jean-Jacques Lescure, Franciszka Lesniak, Olaf Lesniak, Alexander Limb, Katharine Limb, Rachel Limb, Sarah Limb, Hanna Lindley- Jones, Jonathan Lipton, Elizabeth Lleshi, Susan Long, Jennifer Lord, Lindsey Lovatt, Graham Lovell, Jonathan Lovett, Robyn Luckham, Sophie Luker, Emily Luong, Colin Mabey, Vincent Macias, Nicholas Mackay, Clare Mackmin, Jasia Macmeikan, Katherine Makulska, Dorcas Malemba, Rami Malik Chowdhury, Marcie Mallea, William Maloney, Simone Mameli, Emmanuel Mandangi, Sinead Mandlik, Brian Manning, Elayne Manton, Hannah March, Madeleine Marshall, Lucy Marti, Atiya Martins, Duke Maselino, John Maskell, Paul Massey, Tyrik Matthews, Zara Matthews, Chikara Mbakwe, Rosanna Mcdonald, Belinda McFarlane, Estie Mclaurin, Maxine Mcminn, Constance Meade, Cristian Medeiros, Richard Merrick, David John Miller, Paul Milner, Joshua Mintori, Jasu Mistry, Debjani Mitra, Jasdeep Mlait, Conti Moll, Moganie Moodley, Russell Moon, Christine Moore, Angela Morgan, Caterina Moropoulou, Samuel Morson, Elena Mortelliti, Sam Moutet, Kabir Mughal, Lesley Murphy, Zara Mutabazi, Ed Naish, Surinder Nandra, Tasha Nelson, Sheridan Nelson, Tarundeep Neta, Guneet Neta, Catherine Neufeld, Hazel Neville, Tom Newman, Sofina Nichollis, Leigh Norgrove, Alun North, Jevan Nuby, Pamela Nuttall, Stephen Oatley, Ciara O'Brien, Fintan O'Connor, Kate O'Connor, Shanaya Ojeda, Christian Okadigbo, Olurotimi Oke, Lorenzo Okpewo, Ebenezer Okyere-Mireku, Libby O'Leary, Emmanuel Omogbai, Rachel Omogbai, Osas Omorodion-Umaru, Deborah Omoruanzoje, Safiyya Onanuga, Ilze Ose, Adebukonla Osinusi, Noel Otley, Fureel Otubu, Faith Oyegun, Stanley Padmore, Archie Page, Emily Palmer, Kathryn Papworth-Smith, David Parker, Melissa Parmar, Tracy Parr, Ann Parsons, Lesley Parsons, Marion Pastellas, Maariyah Patel, Rubina Patel, Alan Paterson, Alan Patient, Kasper Pauley, Siobhan Paull, Aoife Pearson, Maria Pedraza, Yun Yun Pei, Linyu Peng, Lara Perkins, Mark Peters, Jayne Phillips, Clare Pike, Sajeevaney Pillai, Jeanette Pinho, Kenni Poulsen, Nyima Pratten, Helen Preston, Charlotte Priestley, Dalia Puertas Jimenez, Charlotte Pye, Laurent Quenelle, Sarah Quinn, Christine Radu, Fawziyah Rafique, Mahdhi Rahman, Zia Ralston, Jenny Rampling, Steve Ranford, Jen Rankin, Ali Rashid, Alex Read, Olivia Reardon, Alison Redford, Alex Reece, Paris Reefer, Selvin Reid, Sarvjit Renoo, James Rhodes, Allan Richards, Liz Ridgewell, Marc Ridley, Oscar Ridout, Julia Ridout, Mya Robert, Adam Robertson, Paul Robinson, Chris Rogers, Phil Rosenberg, Matt Ross, Christine Ru Pert-Em-Hru, Gerald Ruddock, Jennifer Ruffell, Kareena Rummun Soobaraydoo, Kieran Rushton, Terence Russ, Jo Ryan, Tim Ryan, Serhad Sahin, Nick Sait, Bolaji Salokun, Jolene Sampson, Joseph Sanders, Tony Sanders, Lee Sargent, Annapoorany Sathiyamoorthy, Jimmy Savvas, Chris Scott, Vanessa Scott, Heather Scratcher, Lesley Anne Scutter, Chloe Selby, Alpha Sesay, Anna Sewell, Atifah Shah, Idris Shaikh, Zeenat Shaikh, Joseph Shambrook, Maisie Sheehy, Esther Shepherd, Magdeline Shepherd, Ruth Shepherd, Oliwia Siemion, Andrew Sigley, Gabriel Silveira, Chrissy Simmonds, Miriam Simmons, Alexis Simpson, Gerald Simpson, Natalie Simpson, Martin Skipper, Bartosz Skonieczny, Annetta Slade, Kungwa Small, Natalie Smellie, Alfie Smiley, David Smith, Elaine Smith, Jaheem Smith, Sarah Smith, Ann Snell, Lesley Snelson, Rick Snow, Bernie Solly, Leah Spence, Simon Springall, Chris Stacey, Daniel Stacey, Glenda Stamp, Oksana Stasyuk, Mark Stephenson, John Stewart, Coby Stickland, Demi Stickland, Claire Stone, Graham Storey, James Storm, Craig Strachan, Sam Stutterheim, Charlotte Sutton, Miriam Swainsbury, Hannah Sweeney, Yvonne Swift, Josephine Swindell, Thomas Swindell, Bellmani Takueni, Sophie Tamlyn, Mackenzie Tang, Stephen Tang, Nikki Taylor, Susan Terenzio, Ewoenam Tetteh, Johanna Tewolde, Maria Tewolde, Mary Thomas, Samuel Thomas, Thugipa Thurendiran, Kate Thurlow, Kerry Tokley, Susannah Traill, Georgia Tredgett, Amanda Truelove, Chris Truscott, Anne-Marie Tucker, Robert Turner, Kayla Tyson, Maria Uddin, Ashiana Umarji, Ibrahim Umer, Jennifer Usman Vargas, Lara Varga, Non Vaughan-O'Hagan, Sandra Vince, Andrew Vourdas, Jennifer Wade, Patrick Wagstaff, Patricia Wakefield,

Tim Wakeling, Chelsea Walker, Michelle Walker, Heather Wallington, George Walsh, Grace Walsh, Patrick Walton, Cecilia Ward, Hana Ward, Andrew Warren, Flavia Watts, Lara Wear, Charlie Webb, George Webb, Joseph Webb, Sam Webster, Marina White, James Whittington-Phillips, Ruan Whyler, Shannon-Louise Whyte, Diana Williams, Florence Williamson, John Wilson, June Wilson, David Worswick, Rachel Wray, Emma Wyton, Linda Patricia Wyton, Tommy Wyton Wyton, Aki Yamamoto, Udara Yapa, Carlos Yebra López, Canev Yorganci, Rosemary York, Mert Zeytun.

Pandemonium Derek Abbey, Ian Abbott, Laura Abbott, Zenab Abdirahman, Zak Abdullah, Lynsey Abernethy, Joyce Abosi, Massimo Acquisto, Glen Acton, Acuña Acuña Quintana, Daniel Adaja, Dominic Adaja, Jane Adams, Mosun Adebayo, Victor Adedayo-Ogunruku, Cornelius Adenekan, Tolu Adepegba, James Adutt, Otibho Agbareh, Abiodun Agbeleye, Solomon Aggninie, Andrea Agrell, Angela Agyei, Des Agyekumhene, Patrick Ahern, Shamsuddin Ahmed, Marcus Aitman, Abdu Akemel, Adeola Akitoye, Rimi Aktar, Imad Al Dakkak, Rafiqul Alam, Javier Albarracin Perea, Alister Albert, Charles Albert, Rachel Alcock, Kelly Al-Dakkak, Charlotte Aldhouse, Julie Aldred, Holly Alexander, Karen Algacs, Peter Algacs, Mehmet Ali, Mohammed Ali, Seb Alias, Sudheer Alladi, Claire Alleguen, Brian Allen, Jim Allen, Jonny Allen, Michael Allen, Steven Allen, Barney Alley, Laura Alleyne, Tom Allin, Amonn Al-Mahrouq, Ed Alton, Nazare Alves, Dilesh Amlani, Zahra Amlani, Beverley Amoah, Ryan Amstad, Sabrina Anderson, Sean Anderson, David Anderton, Rene Andrew, Thomas Andrews, Matthew Anello, Karl Anns, Angelina Ansah, Marius Antanavicius, Gerard Antony, Sally Antwi, Veronica Apolinario, Lucy Appleton, Dejaar Arabshahi Fard, Baven Arasaretnam, Ricardo Araujo, Kathleen Arbuckle, Alan Archer, Gabrielle Archer, Emma Arden, Stefan Arestis, Kate Argent, June Arinze, Toni Armiger, Keith Armour, Alex Armstrong, Ben Armstrong, David Armstrong, Amanda Arnold, David Arnold, Hamilton Arroyo Ospina, Samuele Aru, Michael Arulanantham, Ravi Arya, Khelisyah Ashamu, Ewan Ashburn, Ian Ashby, Thomas Ashcroft - Nowicki, Andrew Ashford, Peter Ashley, Stella Asonye, Susan Aspinall, Gina Atherton, Steve Atkins-Steel, Greta Attridge, Gill Attrill, Usharani Augstine, Omar Augustus-Brown, Amit Aujla, Ashley Austen, Fabio Avarello, Lawrence Ayeni, Alastair Ayliffe, Shervin Azarian, Subash Bacheta, Jimmy Badal, William Badham, Alex Badrick, Abenaa Baffoe, Kirsty Baffour, Muhammed Bah, Joe Bai, Richard Bailey, Anthony Bailey, Alasdair Bain, Stephen Baines, Tejvir Bains, John Bainton, Alex Baker, Alexandra Baker, Cheryl Baker, Emily Baker, John Baker, Richard Baker, Maathini Balachandran, Vicki Baldwin, Laura Bale, David Balfour, Liz Ball, Steve Ball, Charlotte Ballard, Haiko Ballieux, Bernie Bane, Morli Bangura, Susan Banks, Andrew Bannister, Judy Bannister, Kevin Bannister, Amrit Barard, Karen Baratram, Marvin Barbe, Yvanna Barbe, Martyn Barber, Geoff Bargas, Jennie Barham, Tuahid Barik, Lynn Barker, Clive Barley, Jason Barlow, Matthew Barnes, Rachael Barnes, Peter Barnett, Virginia Baron, Tim Baros, Denise Barr, James Barr, Susan Barr, Lisa Barrett, Kathryn Barriskill, John Barron, Kieran Bartlett, Jo Barton, Sally Barton, Arafat Bashir, Corinne Bass, Edward Bateman, Arthur Bates, Helen Bates, Greg Battarbee, David Batten, Hepburn Battersby, Roy Batty, Erik Baurdoux, Audrey Baxter, Ole Baxter, Neil Bayley, Tristan Baylis, Matthew Bazeley, Anthony Bealing, Mark Bealing, Nick Beat, Kat Beaty, Mark Beautement, Sven Becker, Alexander Beckett, Garrath Beckwith, Phil Bedwell, Volker Behrends, Hiruy Belaye, Timothy Belcher, Martin Bell, Rashidat Bello, David Belnick, Volodymyr Bendikov, Conrad Benjamin, Gillian Bennet, Charlotte Bennett, Clive Bennett, Daryl Bennett, James Bennett, Simon Bennett, David Benny, Hilary Benson, Tim Benson, James Benwell, Niv Ben-Yehuda, Lucy Beresford-Knox, George Beretas, Carolyn Berkeley, Birte Berlemann, Matt Bernard, Sally Berridge, Adam Berry, Daniel Bessong, Melissa Bethune, Katrina Betteridge, Valeria Bettini, Mark Bevan, John Beveney, Tim Beveridge, Harpreet Bhal, Jasmeet Bhambra, Bhav Bhawsar, Bhundia Bhundia, Jamie Biddle, Adam Biggs, Dave Biggs, Gary Biggs, Sammy Bikoulis, Annie Billing, Kate Binchy, Jean Bincliffe, Caroline Bircham, James Bird, Katie Birmingham, Kathryn Birrell, Dav Bisessar, Emily Bishop, Konrad Bishop, Rodney Bishop, Steve Bishop, Liz Blackburn, Alan Blackmore, Ian Blackshire, Katie Blake, Nathaniel Blake, Padraig Blake, Angela Blakemore, Paul Blakemore, Rob Blakemore, Emma Blamey, Tibor Blok, Adam Joseph Bloomfield, Chris Bloomfield, Thomas Bloomfield, Darren Boakye-Adjei, Peter Boakye-Wreh, Margaret Boden, Paro Bodini, Bertrand Bodson, Jemma Bogan, Nadine Bogan, Jon Bola, Sylvie Bolioli, Clive Bolton, Sumanth Bommarthi, Helen Bond, Cynthia Bonds, Kaysea Bonds, Elena Bonfiglio Esper, Sophie Bonnefoi, Jodie Borer, Murray Borthwick, Thomas Borwick, Jo Bott, Jenn Botterill, Andrew Bottomley, Adrian Bouillin, Natasha Boult, James Bourton, Barbora Bousova, David Bower, Fredrica Bowkett, Sean Bowles, Nicholas Bowman, Ian Boyd, Sean Boyle, Vicky Boyle, Rich Bradish, Shaun Brannigan, Becky Brass, Martin Braund, Philip Brecht, Philip Bremang, Laura Brennan, Simon Brett, Steve Brett, Rachel Brewer, Cathrine Bright, James Bright, Tristan Bright, David Brighton, Jayson Brinkler, Nigel Brinklow, Steve Broad, Phyllis Broadbent, Joe Brookman, Laura Brooks, Jonathan Brooks, Beccy Brown, Ben Brown, Cathy Brown, David Brown, Delroy Brown, Jen Brown, Karen Brown, Kat Brown, Lennox Brown, Louise Brown, Robert Brown, Sarah Brown, Scott Brown, Stuart Brown, Susan Brown, Bernita Brumant, Elvena Brumant, Evangelica Brumant, Sylvester Brumant, Keith Brunger, Keith Bryan, Deborah Bryant, Ben Buckby

Jones, Kathy Buley, Stephen Bulfield, Julia Bull, Clare Bullen, Jenny Bunclark, Caroline Bunker, Sally Bunker, Catherine Bunten, Deborah Burke, Paul Burne, Penny Burrows, Sophie Burrows, Michael-Deon Burton, Olivier Buschino, Andrew Butler, Grant Butler, Sarah Butler, Tom Butler, Stephen Byrd, Bruce Cade, Michael Cafferkey, Xinzheng Cai, Stefan Caiafa, Asa Cairns, Allan Callaby, Alex Callaghan, Jonathan Calvert, Candy Calvert-Ansari, Adrian Calvo Valderrama, Daniel Cameron, Kadian Cameron, Melanie Cameron, Samuel Cameron, David Cammock, Hollie Campbell, Sean Campbell-Hynes, Scott Campling, Vikki Canniford, Ben Canning, William Cantwell, Orlando Capitanio, Robert Capper, Benedict Carandang, Ben Carpenter, Carol Carr, Melanie Carr, Eliene Santana Carreiro Carreiro, John Carstairs, Jason Carter, Anne-Marie Carter, Adam Cartwright, Diogo Carvalho, Maureen Carvana, Anucska Case, Michael Casey, Sony Castillon, Joanna Cavan, Louise Cave, Omer Cavusoglu, Scott Cawley, Valeria Cazas, Anxo Cereijo Roibas, Richard Chadwick, Dia Chakravarty, Ruth Chalke, Liz Chamberlain, Rebecca Chamberlain, Richard Chamberlain, Chris Chambers, Philip Chambers, Mark Champion, Sylvia Chan, Harsharan Chana, Kenneth Chapman, Noor Charania, Andrew Charles, Darius Chatfield, John Chatfield, Kakia Chatsiou, Leo Chauhan, Vinesh Chauhan, Tarun Chavda, Raj Rani Chawla, Will Chegwidden, S Chelvan, Donald Chen, Kahtoong Cheong, Robert Cherry, Suet Yee Cheung, Chinenye Chigbu, Raymond Chihata, John Child, Nick Childs, Peter Childs, Brandon Chin, Marianne Chipperfield, Chiutsu Chiutsu, Arfuman Choudhury, Shaz Choudhury, Beverly Christie, Daniel Chu, Sandy Chui, Trevor Church, Rosa Cisneros, Matt Clack, Anne Clark, Charles Clark, Elaine Clark, Hugh Clark, Ian Clark, James Clark, Nick Clark, Hayden Clarke, Phil Clarke, Ricardo Clarke, Simon Clarke, Wesley Clarke, Katie Cleanthous, Christine Cleaver, Trevor Clitheroe, Marion Close, James Clossick, David Coatesworth, Rachael Coggins, Joseph Cohen, Heather Coke, Christina Coker, Foluke Cole, Jonathan Cole, Neil Coleman, Eddie Coleman, Ashley Coleridge, Nicola Coles, Chris Collier, Lynn Collier, Mark Collins, Gail Collins, Kieran Collyer, Michael Colman, Carla Colquhoun, Mark Philip Compton, Paul Conlan, Eki Connolly, Patrick Connolly, Amy Connor, Scott Connor, Amelia Cook, Stephen Cook, Declan Cooke, Simon Cooksey, Matthew Cooksey, Lisa Coomey, Jamie Cooper, Natalie Cooper, Matthew Copeland, Julia Copeland, Paul Copeland, Andrew Copley, Mathew Copping, James Copple, Raymond Corder, Simon Cork, Thomas Cornell, Peter Cornford, Roy Correa, Simona Costanzo, Chris Costello, Jim Costello, Josie Coster, Marie-Caroline Cotel, Susan Cotton, Lesley Covington, Alistair Cowan, Anthony Cowan, Christopher Cowan, Iain Cowell, Janine Cowie, Annette Cox, Daniel Cox, Ian Cox, Colin Coxall, Philippa Cradock, Ross Craib, Gareth Crane, Steven Crane, Alec Creed, Nick Creed, Andres Crespo, Nicholas Creswell, Terrie Creswell, Blair Crichton, David Crick, Darren Crisp, Suzanne Cross, Gillian Crow, Keith Crowe, Shannon Crowe, Sharon Crowe, Simon Crowhurst, Shaun Crowther, Pez Cuckow, Danielle Cudjoe Vincent, Christopher Cudmore, Martin Cullen, Andrew Culpan, Brian Cumming, Nadia Currie, Sarah Cusack, Victoria Custerson, John Cuthbert, Rodney Da Silva, Vander Da Silva, Vena Dacent, Neerav Dahya, Vince Dalaimo, Peter Dale, Kwabena Dallaway, Michelle Dalmacio, Adam Dalton, Barbara Dandy, Christopher Daniel, Chris Daniels, Tunde Danmole, Susmita Das, Adam Davey, Peya Davidovic, John Davidson, Lorna Davidson, Chloe Davies, Jill Davies, Mark Davies, Meryt Davies, Michael Davies, Peter Davies, Phill Davies, Toby Davies, Wendy Davies, Christine Davis, David Davis, Havva Davis, Jan Davis, John Davis, Thomas Davis, George Davison, Kathy Davison, Paul Davison Davison, William Davison, Sally Daw, Adam Dawes, Hayley Dawson, Phil Dawson, Jacqueline Day, Alexandre Yemaoua Dayo, Raquel De Almeida, Leonardo De Almeida Pancione, Scott De Blasio, Silvia Maria De De Mello, Carlos De Oliveira Gomes, Kim De Ram, Pedro De Sousa, Rene De Sousa, Carla De Sousa Coutinho, Charles Dean, Helen Dear, Samuella Dedji, Alesha De-Freitas, Matthew Deighton, David Dellaire, Patrick Dempsey, Emma Dengate, Rob Dennett, Christopher Derbyshire, Julius T Dete, Annick Devillard-Pickavance, Ruth Dewdney, Emma Dewhurst, Kevin Hugh Deyna-Jones, Mani Dhani, Mohan Dhar, Jag Dhesi, Nuno Dias, Jairo Diaz, Rimini Dick-Carr, Guy Dickens, Roger Dickson, Gillian Dinan, Chan Divani, Ben Dixon, Marina Dixon, Nigel Dixon, Sam Dixon, Amanda Dodd, Michael Dodd, Dennis Dolina, Jessykar Donald, Oliver Donaldson, Peter Donn, Carl Donoghue, Catherine Dook, Maria Dos Santos Veiga, Imran Dosani, Emily Douglas, Sue Douglass, Colm Downes, Frederick Dows, Beverley Drain, John Dray, Phill Drew, Dmitry Drozdov, Kathleen Drum, Chris D'Souza, Miriam Dubois, Peter Dudas, Mark Dudley, Gwyneth Duhy, Fiona Duncan, Holly Dunlop, Ross Dunning, Dave Duxbury, Stephen East, Daniela Eavis, Vicki Eddens, Iain Edmondson, Talya Edmondson, Michelle Edney, Rebecca Edwards, Tom Eeles, Jonathan Efoloko, Elizabeth Eley, Henry Eliot, Penny Elkins, Nicola Elliott, Thomas Elliott, Adrian

Ellis, Chris Ellis, Philip Ellis, Sophie Ellis, Jennifer Emerson, Russell Endean, Nicole English, Shane Enright, Ryan Epps, Anna Eriksson, Patrick Erni, Giles Ernsting, Taiwo Eshinlokun, Rahim Esmail, Rachel Espeute, Louise Etheridge, Marc Etherington, Russell Eubanks, Adrian Evans, Cheryl Evans, David Evans, James Evans, Jim Evans, Mark Evans, Rachel Evans, Richard Evans, Lauren Eve, Simon Evison, Elke Fabian, Zuza Fabiszak, Remi Fadare, Felipe Fagundes, Marcos Fagundes, Richard Fairs, Yuan Fang, Michelle Farber, Julia Farestvedt, Matt Fargie, Ana Clara Faria Do Amaral, Margaret Farmiloe, Susan Farnsworth, Alison Farrell, Rebecca Farrow, Del Fay, Ann Feloy, Carol Felton, Carol Felts, Gary Fentiman, David Fenton, Harris Fenton, Colin Fergusson, Peter Ferguson, Denis Fernando, Fernando Ferreira Dos Santos, Jack Ferro, Rebekah Fielding-Haynes, David Figg, Caroline Firman, Caroline Fisher, Sarah Fisher, Simon Fisher, Gill Fitnum, Alistair Fitzpatrick, Liam Fitzpatrick, Martin Fitzgerald, Preston Fitzgerald, Jazz Flaherty, Jim Fletcher, Nicolas Fleury, Peter Flew, William Flinn, Adriana del Carmen Florez Lopez, Jan Flower, Katherine Fodor, Ian Foley, Paul Foley, Timothy Foley, Matthew Folson, Richi Fontaine, Oliver Foot, Scott Forbes, Aundray Forde, Judith Forde, Michelle Forde, Andrew Forey, Paolo Fornasiero, Elliot Forward, Bray Foster, Colin Foster, Cru Fox, Hugh Fox, Steve Fox, Sue Foyle, Gregory Frame, Phil Francis, Roy Francis, Otis Leroy Francis, Craig Francis, Miriam Franz, Giuseppe Fraschini, Emma Frayne, David Freeborn, Bill Freeman, Shaun Freeman, Claire French, James French, Jonathan French, Sergio Freschi, Michael Frewin, Scott Friesen, Graham Frosdick, Christopher Frost, Robert Frost, Matt Frye, Dancemastergozi Fulani, Sean Fullerton, Polly Fung, Lorraine Furneaux, Justin Fynes, Henry Fynn, Anvar Gabidullin, Christian Gabriel, Jemima Gaddam, Matt Gage, Charlie Galarza, Emma Gale, Chris Galloway, Cordula Galster, Ej Gamboa, David Gamez, Dimisha Gami, Christian Gangeri, Poushali Ganguli, Duncan Ganley, Bin Gao, Qinquan Gao, Manuel García Sanchez, Kathryn Garden, Karen Gardiner, Charlotte Garey, Simon Garlinge, Christian Gastaldello, Sonia Gaus Agusti, Lucia Gavalova, Claude Gayle, Andrea Gazzola, James Gbadamosi, Jennifer Geary, Amanda-Jane Geddes, Andrew Geddes, Lara Gee, Thomas Gell, Tina Gellie, Cally Gentle, Jackie Gentle, Simon Gentry, Lorraine George, Velko Georgievski, Theodosis Georgiou, Lisa Gervais, David Gethin, Lee Gibbons, Joyce Gibbs, Julian Gibbs, Bramwell Gibson, Nick Gibson, Jagjit Gidda, Kieran Giffen, Howard Gilbert, Chris Gilchrist, Justin Giles, Chris Giles, Adrian Gill, Robert Gill, Sukhdev Gill, Sean Gillen, David Gillson, Gilly Gilmour, Luke Girvan, Shaz Gitay, Danny Gleeson, Denesh Gnanalingam, Darren Goad, Bryan Goddard, Tim Goddard, Aidan Godwin, Michelle Goel, Sandeep Gohil, Suzanne Goldberg, Janine Goldblatt, Doreen Golding, Max Goldman, Chris Gomersall, John Gomez, Nestor Raul Gomez Usme, Joseph Gonzales, Alina Gonzalez, Leo Gonzalez, Maria Goodall, Dan Goodhind, Peter Goodrick-Clarke, Renee Goodwin, Dennis Gordon, Justin Gordon, Peter Gordon, Malcolm Gorrie, Stewart Goshawk, Lydia Gosnell Dougan, Himanish Goswami, Amanda Gotham, Philip Goudal, Keef Gould, Marilyn Gould, Neil Goulder, Raju Govindasamy Muthuswamy, John Graddon, Matthew Graham, Bruce Graham, Eric Grainger, Pietro Grandinetti, John Grant, Andy Gray, Julius Gray, Lizi Gray, Felix Greaves, Matthew Green, Robert Green, Sadeysa Greenaway-Bailey, Vistra Greenaway-Harvey, Elisabeth Greenbank, Roberta Greenhalgh, Daniel Greenhow, Alison Gregory, James Gribble, Kim Griffiths, Lynda Griffiths, Laura Grist, Antti Gronlund, Victoria Groves, Alan Guest, Xiaofei Gui, Louisa Gummer, Amanda Gunn, Yan Guo, Anil Gupta, Rajeev Gupta, Alaettin Gurarslan, Kiran Guraya, Abigail Gurr, Keiji Gurung, Mike Guy, Guzman Guzman Gonzalez, Jo Gweshe, Elsa Gwilliam, Keif Gwinn, James Gwynne, Carol Gysin, Peter Hackmann, Aceil Haddad, Kie Haddow, Loretta Hadjikoumi, Emina Hadzifejzovic, Nick Hafezi, John Hail, Helen Haile, George Hajiantonis, Matthew Hale, Stef Hale, Rebecca Hales, Alison Hall, Joey Hall, Phill Hall, Thomas Hall, Will Hall, Muj Hameed, Beverley Hamilton, Craig Hamilton, David Hamilton, David Hampson-Ghani, Edward Han, Ian Hancock, Diana Hancox, Steven Handley, Christopher Hanratty, Carol Hanson, Flo Hanson, Ryu Harada, Jonathan Harbourne, Daniel Harding, Tamsin Harding, Phil Hardisty, Joshua Hargense, James Hargreaves, Anjali Hariharan, Dorinia Harley, Kenneth Harlick, Jordan Harold, Melanie Harper, Roachelle Harper, Edward Harris, Jack Harris, James Harris, Judith Harris, Richard Harris, Rob Harris, Bridget Harrison, Nancy Harrison, Richard Harrison, Stephen Harrison, Kim Hart, Gideon Hart, Lucy Hartley, Ben Hartley, Robert Hartop, Jamie Harvey, Kate Harvey, Paul Harvey, Syed Raza Hasan, Stephen Haskins, Douglas Hassal, Arthur Haste, Oluseghun Haughton, Tom Haughton, Paul Hawes, Virginia Hawke, Peter Hawker, Catherine Hawkes, Matthew Hawksworth, Andrew Hawtin, Marge Hay, Kevin Haycock, Richard Hayes, Ben Hayter, Lesley Hayward, Dominic Hayward-Peel, Sijin He, Janet Head, Tim Hearn, Nicola Heather, Jo Hedges, Peter Hegan, Alex Henderson, Liam Henderson, Shirley Henry, Anne Henwood, Brad

Hepburn, David Hepburn, Ferenc Hepp, Gavin Heppelthwaite, Ruth Herbert, Fabian Hermosa Alarcon, Henry Herrera, Tobias Herrmann, Cristina Heselden, Andrew Hesselden, Jason Hewitt, Jonathan Hewett, Stephen Hewitt, Max Heywood, Kathleen Hicks, Mandella Higgins, Karl Hildebrandt, Dave Hill, Nicola Hill, Tim Hill, Louise Hilliard, Catherine Hillis, Steve Himbury, Kirsty Hinchliff, Wayne Hincks, Felicity Hindle, Doug Hing, Rich Hinwood, Graham Hirst, Alex Hirst, Naomi Hiscock, Martin Hissey, David Hitchen, Louisa Hitchen, Stephanie Hitchins, Sarah Hixson, Andrew Hodges, Janet Hodgson, Nicola Hogg, Nick Hogwood, Wilfred Hohenkirk, Janet Holden, Emma Holden, Laura Hollands, Marica Holliday, Chris Hollis, Zoe Holloway, Alex Holmes, Andy Holmes, Catrina Holmes, Matthew Holmes, Michael Holmes, Jeffrey Holt, Lewis Holt-Brown, Jenny Honeybill, Bhupinder Hoonjan, Barry Hooper, Clifford Hopes, Ildi Horvath, Julie Horwood, Helen Hosking, Manzor Hossain, Peter Hotchkiss, Christine Houghton, Chris Houston, Edward Howard, Howell Howell, Max Hoy, Chris Hoye, Sylvia Hoye, Michal Hrncir, Matt Hryciw, Boyi Huang, Jane Huang, Zixiang Huang, Raymond Huggins, Dorothy Hughes, Katrina Hughes, Keith Hughes, Richard Hughes, Jill Huguet, Meleta Huie - Drummond, Charlie Huins, Anthony Hull, Nathan Humphreys, Nigel Humphriss, Robert Hunt, Tim Hunt, Robin Hunte, Drew-Levi Huntsman, Paul Hurford, Chris Hurst, Darren Hurst, Josue Hurtado, Riz Husain, Adal Hussain, Adnan Hussain, Akthar Hussain, Mudaser Hussain, Shaon Hussain, Wasif Hussain, Joshua Hustwick, Moses Hutchinson-Pascal, Jason Huynh, Hadi Ibrahim, Amanda Idowu, Mohammed Idriss, Tina Ilsley, Haider Ilyas, Mary Impey, Jerry Inniss, Vicky Instone, Cyrus Iravani, Stephen Irvine, Matthew Irving, Robert Irving, Helen Isaacs, Alberto Isidro, Nurul Islam, Munira Ismail, Sajith Ismail, Helen Ives, Ben Izard, Chris Jack, Annette Jackson, Karen Jackson, Cristiane Jacobs, Ilan Jadoul, Manish Jagatiya, Milena Jakupovic, Caryl James, Aubrey James, Michael James, Paul James, Roger James, Stephen James-Yeoman, Dzestina Janarauskaite, Stuart Janes, Liam Jarnecki, Zuri Jarrett-Boswell, Gary Jarvis, Sunny Jaspal, Isobel Jayawardane, Loriston Jeakngs, Mark Jeary, Martin Jee, Suzie Jeeves, Monica Jelley, Lewis Jenkins, Pam Jezard, Megha Jhaveri, Jingyuan Jiang, Mohamed Jiva, Genevieve Job, Kulvinder Johal, John John, Angela John-Baptiste, Andrew Johnson, Colin Johnson, Edwin Johnson, Kerrisa Johnson, Larry Johnson, Nathan Johnson, Vanessa Johnson, Mark Johnson-Brown, Adrian Johnston, Andrew Johnston, Carole Jolly, Patrick Jolly, Alexander Jones, Allan Jones, Caris Jones, Charles Jones, Gwendoline Jones, Helena Jones, Jenn Jones, Martin Jones, Matthew Jones, Natalie Jones, Nicholas Jones, Rebecca Jones, Steve Jones, Sue Jones, Suzanna Jones, Beverley Jordan, Christine Josef-Santos, Harold Joseph, Hazel Joseph, Joel Joseph, Judith Joseph, Roshini Joseph, Sandra Joseph, Anil Joshi, Madhuri Joshi, Mukesh Joshi, Nikita Joshi, Helen Jousselin, Cameron Judd, Graham Judge, James Jukes, Grzegorz Junka, Vinay Kabra, Mohau Kachula, Eugenia Kaka, Monika Kalde, Tejinder Kalsi, Lilly Kambo, Maulik Kamdar, Laxmi Kanbi, Daryl Kane, Joshua Kanu, Alice Kaphan, Janikunai Karolina, Carla Kaspar, Sema Kaur, Brian Kavanagh, Grainne Kavanagh, Shelagh Kavanagh, Grant Kay, David Kearney, Romany Kebar, John Keech, Daniel Keen, Alicia Keeping, Joe Keerthiratna, Philip Kelly, Neil Kelsey, Peter Keltie, Alastair Kember, Howard Kemp, Benyam Kenbata, Josie Kennedy, Lindsay Kennedy, Georgina Kennington, Jenny Kent, Katherine Kent, Stephen Kent, Kelly Kenubia, Peter Kenyon, Matt Keogh, Kanji Kerai, Amerz Kerwick, Alex Kessie, Claudia Keston, Catherine Ketsimur, Sam Key, Simon Key, Pareena Khairdin, Cyril Khamai, Jahanzeb Khan, Muhammed Khan, Tariq Khan, Kamal Khaveripour, Kibue-Ngare Kibue, Hilary Kidman, John Kim, Yerrie Kim, Anthony King, Blair King, Kirsten King, Steve King, Warren King, Paul Kingham, Nicola Kingman, Cassie Kingston, Jackie Kinnear, Hellen Kirby, Angela Kiss, Tim Kiss Freitas, Charlotte Kitteridge, Andrea Kitzberger, Carol Kleinschmidt, Elizabeth Kliman, Ryan Kliszat, Chris Knight, Lesley Knight, Eve Knights, Melanie Knoedler, Deborah Knox-Hewson, Zoltan Komlosi, Demetri Komodromos, Liane Kordan, Tyrese Koroma, Amita Kotecha, Arun Kottekudy, Helen Kowald, Luisa Krampoutsa, Lukas Krohn-Grimberghe, Nils Krumrey, Hannah Kubias, Romans Kulikovs, Vinay Kumar, Siva Kumaravel, Alexandre Kündig, Alexander Kustow, Patricia Labro, Olu Ladeinde, Peter Laemmle, Jonathan Lahraoui, Shaun Laird, Kulvinder Lal, Amitabh Lall, Irfan Lamba, Miles Lampitt, Nicholas Lane, Cathryn Langdon, Sarah Langslow, Danny Langston, Jayne Larnie, Richard Larsen, Erika Laszlo, Krishan Lathigra, Alan Lau, Hong-Tin Lau, Natalie Laudat, Ade Lawless, Krishna Lawrence, Maria Lawrence, Nigel Lawrence, Jan Lawry, Laura Lawson, Samantha Lawson, Joseph Lawton, Gary Laybourne, Matty Laycock, Dea Le Bargy, Emmanuelle Le Drian, Kieran Leahy, Welber Leao, Gary Joseph Learmonth, Victoria Lebor, Yann Leclercq, Sunee Lee, Andrew Lee, Christopher Lee, Le Kai Lee, Brian Leggett, Andrew Lennard, Nicholas Lennon, Oliver Leonard, James Leppard, Lee Lester, Jessica

Leung, Itay Levin, Angela Lewis, Desmond Lewis, Leonie Lewis, Lewis Lewis, Mark Lewis, Michael Lewis, Naomi Lewis, Travers Lewis, Yang Li, Ying Li, Shuang Li, Yunlu Li, Huai-Chih Liang, Bo Li-Bean, Jakub Lichota, Cary Lied, Elsa Lignos, Wendy Lim, Yihsien Lin, Ming Lin, John Lines, Stanley Malcolm Lippeatt, James Lister, Kevin Liu, Jianning Liu, Ben Liu, Campbell Livingston, Andrew Livingstone, Alison Lloyd, Gary Lloyd, Bradley Lloyd-Prest, Simon Loach, David Lobley, Anthony Lobo, Chris Locke, Andrew Lockett, Keith Lockwood, David Lockwood, Mark Londesborough, Marie Lonergan, Stephen Long, Dave Longman, Michael Longridge, Rafael Lopez-Bravo, Vicky Lord, Katie Louch, Derek Love, Jeffery Lovejoy, Sarah Lowes, Dominic Lown, David Lozano, Zhiyuan Lu, Xialan Lu, Brett Lucas, Adam Lucas, Angela Lucas, James Lucas, Robert Lucas, Terry Luddington, David Lumby, Michael Wai Ko Lung, Priscilla Lungu, David Lyon, Lynne Lytton, Zibi Maciag, Elizabeth Macintyre, Peter Mack, Matthew Macmorland, Alan Macpherson, Hugh Macpherson, Reddy Madadi, Vaishnavee Madden, Chris Madell, Peter Magee, Sophie Maggs, Vasili Magnis, Deborah Magri-Overend, Shaun Maguire, Gary Mahoney, Jock Maitland, Stefan Majczak, Kevin Makepeace, Paras Malde, Sepehr Malekahmadi, Duncan Mallison, Malloy Malloy, Sally Manderson, Stephen Mangiurea, Geoff Manley, Chloe Mann, Andrew Manning, Annabel Mansell, Kevin Maple, Luke Mappley, Lilian Maranciuc, Darren Marash, Rebecca Marcano, Hannah Marcazzo, Michele Marchionni, Roman Marie, Cassandra Marillier, Max Marino, Andrew Mark, Dominic Markes, Sarah Marks, Emily Marrison, Carlos Marroquin De La Cruz, Alex Marsh, Simon Marsh, John Marshall, Steve Marshall, Tracey Marshall, Elaine Martel, Leonard Martin, Lynda Martin, Wendy Martin, Louis Martinelli, Sara Martins Martins Pereira Duarte, Milena Marucci, Darren Mason, Nadeem Masood, Heather Mathew, Michaela Mathieu-Marius, Oliver Matjasz, Alistair Matson, Mutsumi Matsuba, Ellie Matthews, Helen Matthews, Melissa Matthews, Nicky Matthews, Peter Matthews, Philip Matton, Sally Maxwell, Christopher May, Rachel Mayes, Henry Mayhead, Darren Mccabe, Sarah Mccaffrey, Judeth Mccall, Acquaye McCalman, Lionel McCalman, Robert Mccamon, John Mccann, Matthew Mccourt, Michael Mccoy, Charmaine Mccracken, Paul Mccrudden, Raymond Mccullagh, John Mccusker, Ewan Mcdonald, Oprah Mcdonald, Edward Mcdonald-Toone, Easton Mcewan, Timothy Mcgeever, Rowlands Mchale, Rachael Mcilroy, Tim Mcinerny, Ian Mcinnes, Martin Mckechnie, Sue Mckenzie, Conor Mckeown, Mark Mckinnon, Hugh Mclaren, Katherine Mclean, James Mcloughlin, Daniel Mcloughlin, Sean Mcmanus, Emma Mcpeake, Warren Mcwilliams, Lucy Meachen, Robert Mead, Jillian Meadows, Gemma Mears, Roopal Mehta, Christopher Melia, Giuseppe Membrino, Shauna Mennis, Seema Menon, Emmanuel Mensah, Leandro Mariano Mera Otero, Rachel Merrett, Caroline Merritt, Nick Metcalf, Yan-Ping Mew, Jane Michele, Kate Middleton, Keith Middleton, Katherine Midgley, Paul Milford, Wendy Millar, Graham Miller, Alex Millington, Carl Mills, Juliana Mills, Stephanie Mills, Rob Millwood, Adrian Milner, Ben Milway, Raj Mistry, Jonathan Mitchell, Kev Mitchell, Kurt James Mitchell, Liz Mitchell, Neil Mitchell, Paul Mitchell, Bradley Mock, Ranjit Modhawadia, Ahmed Mohideen, Jonny Molloy, Dominic Moloney, Andrew Mondia, George Monisse, Annabelle Monks, Clyde Monserrate, Waleed Montasser, Hannah Montrose, Jack Moody, Steve Moody, Simon Mooney, Katharine Moore, David Moore, Kevin Moore, Anthony Moran, Daniel Moravanszky, Alexandre Moreau, Alexandra Morgan, Liz Morgan, Alex Morgan, Kathy Morley, Katie Morris, Ruth Morris, Tim Morrish, Alan Morrison, Anya Morrison, Ian Morrison, Mac Morrison, Kristofre Morton, Juliusz Mosek, Rachel Moses, Sarah Moss, Celia Moutell, Thandie Moyo, Ann Moyse, Marcus Mozley, Lawal Muhammad, Dennis Muir, Laura Muir, Martin Mulgrew, Joe Mulkerrin, Thomas Mullaney, Stephen Mulley, Babita Mundra, Jim Munro, Jean Wangari Muoria-Sal, Sid Murad, Francesca Muro, Mary Muro, Claire Murphy, Jacqueline Murphy, Linda Murphy, Murphy Murphy, Sam Murphy, Joe Murray, Philippa Murray, Daniel Musikant, Clare Myers, Janet Naghten, Zoltan Nagy, Samra Naim, Rosemin Najmudin, Angela Nascimento, Nisha Natalia, Aseem Natekar, Manjula Natkunan, Dave Nattriss, Eileen Naughton, Andrew Naylor, Russell Neal, Tom Needham, Susan Nelson, Sonia Nelson-Williams, Tim Neumann, Stephen Neville, Tim Newbould, Annabel Newell, Alastair Newens, Andy Newman, Ross Newsome, Veronica Newson, Ellis Ngui, Margaret Ngui, Beth Nguyen, Katie Nicholas, Richard Nicholson, Sue Nicholson, Lauren Nickless, Gerhardus Niemand, Mauro Niewolski, John Nixon, Phil Nixon, Tristan Noakes, Marianna Nodale, Atsuhiro Noguchi, Craig Nolan, Abdud Nordien, Allison Noreiga-Clarke, Carolyn Norgate, William Norris, Inderjeet Notta, Elia Ntaousani, Deirdre Nugent, Jaime Nunez-Lopez, Stephen Nunn, Aileen Nurse, Victor Nutakor, Will Oakey, John O'Brien, Sarah O'Brien, Brendan O'Connor, John Odell, Stuart O'Dell, Aderemi Odeniran, Olly Offord, Phil O'Flaherty, Eoin O'Flynn, Steve O'Gallagher, Bernadene Ogle, Neil O'Grady, Paul O'Hara, Peter O'Hare, Mudimo

Okondo, Oritsetimeyin Okoro, Patricia Olabre, Tomasz Olejniczak, Hugo Oliveira, Charlene Oliver, Jarrad Oliver, Peggy Oliver, Ayotunde Olutimehin, Saira O'Mallie, David O'Neale, Sarah Ong, Onkar Onkar, Nigel Oram, Lizzy Orcutt, Louisa Orr, Graham Orriss, William Orrock, Juan Ortiz Fernandez, Takeshi Osada, Rex Osafo-Asare, Lionel Osborne-Wakely, Jonathan Oser, Kieron O'Shea, Siobhan O'Shea, Inka Oshodi, Fiona Owen, John Owen, Nicky Owen, Robert Owen, Thomas Owen, Ayo Oyewusi, Cemile Ozkan, Marcin Pachura, Martin Padilla Borrero, Pedro Pages, Marjorie Palfrey, Monica Palmer, Scott Palmer, Trevor Palmer, Helen Pankhurst, Laura Pankhurst, Verinder Pardesi, Lisa Parfitt, Pauline Park, Claire Parker, Edward Parker, Sally Parker, Deb Parsons, Matt Parsons, Edward Parsons, Parthi Parthipan, Jonathan Partridge, Clinton Pascoe, Neringa Paskeviciute, Bharat Patel, Bhaskar Patel, Nimisha Patel, Prabha Patel, Yatin Patel, Susan Paterson, Padmraj Patil, James Paton, Sharon Paul-Taylor, Adrian Pavia, Peggy Pawlowski, Andy Pawsey, Alan Paxford, Chris Payne, Diana Payne, Douglas Payne, James Peach, Malcolm Peake, Carole Pearce, Christopher Pearson, Robert Pearson, Jan Pearson, Edward Peerless, Dave Peirson, Ben Peng, Natalie Pereech, Charlotte Pereira, Jean Pereira, Randolph Pereira, David Perkins, Jen Perkins, Matthew Perkins, Leslie Perrier, Nargis Persaud, Ann Persson, Tom Peters, Vivien Peters, Theresa Peterson, Kathy Petrakis, Katrina Pett, Philip Pettenuzzo, Rob Petty, Christopher Peugniez, Dominic Pflaum, Daniel Pharoah, Ray Pheasant, Gary Phibbs, Stefano Philand-Maini, Stephon Phillip, Rachel Phillips, Will Phillips, Kirstin Phillipson, Aisha Phipps, Billy Picard, James Pickford, Leigh Piercy, Rebecca Pike, Tashia Pillay, Daniel Pilling, Rolando Pincay Macias, Jessica Pinho, Jonathan Fabian Pinho, Monica Piovesana, Sam Pitt, Angela Plah, Adrian Platt, Billy Plaw, Carol Plaw, Lindsey Plaw, Nikki Plaw, Toni Plaw, Milana Plecas, Andrew Plum, Tito Poblete, Jan Poklewski, Michael Poku, Lukian Poleschtschuk, Deborah Pollard, Glenn Pollard, Georgia Pollock, Mario Polo, Nicholas Poltorak, Anja Pomeroy, Sergei Ponomarjov, Jackie Pooley, Sarah Pope, Louise Port, Gerry Porter, Lucy Porter, Simon Porter, Anna Portosi, Vivienne Potter, Kevin Poulter, Seyedali Poursamar, Daniel Powell, Lee Powell, Zoe Prag, Raj Prasad, Kajann Prathapan, Alistair Prestidge, Paula Preston, Jess Price, Steve Price, Paula Prichard, Lynnette Prigmore, Neil Prior, Tiffany Pritchard, Tom Pritchard, Gavin Pritchard, Annette Probert, Loraine Prokopiou, Christine Prosser, Inderjit Puaar, Liva Puce, Timothy Purcell, Claire Purnell, Gill Purnell, Paul Nino Sunder Purswani, Gemma Putney, Sam Pye, Cornelia Pykett, Zhaoyu Qi, Junyan Qiu, Janeen Quentin, Hannah Quigley, Brendan Quinn, Jonathan Quinn, Noelle Quinn, Ash Qureshi, Sarah Radcliffe, Michel Radermecker, Sonia Rafferty, Sonal Raghwani, Anisah Rahman, Faizur Rahman, Avnish Raichura, Sonia Raichura, Thara Raj, Arti Raja, Louisa Rajakumari, Shamma Rajan, Andrew Raju, Rashmi Rajyaguru, Ruby Rall, Jess Ramasamy, John Ramchandani, Anil Ramdeen, Daniel Ramdeen, Maria Ramdeen, Danilo Ramos, Michelle Ramrachia, Clare Ramsaran, Lindsay Ramsbottom, Alok Rana, James Randall, Rachel Rankin , Wendell Raphael, David Rapp, Jeyakumar Rasaiah, Kabir Rashid, Sarah Ratford, Adrian Raven, Olivia Raven, Kumaran Ravendradas, Alan Rawlinson, James Rawstron, Darryl Rayner, Chris Read, Tim Reading, Kayley Redrup, Wendy Rees, David Rees, Luke Reeve, Michael Reeve, Olivia Reevell, Pier Reid, Lisiane Reis Moura, Ellen Reynolds, Cemi Rhule, Corinna Richards, Helen Richards, John Richards, Julie Richardson, Kate Richardson, Terence Richardson, Thomas Richardson, Tim Richardson, Jean Richmond, Cleo Ridgeway, David Risley, Angela Maxine Risner, Alistair Robbie, Elwyn Roberts, Helen Roberts, Stephen Robertson, Deborah Ann Robinson, Genevieve Robinson, Paul Robinson, Daniel Robson, Rob Rochette, Marek Rodgers, James Roditi, Donna Rodrigues, Paul Roebuck, Aurelia Rogalli, Xavier Roger, Nicholas Rogers, Oliver Rogers, Oliver Rogers, Tom Rogers, Stephen Rolle, Donald Romeo, Lauren Rooney, Chris Roots, Jose Rosa Diaz, Adam Rosbottom, Alan Rose, Joe Rose, Philippa Ross, André Rostant, Peter Rostron, Catherine Roulston, Amy Rowe, David Rowe, Richard Rowe, Scarlet Rowe, Mark Rowland, Christopher Rowland, Dave Rowlands, Tim Rudd, Cerian Rudd, Matthew Ruddick, Emile Ruddock, Ro Ruiz-Ochoa, Nick Rundall, Bridie Rushton, Pete Rusin, Adrienne Russell, Lin Russell, Megan Russell, Christopher Ryan, Carl Ryan, Chloe Ryan, Emma Ryan, Richard Sackey-Addo, Michael Sadan, Emily Sadler, Alex Sadowsky, Cleofe Sagun, Gogi Saini, Tom Sainsbury, Clarinda Salandy, Miranda Salter, Don Samkange, Eskandarian Samsudin, Prad Samtani, Julian Sanchez, Eduardo Sanchez-Seco, Zé Sandell, Ian Sanderson, Julee Sanderson, Simon Sandiford, Grishma Santosh, Ivan Sanz, Gaudi Sareno, Claire Sargent, Jasminder Kaur Satnam Singh, Christopher Savage, Tom Savage, Stuart Savill, Brandis Savizon, Farrida Sawh, Steven Saxby, Anya Sayadian, Katherine Sayce, Andrew Scarborough, Evan Schiff, Toby Schuster, Philippe Schwartz, James Sciberras, Joseph Sciberras Margrie, Albert Scott, Elle Scott, Elliott Scott, Helen Scott, John

Scott, Sarah Scott, Sarah Scott, Charlie Seager, Martyn Seaholme, Ricky Seal, Lewis Searle, Maria Seale, Oliver Sears, Jenny Selden, Amy Sell, Lee Selvarajah, Viki Sena, Derek Senft, Luis Fernando Sepulveda Lopez, Felix Serkis, Jay Serrao, Yvonne Settle, Lis Seymour, Andreas Sfikouri, Carole Shackleton, Mohammed Shafi, Baldip Shah, Haroun Shah, Jatin Shah, Neil Shah, Priya Shah, Anisa Shahid, Melinda Shalet, Rahim Shamji, Kimberley Shamtally, Radhika Shanmuganathan, Colin Shannon, Sara Shao, Simon Sharkey, Jyoti Sharma, Ritu Sharma, Austin Shaun, Rachel Shaw, Neil Shaw-Smith, Phillip Sheahan, Tak Sheikh, Justin Shelley, Bright Shen, John Shepherd, Kitty Sheppard, Nigel Sheppard, Matthew Sherr, Amit Sheth, Andy Shirlaw, Damian Shirley, Jacqueline Shirley, Edward Short, Chris Shoubridge, Yagnesh Shukla, Alessandra Shurina, Siphosenkosi Sibindi, Andrey Sidelnikov, Emilie Silkoset, Victor Silva, Kimbo Silver, Emily Simon Thomas, Natasha Simpson, Thomas Simpson, Peter Sinclair, Grainne Sinclair, Anja Singer, Jaspal Singh, Minda Singh, Munjeet Singh, Paul Singh, Sulesh Singh, Robert Sira, Kasun Siriwardana, Katherine Sivieng, Ben Skelton, Alan Skewis, Mark Skinner, Philip Slade, Natasha Slaise, Alan Slee, Angela Slocumbe, Etan Smallman, Tom Smelovs, Adam Smith, Amanda Smith, Anthony Smith, Caroline Smith, Cedric Smith, Daniel Smith, David Smith, David Smith, Eve Smith, Graham Smith, Hannah Smith, Helen Smith, Janine Smith, Joanna Smith, Kay Smith, Neil Smith, Rob Smith, Russell Smith, Sam Smith, Sandy Smith, Susan Smith, James Smy, Barry Smyth, Marc Snell, Chris Snow, Bhavesh Solanki, Jay Kumar Solanki, Tim Sole, Desmond Solomon, Yading Song, Yuchen Song, Bola Sonola, Olly Soper, Marvin Soriano, Luisa Sotgiu, Jose Soto, Robert Sparrow, Todd Speakman, Ezra Spearpoint, Alec Spence, Dan Spence, Amy Spencer, Graham Spencer, Jill Spencer, Mark Spillane, Ruth Spokes, Justin Spray, Matt Squires, Nurinder Srao, Mark Stanborough, Kimberley Stanislas, Karen Stead, Roy Stead, Andrew Steavenson, Ashley Leanne Steed, Chloe Stephens, Richard Stephens, Simon Stephens, Katie Stephenson, Paul Stevens, Ted Stevens, Nigel Stevenson, Duncan Stewart, Michael Stickland, Andy Stillwell, Andrew Stimson, Emma Stoffer, Rhona Elva Stokes, Emma Stone, Peter Stone, Rodney Stone, Graham Stoner, Peter Stoyanov, Linda Strachan, Barbara Stryjak, Elena Sukhova, Sahil Suleman, John Sullivan, Mark Sullivan, Jack Summerfield, Richard Summers, Alan Sunny, Roberto Surace, Raman Suri, Simon Surtees, Carole Anne Sutcliffe, Chris Sutton, Chris Swain, Tommy Swale, Kate Swallow, Laurie Swan, Walter Swan, Dan Swann, Jake Swan-Walters, Elliott Swatton, Kelly Sweeney, Rebecca Sweeney, Susan Sweeney, Kathryn Sweetman, Matt Swinnerton, Bohus Sykora, Peter Szabo, Zsolt Szabo, Terrance Szulc, Taj Taak, Deepak Tailor, Motiur Taj, Toyomi Takeda, Paul Talman, Kai Yuan Tan, Aaron Tanice, Nicola Tanner, Martin Tatem, Jessica Tatnell, Regan Tauton, Isabelle Tawil, Joanne Tay, Alastair Taylor, David Taylor, Dougal Taylor, James Taylor, Julie Taylor, Kishore Taylor, Nadia Taylor, Siobhan Taylor, Tony Taylor, Victoria Taylor, Adele Teague, Herberto Tedaldi Di Tavasca, Roger Tedder, John Telfer, Roydon Temple, Sera Terry, Bharat Thakore, Lekh Raj Thaper, Thaya Thayaparan, Leslie Thelwall, Oliver Thelwall, Della Thielamay, Abraham Thomas, Alastair Thomas, David Thomas, John Thomas, Peter Thomas, Robert Thomas, Sophie Thomas, Steven Thomas, Alex Thompson, Andrew Thompson, David Thompson, Steve Thompson, Trevor Thomson, Richard Thornhill, Mary Thorogood, Joanne Thorpe, Helena Tidey, Wayne Tieken, Mark Tierney, Martin Tilling, Andreas Timm, Philippa Tipper, Gerry Tissier, Aileen Toal, Areta Toalima, Joshua Tomkins, Shirley Ann Tomlinson, Carlos Torres Torres Bujanda, Paul Torry, Frances Touch, Gary Tough, Liam Tracey, Jody Tranter, Carl Treddenick, Shyvonne Trench, Jamie Trentham, Fatima Tribak, Joanne Trim, Roderick Trim, Giulio Troccoli, Patricia Trott, Paul Trumble, Clare Tsangari, Shingo Tsuchiya, Stratos Ttofis, Joshua Tucker, Martin Tugwell, Saw Tun, Paul Tunnell, Susanne Tunnicliff, William Turnbull, Clare Turner, Jordan Turner, Mike Turner, Sam Turner, Shreena Turner, Yvonne Turner, Suzanne Turvey, Michael Tushaw, Alexandra Tutty, Kathleen Tutty, Laura Tutty, Jo Twyman, John Tyler, Mark Tyler, James Tyrell, Russell Tysoe, Agatha Uchendu, Mohammed Uddin, Nonyerem Udeh, Jonathan Underwood, Calum Upton, Umut Uysal, Nicoleta Uzorka Ion, Preeti Vadgama, Alex Vaks, Ella Vallely, Mia Vallely, Stewart Vallely, Vanessa Vallely, Sree Vallipuram Vallipuram, John Vallis, Ayanna van der Maten, Kimani van der Maten, Mario Van Poppel, Alice Van Sertima, Simon Vandepeer, Aisha Varachhia, Nicolas Vasseur, Jess Veale, Jan-Vincent Velazco, Thassiano Verissimo Bueno Pona, Andrew Verney, Rosemary Vidad, Marian Vidra, Elisenda Vila Basté, Sunny Virdee, Ella Virr, Rohan Vithlani, Brian Voakes, Arnie Voysey, Pierluigi Vullo, Mahesh Vyas, Karen Wainwright, Jacek Wajer, David Walach, Wendy Walach, Tasha Walden, Elijah Walker, Ann Walklet, Jason Wallace, Owen Wallage, Thomas Walmsley, Nikki Walpole, Adam Walsh, Deryl Walsh, Peter Walsh, Robert Walsh, David Walter, Mark Walters, Dawn Walton, Kim Wan, Yu

Wang, Shukai Wang, Chris Ward, Harry Ward, Stephen Ward, Victoria Ward, Simon Wardley, Steve Ware, Roy Wareham, Lester Warwick, John Watkins, Rod Watson, Ewan Watson, Tom Watson, Chris Watt, Ray Watters, John Watterson, Richard Watts, Alfie Watts, Teresa Watts, Osy Waye, Thomas Wearne, Chris Weber, Lisa Webster, Roger Webster, David Weinstein-Linder, Christine Weir, Christopher Welch, Amber Wells, Andrew Wells, Lorraine Wells, Michael Wells, Andrew Welsh, Dionne West, Emma West, Leonard West, Melanie West, Katie Westgate, Dan Weymouth, Christopher Whalen, Stuart Whatmore, Stu Whatton, Ian Wheeler, Will Wheeler, Barbara Whilds, Kate Whitaker, Stephen Whitcroft, Christopher White, Ruth White, Sally White, Jonny Whitmore, Pamela Whitter Whitter, Chris Whyley, Sue Whyte, Keith Wickham, Elisabeth Wicksteed, Lettice Wigby, Lesley Wigham, Hemal Wijesuriya, Peter Wildman, Laura Wiles, Clifton Wilkinson, Linda Wilkinson, Roger Wilkinson, Dean Willars, Anthony Williams, Ben Williams, Cat Williams, Deren Williams, Gareth Archard Vaughan Williams, Jane Williams, Jonathan Williams, Joseph Williams, Peter Williams, Roger Williams, Spencer Williams, Tracey Williams, Nick Williamson, Georgette Wills, Pauline Willis, Robert Willis, Mitchell Willshire, Rudi Wilms, Dave Wilson, Hylda Wilson, Jane Wilson, Peter Wilson, Phi Wilson, Cecil Wimbridge, Gavin Winbanks, Deborah Winchester, Emma Winchester, Roger Winfield, Ellie Wingett, Jim Wingfield, Margaret Winniak, Luke Wisdom, David Wiseman, Lewis Withey, Neil Wolfson, Torsten Wolter, Ekie Wong, Andrew Wong, Tsz Wan Wong, Adam Wood, Bernard Wood, Henry Wood, Jeremy Wood, Natasha Wood, Paul Wood, Tim Woodhead, Annette Woods, David Woods, Patricia Woods, Joe Woodward, Peter Wooldridge, Joshua Woolery-Allen, Steve Woolmore, Mark Wootton, Robert Wormald, Michael Worthington, Jay Worthy, Tom Wotton, Gavin Wrangles, Becky Wright, Dave Wright, Derek Wright, Gillian Wright, Jason Wright, Noah Wright, Bian Wu, Gilbert Wu, Zhuoer Wu, Luke Wyeth, Emily Wynne, Wei Xiang, Zhiqiang Xiao, Siyao Xing, Chao Xu, Shengda Xu, Taylor Xu, Jing Yang, Tao Yang, Terry Yang, Xiaoqian Yang, Rukhsana Yaqoob, Ray Yates, Iris Yau, Mahmoud Yazdanpanah, Grafton Yearwood, Cheng Hiang Yeo, Ting Yeung, Hon Mo Yip, Wai-Lun Yip, Nava Yoganathan, Elaine Young, Nicholas Young, Paul Young, John Youngs, Vera Yu, Omolara Yusuff, Salik Zahid, Kamruz Zaman, Jose Zambrano-Navarro, Tomek Zarebski, Aivars Zarins, Mayur Zaveri, Rytis Zayancakauskas, Vakaris Zayancakauskas, Daniela Zebisch, Adriana Zermeno-Eternod, Chen Zhang, Lisa Zhang, Qingshan Zhang, Qinhan Zhang, Xinran Zhang, Yunqian Zhang, Tommi Zhou, Bo Zhu, Lucy Zidour Mcstravick, Preslav Zimnikov, George Zittis, Deborah Zrostlik **Happy & Glorious** Surah Ahmed, Juan Aimur, Mustafa Berk Ak, Oreoluwa Akinfemiwa, Androulla Andrews, Mariana Astudillo, Victoria Badcott, Frank Barber, Oliver Barron, Nicole Beattie, Molly Bloom, Migena Boda, Lillian Boothmam, Alice Brown, Sania Butt, Angela Cabey, Maisie Campling, Maimoon Chowdhury, Ella Clements, Susan Cole, Elizabeth Cooney, Ruby Cowan, Julia Coyne, Gemma Crossland-Lee, Sanam Dana, Grace Davey, Suzannah Davies, Alaine Demosthenous, Anwen Donlon, Selin Dursin, Shantae Elder, Shian Elder, Aidan Etchells, Cameron Etchells, Jenae Feisal, Katherine Finn, Richard Free, Rachel Glasstone, Ieaysha Goodridge, Sabaa Hamiyou-Alam, Carline Ikoroha, Joseph Jacobsen-Laws, Luka Jovanovic, Mohamed Khadar, Anna Kinsella, Matilde Leaver, Maria Lee, Den Levett, Isabel Levine, Walter Lomas, Lisamarie Mcdonagh, Eva Mcneill, Christine McNeill, Jacob Mellor, Marie Meyer, Catriona Minty, Isabel Minty, Martine Monksfield, Kalid Nasser, Daniel Noble, Efemona Omonoseh, Jack O'Neill, Alexandra Parrish, Christine Parrish, Aaliyah Perfect, Kiera Perfect, John Pickett, Lauren Pierce, Athena Pieri, Joseph Jean Rayapen, Joshua Ralph Rayapen, Liberty Reason, Sam Redfearn, Adina Reid, Ilana Reid, Teone Reid, Claire Reilly, Eleanor Reilly, Thalia Saber, Joseph Screene, Cassius Shanahan, Aleata Simpson, Claire Skinner, Anna Smith, Grace Spencer, Jane Spencer, Coco Sterr, Holly Strawson, Madeline Strawson, Lorna Stubbs Davies, Naomi Thomas, Tessa Thomas, Carys Thomas-Hargreaves, Rosa Thorlby, Zara Thorlby, Alice Tiernan, Elizabeth Tiernan, Georgia Timothy, Jessica Tolley, Nichola Tolley, Rebecca Tolley, Susan Tripp, Rayyan Uddin, Connor Vincent, Kathleen Waters, Florence Weston, Georgina Weston, Ella White, Alison Wood, David Wood.

Second to the right, and straight on till morning Zakariyya Abdul-Hannan, Shalom Abe, Rita Aboagye, Zubayr Absiye, Momammad Abu Tahir, Jessica Adams, Toni Adams, Enkeleda Ademaj, Sahra Aden, Walter Adjei, Olayiwola Adunola, Hannae Afellad, Daisy Agidi, Tasneem Ahamed, Stephanie Ahern, Anas Ahmed, Ann Ahmed, Ayesha Ahmed, Chaudary Ahmed, Fabbiha Ahmed, Ilyas Ahmed, Isha Ahmed, Mujahid Ahmed, Nafisha Ahmed, Niyaz Ahmed, Rahma Ahmed, Rahul Ahmed, Sayeba Ahmed, Tanvir Ahmed, Wasif Ahmed, Oluwanifemi Ajayi, Alexander Ajilore, Mandip Ajimal, Johnson Akadiri, Adeola Akande, Tahira Aktar, Christalene Alaart, Ibrahim Alam, Nusrat Alam, Karin Albani, Liz Alderton-Ford, Christine Alexander, John Alexander, Jessica Ali, Mahfuz Ali, Sumayya Ali, Zahra Ali, Nkechi Aligbe, Hayley Allen, Lucy Allen, Kathryn Alley, Yasin Alom, Yunus Alom, Daniel Alvaro, Angela Amegadzi, Rebecca Amissah, Antonia Anderson, Deanne Anderson, Jemoria Anderson, Sally Anderson, Matt Andrews, Luke Anns, Sammy Junior Anwuzia, Ernesta Apanaviciute, Azel Appiah, Lisha Archer, Louise Archer, Sara Arenas-Lopez, Zehra Arkir, Ashvini Arulrajah, Anand Arya, Daniella Asante, Munira Asaria, Nikita Asher, Sara Ashlea, Asrress Asrress, Benedict Atkinson, Diane Atkinson, Ruth Atkinson-Wilks, Natalie Atmore, Sivakulan Atputhachelvam, Carolyn Avery, Margaret Avery, Toritse Awani, Wilbert Ayap, Muhammed Ayazi, Laura Aylett, Khadija Azad, Patrick Babb, Mawgen Baber, Joyce Babirye, Gustavo Bacchetti, Margaret Bacon, Annmarie Badchkam, Oluwatobiloba Badero, Alexis Badger, Khadijah Bah, Kristopher Bahadur, Harry Bailey, Dora Bakaity, Matt Baker, Nicola Baker, Nojus Balciunas, Allan Ballesteros, Alise Balode, Carys Bampoe, Mustari Bangladesh, Claire Bangs, Rachel Banham, Claire Banks, Jan Bannister, Harjit Bansal, Sharon Barbour, Abigail Barden, Karen Barkway, Cheryl Barlow, Kimberley Barnes, Stephanie Barnes, Lamin Barrow, Katy Barton, Alison Basa, Adila Bashir, Gillian Basnett, Maria Bassett, Jashandeep Bassi, Rosemary Bate, Emmeline Bathurst, Tanveer Batool, Rosemary Beale, Lucy Beasley, Catherine Beaton, Nicola Beattie, Ghislaine Beauce, Rashmi Becker, Joanne Beckett, Sharon Beckford, Gabrielle Bediako, Alex Beech, Fatima Begum, Jasmin Begum, Lana Begum, Rima Begum, Shupa Begum, Gintare Beinoraviciute, Nas Bello, Ella Bentin, Otilia Beres, Jerome Bernard, Andrea Best, Ronald Betco, Aaliyah Bevan, Lali Bhaga, Mandy Bhattal, Yousuf Bhatti, Kathryn Bhola, Shriya Bhudia, Muskaan Biban, Nicki Bickford, Justyna Bieniek, Craig Binch, Denise Bingham, Liya Bint Hussain, Theresa Bintoh, Kavirang Biswas, Charlotte Blyth, Nicole Bobb, Natalie Bodden, Callum Bonetti, Harrison Booth, David Boothey, Eliza Borek, Samuel Bourgein, Corinna Bourke, Cydney Bourne, Niamh Bowdler, Tan Bowen, Simone Boyd, Christine Boyle, Rachel Bradbear, Annabel Bradburn, Lisa Bradley, Tiago Bravo, Elyse Braysher, Teresa Bredl, Shirley Bridge, Beverley Brierley, Julia Briggs, Leanne Brisland, Rhonda Bristol, Tracey Brito, Aimee Broadbent, Ruth Brock, Ashley Brown, Darren Brown, Kate Brown, Kim Brown, Loretta Brown, Patricia Brown, Zachary Brown, Barbara Browning, Rebecca Bruce, Glen Bryan, Theresa Bull, Alex Bultitude, Katherine Bunch, Arune Buragaite, Carina Burgess, Michelle Burnett, Felitta Burney-Nicol, Jane Burnham, Rebecca Bygrave, Mary Caddies, Duncan Callis, Aisha Camara, Abigail Campbell, Angela Campbell, Eileen Campbell, Louella Campbell, Pauline Campbell, Lucinda Campbell-Jackson, Julie Cardwell, Sarah Carmichael, Stephanie Carolan, Ellen Carr, Simon Castle, Graeme Caul, Selin Celik, Aviva Cerner, Caroline Chambers, Fiona Chance-Larsen, Helen Chapman, Ruth Charles, Hana Charlesworth, Robert Charnley, Fong Chau, Scott Cheek, Yu Han Chen, Jing Chen, Katja Chessis, Lisa Chishaka, Sean Chitongo, Patricia Chiwapu, Whitney Chobbah, Olivia Choong Gregory, Nadia Choudhury, Athikur Rahman Choudhury, Arpita Chowdhury, Fawziya Chowdhury, Sahat Chowdhury, Christian Christian, Jake Christie, Nila Chudasama, Vivienne Chusney, Julia Clague, Althean Clarke, Janet Clarke, Monica Clarke, Rosemarie Clifton, Amanda Clotworthy, Gillian Cluckie, Claire Cohen, Sheila Cohring, Jenny Collier, Jeni Colton, Holly Conway, Yvonne Conway, Emily Cook, Chris Cooke, Lyn Cooke, Victoria Cooney, Tommy-Jack Coppin, Jan Cornish, Rebecca Corns, Joshua Costa, Rosemary Cowan, Maxine Cox, Trevor Cox, Louise Coyle, Tracey Coyne, Barry Crabtree, Kevin Crabtree, Jennifer Crane, Sarah Crocker, Meryn Crocker-London, Zoey Cross, Audrey Crossdale, Irene Crowley, Rebecca Cuffy-Oliver, Shuo Cui, Roweena Cummins, Faye Curley, Kyron Curtis, Eva Cyhlarova, Miguel Da Silva, Ibukunoluwa Dada, Elizabeth Dada, Tolula Dada, Marianna Dadejova, Jo Dafforn, Michael Daley, Emily Daniel, Sachin Daniels, Usman Fida Dar, Julie Darnell, Renu Daryanani, Priyam Das, Theresa Dauncey, Naomi Davie, Ayo Davies, Juliena Davies, Yvonne Davies, Alisha Davies-Reaz, George Davis, Nicole Davis, Sally-Ann Davis, Caroline Dawes, Leonie Dawson, Julia Day, Sarah Day, Lisa De Jonge, Bradley Deacon, Mandy Deer, Melinda Del Mundo, Edwin Dela Cruz, Linda Deleon, Merlyn Demaine, Mert Demiralay , Patricia Denhard Rae, Tanisha Dennett, Polly Denton, Shaheda Desai,

Usha Desai, Lucia Devine, Nus Devon, Harman Dhesi, Sukie Dhesi, Adama Diallo, Anne Diamond, Laurie Diaz-Steptoe, Rayanna Dibs, Joyce Dimen, Alison Dines, Justine Dingli, Ria Diop, Sheryl Diprose, Naemma Diria, Rachel Dobbin, Jenna Dodd, William Doga, Lauren Domfe, Jade Dowie, Mollie Downing, Holly Drewett, Nicola Dryland, Drusilla Duke, Riley Dunmore, Jane Dunton, Anne Durell, Jasmine During, Uloma Duru, Sarah Duvigneau, Vakaris Dziugys, Pepper Eadie, Victoria Early, Charlotte Eccles, Kerina Edge, Kelly Edmead, Natascha Ehlert, Silvia Eiden, Anna Eka, Abitha Elangovan, Patricia Elcock, Idaho Eley, Sarah Elghady, Kathryn Elliott, Darnelle Elliston, Nabila El-Zanaty, Sue Emson, Tracey England, Victoria English, Taibat Enifeni, Jonathan Espie, Sara Essa, Mame-Esi Essilfie-Bondzie, Tyler Eugene, Fatima Evans, Jane Evans, Chloe Evans Purnell, Rachael Everitt, Kelly Evershed, Astrid Fadare, Phillip Fagcang, Bess Fairfax, Elena Falleti-Hill, Kirsty Fallow, Kate Faragher, Kelsey Farragher, Elaine Farrell, Shaun Farrell, Leonie Felici, Fiona Felix, Susan Fell, Katie Feltham, Olivia Fenton, Helen Ferber, Senith Ferdinand, Ada Ferenkeh-Koroma, Lois Fergusson, Sonny Ferrier, Olivia Festy, Adenamola Feyisetan, Richard Finley, Rose Fish, Joe Fisher, Bobby Fitzgerald, Rachael Fletcher, Sheila Fletcher, Glendelyn Flores, Niamh Flynn, Orla Flynn, Deborah Fofana, Venand Fonkon, Eve Forster, Janice Fortune, Anna Fortuny Torruella, Candice Foster, Fiona Fox, Greeta Franklin, Paula Fray, Gemma French, Deana Frost, Chinye Furner, Chris Gadney, Fainaan Gado, Anna Galasheva, Natalia Gallagher, Aoife Gannon, Alice Gardner, Pat Garner, Fatumata Gassama, Chantelle Gaston, Sulaja Gautam, Cymbeline Gaynor, Lisa Gee, Simone Gelinas, Ricky Gellissen, Kristina Gemkow, Jake Gibbons, Emma Gibson, Alexander Gifford, Nadia Gildeh, Freyja Gillard, Tegan Gilham, Kimberley Gilmour, Nicola Gilmour, Lauraine Gilson, Ilaria Giudiceandrea, Dawn Glover, Alison Goddard, Michelle Gollan, Claire Goodchild, Ryanne Goodman, Louise Gordon, Samantha Gore, Mary Gough, Janine Gower, Diane Gowers, Ann Granger, Annelise Grant, Elaine Gray, Joanne Gray, Doireann Greaney, Sophie Green, Marcus Greenslade, Melodie Greenwell, Hilda Greenwood, Evelyn Griffiths, Sophie Griffiths, Sergio Guimaraes, Lina Gulhane, Rita Gupta, Mariya Gurina, Valentina Hadome, Anthea Hall, Lesley Hall, Maisie Halls, Sarah Halton, Shifna Hameed, Linda Hammett, Katie Hammond, Naomi Hammond, M'Med Ali Hamza, Maria Hanna, Shenai Hannan, Emma Hannibal, Kerry Hanson, Hamza Haque, M'Mad Areeful Haque, Isma'Eel Haque, Shahida Haque, Victoria Harding, Trish Hardy, Claire Harries, Antoinette Harrison, Lorna Harrison, Toni Harrison, Vicky Harrison, Jack Hartland, Olivia Harty, Mustapha Haruna, Sarah Harvey, Sabrina Hasan, Yvonne Haskett, Elias Hassaini, Sumaya Hassan, Velda Hassan, Zara Hassan, Jerome Hassib - Allen, Janette Hawkridge, Theodosia Hayalidis, Emma Hayes, Nikki Haynes, Katharine Helps, Cas Hemelryk, Annie Henken, Patricia Henley, Sara Hennessy, Teneiyah Henry, Elle-Mae Hepworth, Harry Herbert, Catriona Heredia, Cemile Heseldene, Rebecca Hewitson, Anya Hewitt, Gemma Hicks, Andrew Higginbotham, Marina Hill, Jessica Hillicks, Edward Hillier, Leo Hillsden, Samantha Hinton, Tayvia Hippolyte, Joy Hjalmarsson, Gemma Hodgson, Natalie Hodgson, Elizabeth Holder, Hilda Holder, Emily Hollands, Sharon Hollingworth, Lavinia Holloway, Pam Hollyman, Janet Holmes, Issy-Trixy Hood, Mohammad Emdadul Hoque, Sam Horrocks, Katja Horsch, Gemma Hoskins, Rhea Houlker, Matthew House, Stacey Howard, Lucy Howes, Katy Hoxha, Linda Hudson, Catherine Hughes, Elle May Hughes, Kiyah Hull, Fiona Hulley, Ellie Hulme, Rebecca Hulme, Annette Hunter, Catherine Hunter, Iain Hunter, Paula Jane Hurrell, Angela Husband, Hafsa Hussain, Iarfat Hussain, Khadra Hussain, Lubna Hussain, Muhammad Hussain, Nasreen Hussain, Syeda Hussain, Thamid Hussain, Mohammed Hussain Jalal, Ihsan Hussain-Espinar, Jordan Hutchinson, Christopher Hyland-McCormack, Marina Iaverdino, Ebenezer Ibeneche, Muhammed Ibrahim, Sophia Ike, Anthony Ikemefuna, Gayathri Ilangairatnam, Elizabeth Ilesanmi, Liz Illman, Yusra Imam, Clare Inglis, Abdi Irad, Aaron Isaac- Hamm, Nazia Ishaq, Adam Ishaq, Jasmine Islam, Rejwana Islam, Suim Islam, Aaisha Islam Rakibul, Shuaib Mohamed Ismail, Galina Ivaciova, Wendy Ives, Katie Jackling, Keri-Louise Jackson, Lorna Jackson, Daud Jama, Drew James, Joan James, Heila Jansen Van Vuuren, Sharon Jarlett, Sabariya Javed, Lena Jawad, Zoe Jefferson, Susannah Jenner, Rickie Jennings, Emelie Jensert, Ceejay Jepson, Frances Jessie, Jennie Jethwani, Johan Tahaafe Johansson, Adele Johnson, Beverly Johnson, Donna Johnson, Lorraine Johnson, Penny Johnson, Alison Jones, Charlotte Jones, Christine Jones, Kelly Jones, Lizzie Jones, Nicholas Jones, Rosie Jones, Sarah Jones, Eveline Jonkute, Marsha Joseph, Nishka Joshi, Pushpsen Joshi, Jack Jugurnauth, Ayoola Kabara-Clarke, Shirleen Kadje Nguethe, Lyande Kai Kai, Elif Kalaycioglu, Nikhita Kalsi, Meeta Kalyanji, Michelle Kanalas, Kajipa Kandiah, Stephanie Kane, Jemi Kanjia, Rita Karaliene, Joseph Karanja, Tahirjan Karimov, Vidhyalakshmi Karthikeyan, Kayina Katalayi, Mandeep Kaur, Serender Kaur, Katherine Kay, Yelda Kaya, Junior Kazumba,

160

Jillian Kee, Laura Kelland, Richard Kendall, Katy Kennedy, Hannah Kermeen, Agnieszka Kertynska, Eshal Khan, Hazera Khan, Rubina Khan, Tanvir Khan, Angelique Khan, Rahena Khanam, Rashida Khanom, Sawdha Khanom, Aklima Khatun, Ayshah Khatun, Jareen Khatun, Sumaiya Khatun, Christian Kimbugwe, Aimee Kimerling, Martina King, Keith King, Roland Kirkby, Frances Klemperer, Lizzie Klotz, Caroline Knight, Michelle Knight, Imelda Koch, Mojerioluwa Koleowo, Anja Konter, Ligia Kowalska, Gunta Kretova, Gabriele Kripaityte, Maithri Krishnan, Sabina Kurieniuviene, Adelina Labriola, Abelaine Ladinez, Meenu Lakhani, Anita Lalji, Poonam Lall, Dennis Lalusis, Sukwant Landa, Katherine Laporte, Fernanda Lara, Brandon Lasmel, Susan Lauder, Helene Laurent, Betsey Lau-Robinson, Mazeedat Lawal, Johanna Lawrence, Jenny Leach, Danielle Leacock, Laura Leadsford, Janet Lee, Katie Lee, Jo Lenchner, Rhielle Lerendu, Helen Leslie-Smith, Sharon Lester, Mandy Levy, Dominic Lewis, Lizzie Lewis, Stella Lewis, Chi Yan Lilian Li, Angela Lim, Chris Lincoln, Sarah Lindsay, Magda Ling, Christiane Link, Natalie Loader, Jane Lynne Logan, Humnaa Lokasher, Christine Lomas, Julie Loosley, Kathleen Theresa Lord, Asheley Lotter, Jackie Lowe, Estrella Luna Vera, Giuliano - Adrian Lupu, Sarah Luscombe, Alessandra Lustrati, Bach Luu, Diana Luu, Rachel Ly, Simeon Lynch-Prime, Ella Macaulay, Margaret Macdonald, Peigi Mackay, Elizabeth Mackie, Ella Macks, Margaret Macqueen, Neil Madden, Stella Mageto, Polly Maggs, Laura Maher, Teresa Mahoney-Bostridge, Manahil Malik, Asif Malik, Hakim Malone, Sam Malpass, Kudzai Mangwende, Avneet Manku, Ayesha Mannan, Emily Manning, Maja Manojlovic, Larissa Manyasi, Rajinder Marbay, Elizabeth Marchant, Wynford Marfo, Karen Marks, George Marshall-Childs, Harry Marshall-Childs, Bailey Martin, Carmen Martin, Chloe Martin, Linda Marulanda Beltran, Dipa Masud, Lizzie Mather, Sumiaya Matin, Denise Matthews, Holly Matthews, Judie Matthews, Linda Matthews, Mark Matthews, Matilda Maxwell, Robin Mayers, John Mayson, Ajay Mazumdar, Farhat Mazumder, Maggie Mbelo, Gladys Mbenga, Ariella Mbuyi, Sean Martin MC Ateer, Jacob Mcalinney, Courteney McCabe, Dylan Mccarroll, Jessica Mccarthy, Jenny Mcclure, Janet Mccormick, Claire Mcdonald, Keith Mcgee, Mark Mcglinchey, Joanna Mcglynn, Mark McGovern, Ryan Mcgowan, Kelly Mcintosh, Jade Mcintyre, Victoria Mckennell, Keanu Mckoy, Helen Mclean, Linda Mcleod, John Mcminn, Caroline Mcnamara, Jean Mcnamara, Marie Mcnulty, Laura Mcpartlan, Catherine Medcalf, Rory Mee, Isabella Mees, Tessa Mellow, Camelia Melody, Emiro Mendoza Enciso, Nannah Mends Buah, Abid Menezes, Lilian Janet Menezes, Trudi Mercer, Dominique Merlande, Samuel Metcalf, Katja Metz, Bana Mhaldien, Anib Mhamud, Hakim Miah, M'Med Mikdad Miah, Muhammad Miah, Nadirah Miah, Nasim Miah, Sameera Miah, Sophie Michael, Carita Middleton, Catherine Milabo, Lesley Miles, Derek Miller, Rebecca Mills, Tara Mills, Tim Milne, Abdur Minhaj, Esther Missengue,

Sangeeta Mistry, Nadim Mobasser, Amin Mohamed, Halima Mohamed, Mahamood Mohamed, Mahir Mohamed, Shafina Mohamed Yousuff, Hamidah Mohammed, Jamal Mohammed, Sushmita Mohapatra, Cecilia Mojzes, Nneka Molokwu, Anisha Mondair, Patrizia Monteleone, Astrid Moore, Jutta Moore, Zoe Morey, Domas Morkunas, Gayle Morris, Lesley Morris, Sophie Morris, Noeleen Morritt, Natasha Louise Morrow, Denise Mortimer, Alicia Morton, Shazia Mowlabaccus, Ruth Mudiandambu, Krishna Mudra, Lizzy Muggeridge, Samirul Muhit, Cath Mummery, Gerry Munisteri, Fahin Muntasir, Beveline Mupata, Tari Muringai, Emma Murphy, Dana Murray, Laura Murray, Emily Muscatt, Robb Musgrave, Gemma Muskett, Sally Mussellwhite, Louise Must, Imran Naaji, Rachel Nabudde, Amina Nabukenya, Yusuf Naeem, Ashitha Nagesh, Bruntha Narendran, Sarah Naser, Nurani Nathoo, Rohan Nauth-Misir, Ana Navarro, Ammaarah Nazeer, Hilary Neal, Richie Neary, Kristijonas Nekrosevicius, Dante Nelson, Gamze Newell, Lucy Newman, Yasmin Newport, Helen Nicholson, Sue Nicholson, Christie Nixon, Suzannah Nobbs, Frankie Northfield, Abya Nouar, Kim Novak, Panayotis Ntourntoufis, Abian Nur, Afulenu Nwabuzo, Jonathan Nyong, Kasia Oberc, Caitlin O'Brien, Chris O'Connor, Niamh O'Connor, Jeremiah Odubade, Olusola Ogbajie, Miriam Ogbonnaya, Tola Ogidan, Tobi Ogumjimi, Solomon Ogundana, Leon Ojukwu, Fabian Okabe, Helen O'Kelly, Ugo Okonkwo, Florence Okorocha, Tina Okpodike, Ivie Okwuegbuna, Olusola Oladoyin, David Olajorin, Adaora Oli, Samuel Olley, Jamie Olney, Marvell Oluwaleye, Korlei Omaboe, Siobhan O'Neill, Michelle Onwusiri, Shanae Onyeka, Josie Oppong, Tase Oputu, Amanda O'Regan, Donna O'Reilly, Emanuela Orlandi, Chisolum Orliaku, Georgia Orunmuyi, Sarah Osborne-Fender, Victor Osei, Noirin O'Sullivan, Alice Outen, Anneke Outen, Sarah Owen, Deniz Ozdemir, Emma Page, Arun Pall, Christine Palmer, Hazel Palmer, Helen Palmer, Tyrone Palumbo, Ankit Pandey, Bina Pandya, Dharmana Pandya, Matthew Panter, Luca Paolone, Penelope Parisi, Katie Parks, Ellen Parnavelas, Azra Parveen, Iram Parvez, Maxine Passley, Stella Paszkiewicz, Afrin Patel, Deepa Patel, Minu Patel, Shreema Patel, Muhammed Patelia, Lynne Paterson, Sheliya Paul - Swaby, Rosalind Payne, Eve Pearson, Jessica Peek, Bruno Pereira, Tamasin Perkins, Terri Perrin, Anisha Pervin, Samantha Pescott-Frost, Julia Peters, Marcia Phillips, Maureen Philogene, Alex Philpott, Lesley Pick, Aaliyah Pierre, Amy Pieterse, Chris Pigram, Miloslava Pilatova, Faye Pincott, Nuno Pinheiro, Charlotte Pink, Aaliyah Pipe, Alexander Plank, Juanita Plaza, Janine Plummer, Angela Poku, Lanier Pole, Hugh Pomells, Sarah Porteous, Destiny Porter, Laura Porter, Victoria Porter, Aimee Porter-Smith, Clare Portman, Farzana Potter, Barbara Powell, Connor Power, William Power, Tracy Poyntz, Katherine Prees, Janine Prever, Alice Prevezer, Carlynne Preville, Michaela Prew, Callum Price, Lisa Price, Chris Prior, Judith Procter, Anjohleen Prozhmi, Amanda Pun, Deborah Purseglove, Samantha Purser, Muhammad Qadder, Paula Quigley, Mehrun Rabbani, Shagufta Rafiq, Abidur Rahman, Ali Awwal Rahman, Amanur Rahman, Anis Rahman, Fahmid Rahman, Mahdiur Rahman, Sadia Rahman, Abir Raj, Raghini Rajaram, Raquel Ramos Fraga, Paulina Ramos-Irele, Johannah Randall, Michael Ranft, Aysha Ranny, Alice Raper, Katie Raven, Bryce Raymond Da Silva, Kelly Read, Sue Reader, Helen Reed, Sarah Reeve, Yasmin Rehman, Sally Reichardt, Kiya Reid, Lisa Reid, Khepera Reid - Wynter, Grace Ren, Mignon Reynolds-Hall, Sandrine Ribeiro, Karen Richards, Matthew Richards, Melissa Richardson, Sarah Richardson, Linda Ridgwell, Daniel Robb, Carlene Roberts, Emma Roberts, Jasmine Roberts, Kaiya Roberts, Lorraine Roberts, Zoe Roberts, Vikki Robins, Hollie Robinson, Isobel Robinson, Elaine Rodrigues, David Rogalski, Constance Roger, Sheila Rogers, Helen Rogerson, Anna Rolfe, Brandon Rolle, Joanne Rooney, Ana Maria Rosales Hernandez, Amy Rose, Marina Rova, Rayhan Rumel, Denise Rushen, Chloe Russell, Jenny Rusyniak, Syed Ryhan, Lisa Sadler, Boothayna Sahnine, Emiko Saito, Anaar Sajoo, Samina Saleem, Danielle Salem-Tedj, Nakai Sambani, Genine Sambile, Catyah Samfat, Hanna Samueal, Justin Samuels, Beverley Samuels-Campbell, Regina San Juan, Lucy Sandford, Richa Sandill, Ayanfeoluma Sanusi, Sumayyah Sardar, Francoise Sargent, Charlotte Sarmiento, Ardchaya Satheskaran, Simona Sava, Nicola Savill, Leanne Saxon, Sinead Scanlon, Mirjam Schuke, Emily Scott, Gemma Scott, Lydia Scott, Lowri Seager, Janet Seeney, Samantha Selmes, Aaron Selvapandiraj, Jackie Serrano, Alecia Sesluk, Rashpal Seyan, Joanne Seymour, Danielle Shadbolt, Nayan Shah, Prisha Shah, Raima Shaheenul, Murshed Shahriyar, Isra Shahzad, Renee Sharkey, Grace Sharp, Hilary Sharpe, Pauline Shaw, Lesley Sheehan, Karen Shevlin, Rachel Shillito, Oly Shipp, Veena Shivnath, Ifaz Shohel, Victoria Shooter, Mehzabin Siddeka, Tia Siddiquee, Edmilson Silveira Neto Guilherme, Shaila Simon, Natalie Simpson, Amritraj Singh, Anas Sinole, Katherine Sissons, Nativel Siu Rodriguez, Tija Skvarciute, Emer Slattery, Aidan Slowie, Jamie Smart, Mia Smerdon, Bex Smith, Christine Smith, Graham Neil Smith, Janice Smith, Leonie Smith, Luke Smith, Michele Smith,

Rashid Smith, Cathal Smyth, Nita Solanky, Irum Sorathiya, Shefa Sorathaiya, Jayson Sousa Vieira, Amandeep Spall, Wesley Spaull, Heather Spence, Alfie Spencer, Pauline Ssemubumbe, Reece St John-Commey, Sharon Stacey, Sinead Stack, Carolyn Stanley, Jacob Stanton, Kasia Stegienta-Toman, Melanie Stein Du Pre, Rosie Stewart, Ceyrone Stokes, Kat Stretch, Chun-Yiu Su, Valerie Suarez, Victoria Sugden, Moaiz Suletch, Humza Suliman, Keely Sunderland, Kashmira Sunni, Kadamban Suntharalingam, Marlo Surath, Katrina Swanston, Aoife Sweeney, Inaya Syeda, Tasnim Tabassum, Rachael Taiwo, Arshad Takun, Tina Tan, Donna Tang, Laiba Tanveer, Zoe Tasker, Gary Talor, Patricia Taylor, Anneliese Taylor, Amy Taylor, Brothers Taylor, Sheila Taylor, Juliet Taylor, Ciska Taylor-Reid, Bhavnita Tejura, Sandria Terrelonge, Linsee Tham, Gemma Thomas, Julie Thomas, Mecia Thomas, Mica Thomas, Dana Thompson, Dionne Thompson, Emma Thompson, Lorraine Thompson, Monica Thompson, Mia Thompson-Semackor, Emily Thomson, Amber Thorne, Andrew Thornton, Emma-Jane Thornton, Lauren Thorogood, Wanda Tiley, Darren Tippetts, Mary Todd, Jessica Tofan, Rachel Tompkinson, Satwinder Tooray, Carole Toth, Leona Tran, Nu Tran, Chitra Tripathi, Neeraj Tripathin, Konstantinos Tsormpatzidis, Orchid Tunaya, Chelsea Tunbridge, Emma Turtle, Anna May Ty, Suraiya Uddin, Nazifa Uddin, Victoria Ugbekile, Evie Ukairo Morris, Mara Ukairo Morris, Pearl Ukairo Morris, Eddie Uku, Zarin Ullah, Nuruzzaman Ummi Kulthoom, Sam Underdown, Verity Upton, Lisa Urbanski, Leah Vadher, Sheila Vanezis, Meera Varsani, Shambai Varsani, Oluwafunmilayo Vaughn, Chelsea Vaught, Laura Venegas, Jaden Victorin, Janina Villalta, Jenny Vincent, Kaitlin Vincent, Ieva Vinciarauskaite, Raquel Vives, Belinda Voos, Jessica Wade, Matthew Wade, Regina Wade, Claire Wadeley, Christine Walker, Gillian Walker, Erin Wallace, Julie Waller, Lauren Walsh, Janet Walter, Caroline Walton, Juliet Walton, Meimei Wang, Jin-Jin Ward, Hazel Ware, Michelle Warnes, Aleeza Wasim, Hannah Waters, Rosemarie Watley, Kayleigh Watson, Tina Watts, Sally Watts, Rebecca Weaver, Beattie Webber, Charlotte Webber, Doerte Weber, Ariadne Welby-Everard, Freda Wells, Rosamunde Wells, Sally Wetten, Hayley Weyman, Paige Wharton Stroud, James Whatley, Emily White, Emma White, Katie White, Shanae White, Wendy White, Jayne Whiteside, Ruth Whitfield, Ailsa Whyte, Josie Wicks, Jamie Wilcox, Jake Wilkes, Rebecca Wilkinson, Angela Williams, Danny Williams, Diane Williams, Indalasha Deer Williams, Jennifer Williams, Kate Williams, Katie Williams, Lindsey Williams, Muna Williams, Rhyanna Williams, Tim Williams, Luke Williamson, Kayleigh Williams-Stubbs, Claire Willis, Anna Wilson, Nicole Wilson, Paula Winter, Michelle Witheriff, Valentina Wong, Nicola Woodruff, Amanda Woods, Sarah Woods, Diana Woodward, Josephine Woolley, Janelle Wyke-Joseph, Julia Wykrota, Kai Yang, Heather Yates, Ezgisu Yilmaz, Karen Young, Fabbihah Ysmin Ali, Muhammed Yunus, J'Nae Zamore, Chenying Zang, Rebecca Zerkani, Zhuying Zhang, Angela Zhou, Marcel Zielonka, Darren Zingoula Dezo.

frankie & june say... Thanks Tim Harriet Abbiss, Kirstie Abbott, Madeline Adeane, Ayisat Adeniji, Elizabeth Adeyemi, Mauricio Affonso, Thelma Agbadze, Alexis Terry Aggett, Kurtis Agyekum, Nona Ahamat, Tahira Ahmed, Jordan Ajadi, Tomi Ajayi, Chim Akah, Sodiq Akanmu, Kenny Akindele-Eshinlokun, Precious Akpokodje, Vera Akuoko Akuoko, Taiba Al Bisher, Sarah Albano, Lorraine Albrow, Annabel Aldridge, Sophie Alexis, Shelina Ali, Motin Ali, Glen Allan, Sophie Allan, Jenni Allen, Kim Allen, Kingsley Alleyne, Harriet Allum, Daniel Alvarez Gonzalez, Lucinda Al-Zoghbi, Daniela Amadio, Chloe Amankwah, Thalia Anagnostopoulou, Matt Anderson, Jessica Andrade, Coralina Andrews, Kate Andrews, Michael Annan, Iain Anstess, Francesca Antonyogarajah, Noel Antonyogarajah, Mehdi Aoustin-Sellami, Dekan Apajee, Katie Appleby, Lizzy Appleyard, Teeyana Araromi, Rafael Cristiam Araujo Ribeiro, Katie Arbuckle, Luke Armstrong, Laurence Arora, Adrian Arroyo, Gabriela Arthur, Ross Arthurs, Tabitha Ashby, Amber Ashby, Dorcas Asuming, Si Austin, Chloe Ayling, Kath Ayres, Patrick Azimi, Daphne Babalis, Jennifer Bacon, Ildiko Bagladi, Louise Bailey, Simon Bailey, Sarah Baily, Katherine Baines, Jennifer Baker, Lauren Baker, Miriam Baker, Rachel Baker, Ruth Baker, Dee Bakre, Francesca Balchin, Hemavli Bali, Marge Banes, Sabrina Bangladesh, Jerrica Bangura, Leonor Barbosa Gonçalves, Shay Barclay, Kimberly Barker, Michele Barker, Rhian Barker, Marc Barnes, Ruth Barr, Catherine Barritte, Keira Bartram, Erica Bartrum, Charlotte Barwick, Danielle Barwick, Lucy Basaba, Ethan Bascombe, Kirsty Bascombe, Zoe Basket, Julie Baskett, Sedudzi Basoah- Acolatse, Hannah Batchelor, Susie Bates, Katie Bayfield, Nigel Beard, Jennie Beeson, Rahana Begum, Catarina Beijôco, Aiste Beinoraviciute, Diane Bell, Lizzie Bell, Jane Bellamy, Holly Bellsham, Abena Bentum, Rachel Besley, Michael Bettell, Sej Bhabra, Tav Bhatia, Vipul Bhatti, Daria Bierla, Bryony Billingham, Tobias Bilton, Gina Birch, Emily Birleson, Charlene Bissessar, Laura Blaauw, Amy Joanne Blackburn, Katie Blackwell, Tyler Blackwood, Elena Blanco Alba, Stephanie Blandford, Claire Blatchford, Johanna Blight, Sarah Blow, Tessa Boakyewaa, Charlotte Bocarisa, Jan Bogdanowicz, Troy Bohn, Fiona Bolton, Zoe Bolton, Belinda Bonanno, Adam Bond, Anneka Bones, Katie Booth, Pam Borg, Gabriel Borozescu, Michelle Boswell, Diana Botey, Samantha Bottle, Jane Bourne, Regine Boutin, Elizabeth Bower, Daisy Bower, Robyn Bowers, David Bowers, Jessica Bowles, Kirstin Box, Fidelma Boyd, Courtney Boyle, Gillian Brady, Karen Braganza, Elaine Bramall, Helen Branton, Jasmine Breinburg, Katherine Brenchley, Claire Brennan, Sarah Brett, Claire Brewer, Joanna Bridge, Hannah Bridger, Emma Brigg, Matt Briggs, Samuel Brightman, Brian Brinkley, Matthew Brinkworth, Sophie Brockie, Heather Broderick, Chloe Brooks, Lara Brooks, Michael Brooks, Emma Broom, Laura Broome, Angela Broomes, Emma Broomfield, Amie Brotherton, Alexandra Brown, Katherine Ann Brown, Tyla Brown, Daniel Browne, Roseanne Browne, Richard Brownlie-Marshall, Ashley Bryant, Andrew Bryant- Chesworth, Angela Bucknor, Lucy Bugler, Corinne Bull, Daniel Bull, Ryan Bullman, Katie Bunting, Tamsin Bunyard, Samantha Burden, Alix Burhouse, Andrew Burke, Vicki Busfield, Georgina Bussell, Pauline Byles, Kirsty Byrne, Megan Byrne, Zhenjie Cai, Ria Cajee, Zaja Calder-Grant, Jenna Jay Cameron, Suzie Campbell, Cheryl Cannon, Min Cao, Louis John Capadosa, Chantelle Capstick, Christy Carey, Lauren Carne, Leonie Carpenter, Kyroe Carrington-Mckenzie, Nic Carter, Emma Carter, Josiah Carter, Kimi Carter, Eleanor Carwithen, Chez Cascarino, Maria Cascarino, Emma Casey, Elda Castillo Rivera, Natasha Cesco Gaspere, Deny Chacko, Jennifer Chadney, Laura Chan, Stephanie Chan, Weini Chan, Rachel Chance, Sebastien Chaneac, Angharad Chapman, Caroline Charles, Dikaia Chatziefstathiou, Dylan Chauhan, Leena Chauhan, Haixia Chen, Deborah Chernanko, Pinki Cheung, Rachel Chew, Ama Chin, Jane Chinery, Chris Chinnock, Claire Chin-Sue, Angelina Chudi, Josey Chukwuemeka, Mathurot Chuladul, Emily Churchill, Christina Churchman, Mark Civil, Brian Clark, Tim Clark, Andrew Clarke, Charlie Clarke, Marie Clarke, Victoria Clarke, Zara Clatworthy, Anna Clave Arderius, Becky Clayden, Emma Cleaver, Daniel Clegg, Penny Clements, Anne-Marie Clifford, Lyndsey Clifton, Paige Close, Declan Coates, Tessa Coates, Katie Cockburn-Smith, James Cogle, Sophie Colbourne, Daisy Cole, Nicholas Coley, Gaby Colotto Do Santos, Lauren Concannon, Wan Lu Cong, Sarah Conkling, Lis Cook, Lucy Cook, Kate Cooper, Nicola Cooper, Laura Corbett, Kate Corbett-Winder, Sam Cornelius-Jones, Henrique Costa, Emily Cotter, Laura Cottrell, Emma Cowan, Harriet Cowell, Kate Cowell, Emily Cowie, Farrell Cox, Peter Crawford, Jane Crawshaw, Andro Crespo, Karen Crookes, Jonathan Crowley, Raffaella Cuccia, Jakki Cummings, Tiffany Curtis, Tavy Cussinel, Ayodele Dada, Anna-Marie Dadd, Amish Dahyabhai, Laura Dajao, Joanne Cull Dalton, Cristina D'Andrea, Thuy Quynh Dang, Katie Daniels, Amy Darby, Zoe Darby, Sophie Darrington, Kismet Dauti, John Daveney, Landra Davidson, Katherine Davies, Mary Davies, Philip Davies, Sarah Davies, Sian Davies, Steph Davies, Andrea

164

Davis, Beckie Davis, Leah Davis, Lewis Anthony Davis, Marcelle Davison, Alex Davy, Darrell Davy, Debbie Daws, Laura Day, Filipe De Barros, Jude De Bont, Sebastian De Verteuil, Lucy Deacon, Jody De'Ath, Natasha De-Freitas, Louise Dekker, Felino Antonio Dela Merced, Julia Delaney, Elena Dell'Acqua, Natalia Delmastro, Amanda Dempster, Charlotte Dengate, Amelia Dennehy, Himesh Depala, Camille Desmarest, Tyler Dew, Joseph Dewey, Sophie Dewing, Sonia Dham, Prabhjot Singh Dhami, Veena Dhulipala, Laura Diamond, Amy Dickens, Kate Dickety, Jennie Dickie, Helena Diffey, Kerry-Anne Dignam, Laura Dilloway, Matthew Dilworth, Iliana Dimoni, Xiaotong Ding, Tilini Dissanayake, Alka Dixit, Geeta Dixit, Jamila Dixon, Michala Dobiasova, James Dodsworth, Nathan Donaldson, Marcelo Dos Santos, Gurpreet Dosanjh, Sharan Dosanjh, James Douglas, Elizabeth Douglass, Holly Dover, Tess Dowdeswell, Megan Dowell, Samuel Doyle, Virginia Draper, Nicky Driscoll, Portia Dujon, Matt Dummigan, Rosie Duncan, John - Anton Dunn, Roanna Dunsford, Sruti Dupaguntla, Sultana Dyfan, Sophie Dymond, Katherine Eames, Tina Easteal, Gabriel Eaton, Angela Ebiner, Emma Edwards, Martin Edwards, Michael Edwards, Ryan Edwards, Sally Edwards, Clive Elkington, Catherine Ellis, Charlotte Ellis, Kieran Ellis, Amira El-Shafie, Ijeoma Emeruwa, Diana Endsor, Carly Enstone, Patricia Erdei, Beverley Erogun, Kylie Etherton, Jean Eu, John Evans, Morgan Evans, Rachel Evans, Zoe Evans, Nikita Eve, Karen Ewens, Alexandra Ewing, Femi Fagunwa, Savaughan Fairman-Campbell, Abi Fancourt, Rachel Fanshawe, Marcos Faquer Manhaes, Chantelle Farmer, Katie Farnsworth, Samantha Farnsworth, Emily Farrelly, Jumoké Fashola, Alexandra Feachem, Thomas Feeny, Charlie Fennell, Megan Ferreira Souto Jones, Cadi Fester, Rosa Firbank, Stephanie Firtt, Laura Fisher, Aston Fisher, Michelle Fisher, Rachel Flenley, Zoe Flight, Katie Floyd, Jo Foley, Kane Foley, Aiesha Fontaine, Angharad Forbes, Sam Ford, Mariella Fortune-Ely, Sarah Foster, Robyn Fox, Andrew Francalanza, Shynell Francis-Devaux, Joseph Francois, Audley Franklin, Chloe Franklin, Joshua Franklin, Maylee Fraser, Rupsha Fraser, Victoria Frayard-Smith, Stefanie Freeman, Angela Frost, Wendy Frost, Redz Fulgence, Ayaka Furukawa, Genevieve Fyfe, Megan Gadd, Alexa Gardner, Heidi Hovind Garwood Garwood, Valeria Gasparini, Isabella Gaupmann, Lanre Gbolade, Jazmine Genius, Robert Gentle, Daniel George, Elena Georgiou, Kiri Gibson, Laura Gilbert, Victoria Giles, Juliette Gilford, Lauren Gill, Rebecca Gillett, Monica Gimbernat Alemany, Nathalie Ginvert, Nicole Gipps, Matthew Glenn, Adam Glover, Emily Gloyens, Charlotte Godfrey, Katharine Godfrey, Ellie Goldsmith, Tracie Goldsmith, Anita Gomes, Ruth Gomez, Jennifer Gondola Bokoba, Caroline Gordon, Elizabeth Gordon, Sarah Gordon, Marcella Gordon-Chambers, Rahiem Gordon-Smith, Lucinda Gosling, Georgina Gould, Alistair Grant, Laura Grant, Serena Grant, Edwin Grappy, Maxwell Grappy, Andre Graver, Claudia Gray, Dinah Gray, Gemma Gray, Zoe Gray, Fabio Greco, Natasha Green, Sarah Green, Sue Green, Tanya Greig, Karina Grieco, Lauren Griffin, Jules Griffith, Claire Griffiths, Jessica Griffiths, Rowan Griffiths, Maya Gudka, Nicola Guenigault, Matilde Guerriero, Jo Gunston, Yulia Gusakova, Debbie Gustaffe, David Ha, Sally Hacking, Elena Haddad, Jessica Léa Haener, Hashma Haidar, Claire Haines, Jessica Hajdu, Afia Hale-Abusham, Phil Hall, Teresa Denise Hall, Zoe Haller, Victoria Hambling, Imogen Hamel, Dominic Hamilton, Kirsty Hamilton, Katie Hammond, Vicky Hampshire, Frances Hampson, Caroline Hampstead, Annie Hanafin, Alice Hancock, Lottie Hancock, Felicity Hand, Lisa Hann, Tsugumi Harada, Chloe Harcourt, Alexandra Hardman, Elaine Hargreaves, Elena Hargreaves, Michelle Ellen Harkes , Angelee Harris, Matt Harris, Natalie Harris, Rosemary Harris, Natasha Harrison, Ian Harrod, Ben Hart, Jayne Hartley, Philippa Harvey, Sarah Harvey, Maham Hashmi, Rouzie Hassanova, Gillian Hatherall, Suzy Haven, Sonia Hawkey, Clare Hawkins, Sam Hawkins, Sally Hawkridge, Mike Hawthorne, Harriett Hayden, Laura Hayman, Victoria Haynes, Anders Hayward, Sophie Hayzelden, Ellie Hazell, Kelly Head, Jo Heath, Catherine Hector, Bethany Hedges, Lindsey Hedges, Bal Heer, Kirsty-Ann Heggie, Tamsin Hellier-Hough, Mahalia Henry-Richards, Holly Heron, Claire Hetherington, Rebecca Hickey, Emalene Hickman, Amanda Higgins, Katie Hill, Sian Hill, Verity Hill, Emma Hixson, Chloe Ho, Sarah Ho, Philippa Hobbs, Giles Hockridge, Laura Hodges, Laura Hodgkins, Elaine Holbrook, Anna Holden, Pete Holland, Carrie Holman, Georgia Homewood, Jennie Hone, Louise Hooper, Jezz Hooton, Joanne Hooton, Samuel Hopkins, Rebecca Horgan, Katherine Horsham, Lauren Houlder, Jevan Howard-Jones, Eileen Hsieh, Yibai Hu, Iris Huang, Harriet Hughes, Sally Hughes, Ellen Hunter, Matthew Hunter, Steph Hunter, Stephen Huntley, Jake Hurlock, Alisdair Hurst, Amran Justin Matheo Hussain, Baber Hussain, Sayma Hussain, Kathryn Hyde, Ana Sol Ibanez Wilkinson, Catherine Ibbotson, Caroline Ienne, Luciana Ieno, Lara Inge, Victoria Innes, Anna Marie Iporac, Eshita Iqbal, Daniel Irvine, Louisa , Michelle Jackley, Amber Jackson, Natasha Jacobsen, Adam Jajbhay, Abdul Jalloh, Dean James,

Sarah James, Claire Jared, Alex Jarrett, Paul Jarvis, Kevin Jarvis, Yvette Jarvis, Lasika Jayamaha, Annabel Jeffcoate, Trina Jeffers, Dora Jejey, Kelly Jenkins, Craig Jenner, Tom Jewett, Yu Jiang, Davinia Jimenez, Gwen JnoBaptiste, Savvanh John Leighton, Carrie Johnson, Chloe Johnson, Eleanor Johnson, Sian Johnson, Jonathan Johnston, Patrick Johnston, Alana Jones, Doreth Jones, Emma Jones, Nicola Jones, Nikki Jones, Rebecca Jones, Ruth Jones, Sion Jones, Wendy Jones, Mariem Joof, Jason Jordaan, Sophie Joyce, Paul Judd, Pauline Julian, Chloe Juste, Gemma Elisabeth Kalmakrian, Timea Kalmar, Isata Kamara, Rakeem Kamara, Kenneth Kangethe, Agni Kasparian Saraidari, Salimah Kassam, Irene Kavoura, Leanne Keatley, Sian Keauffling-Burns, Karen Keeley, Sarah Kelly, Clare Kendall, Karolina Kendall-Bush, Stephanie Kenny, Ruth Kent, Mary-Jane Kerr, Sarah-Ellen Kerr, Tristan Kerr, Georgina Ketteman, Lia Khan, Lauren Kidd, Rachael King, Michele Kingston, Amy Kippen, Jennifer Kipphut, Ella Kirby, Tom Kirby, Rhiannon Kirk, Hannah Kiss, Howard Klaasen, Adam Knight, Alison Knight, Phoebe Knight, Daniel Kok, David Kolundzija, Sammy Kong, Merin Kovoor, Maria Kramvi, Elmo Kuang, Madhura Kuduvalli Nagendra, Aaron Kumar, Akwasi Kwarteng, Loriane Laku, Claire Lambert, Siobhan Lambert, Susan Lambert, Audrey Lamptey, Tamsin Landells, Sarah Lane, Tom Langdale, Anneka Lange, Annabel Langley, Eve Langley, James Langridge, Lucy Lapham, Danielle Latimer, Kei Lau, Safiatou Lawson, Ellie Lawton, Paul Lazarus, Hannah Leach, Sinead Leahy, Alice Leake, Edward Lee, Jenny Lee, Rebecca Lee, Sammy Lee, Susannah Lee, Jennie Leggat, Kelly Legrange, Leigh Stevenson Leib, Jamilah Leigh, Amy Lennox, Chris Lewington, Caroline Lewis, Lisa Lewis, Michael Lewis, Kerri Leybourne, Linfei Li, Manyin Li, Marielle Li, Chen Liang, Helena Lima, Lindo Lindo, Christina Lindquist, Helen Line, Grazina Linkeviciute, Sian Lipscomb, Karen Lister, Lu Liu, Yang Liu, Amy Liversidge, Kenzo Liwasa, Lucy Llewellyn, Tahiia Lloyd-Evans, Paige Lockwood, Roberto Lonetti, Georgia Long, Alec Longair, Sarah Longley, Victoria Longmore, Melanie Loudonsack, Nuno Lourenco Rodrigues, Emma Lovell, Robert Lowe, Karolina Lubecka, Jack Ludwig, Stephen Lue, Angela Lurssen, Amelia Lynch, Kat Lynch, Tamira Lynskey, Janita Maaranen, Josephine Maccarthy, Ceilidh Macdonald, Sophie Macken, Eleanor Mackinder, Robert Macnamara, Leanne Mae Macphail, Liam Maddin, Emma Mageean, Holly May Magill, Izabele Maitusyte, Marta Maj, Alena Maksimuk, Anita Makwana, Emily Malcolm, Malina Malina, Pui-Tien Man, Jaini Mandoda, Margarita Maniati, Leanne Manning, Patricia Manning, Rosa Manning, Ibrahim Mansaray, Bethany Manser, Husnara Mansoor, Claudiu Marinescu, Kevin Marlow, Elodie Marques De Oliveira, Laura Marr, Alexander Marsden, Kayleigh Marsh Davis, Gracie Marshall, Claire-Monique Martin, Casey Martin, Georgina Martin, Joanna Martin, Leanne Martin, Rebekah Martin, Leslie Mason, Kevin Matadeen, Katharine Mathers, Kirstie Mathieson, Jermaine Matias, Sophie Matthews, Josh Mayhew, Anna-Louisa Mazzola, Karen Mc Walter, Francesca Mcarthur, Luke McCabe, Paul Mccarthy, Rachael Hannah Mccaul, Tamara Mccombe, Sally Mcconville, Katharine Mcculloch, Frazer Mcdonald, Scott Mcdonald, Lynne Mcdowell, Chloe Mcgregor, Clodagh Mcguirk, Phoebe McIntosh, Alicia Mckenzie, Jessica Mckenzie, Caitlin Mcstay, Kyle Meade, Neil Meads, David Meany, Palma Measho, Aliya Meghjee, Lucy Mellamphy, Precious Meyer, Laura Middleton, Brianna Middleton Macpherson, Inge Midl, Brian Mifsud, Kanna Mihara, Bobby Miklausic, Matt Miller, Nathalie Miller, Rachel Miller, Stephanie Miller, Desiree Mills, Nathan Mills, Remmie Milner, Stephanie Milton, Mila Mincheva, Roberta Miozzi, Sophia Mir, Hassan Mirza, Zee Misikonyte, Punam Mistry, Trusha Mistry, Dennis Mitakos, Will Mitchell, Charmaine Mitchell, Remel Mohammed, Shade Mohammed, Zi Hong Mok, Ingrid Molinos Torres, Joanne Molyneux, Victoria Monaghan, Victoria Moor, Miriam Moore, Elinor Moran, Chahna Morgan, Emma Morgan, Hannah Morgan, Kaneen Morgan, Keisha Morgan, Carlene Morlese, Amber Mortelman, Emily Moss, Olivia Motyer, Adam Moulder, Mareme Mufwoko, Fiez Mughal, Laura Marie Mulholland, Chloe-Louise Mullen, Abbie Munk, Klisman Murati, Steven Murphy, Amy Murray, Martina Murtas, Wendy Musson, Cigden Mustafa, Amanda Myers, Leanne Myers, Nic Myers, Danielle Nadal, Frieda Nakimbugwe, Lauren Nash, Rachel Nash, Samita Nathoo, Harriet Naylor, Ndenko Ndenko Manguntang, Katie Neal, Ciarra Nevitt, Gemma Newby, Karen Newby, Olivia Newey, Grace Nichols, Carla Nicholson, Yang Ning, Hannah Nixon, Kevin Noble, Teresa Noble, Sophie Northmore, Aicha Noui, Amanda Nyandoro Chiyangwa, Nicole Nyemi-Tei, Lise Nymoen, Martha Oakley, Emma O'Brien, Charley O'Dell, Emily O'Donnell, Afie O'Donovan, Gifty Oduro, Andy Officer, Andrea Ogden, Sam Oh, Kiichiro Okano, Brandon O'Keeffe, Joan Okere, Adaku Okoro, Christina Okorocha, Bomi Okuyiga, Tunde Olasupo, Cat Oldham, Diana Olishaba, Luciana Oliveira Sousa Pederzoli, Tolu Oluwadare, Amy O'Malley, Precious Omonuwa, Shreeya Ondhia, Matthew O'Neill, Adaora Onuora, Jia Wen Ooi, Anne-Marie Oreskovich, Rosie O'Rourke, Gem Orthner,

Dana Osadebe, Ryan Osang, Brodie O'Shea, Helena O'Shea, Sheun Oshinbolu, Razak Osman, Emily O'Sullivan, Cheryl Oteng, Michael Othen, Amber Ould, Habib Ouro-Gnao, Amy Owen, Derya Ozbasmaci, Katie Page, Roxanne Page, Sarah Pagram, Samantha Pain, Michal Paker, Jo Palmer, Rebecca Palmer, Stephanie Palmer, Ieva Palujanskaite, Carolyn Panday, Demetriani Pandi, Eleni Papaioannou, Rianna Parchment, Hannah Parker, Rhoda Parker, Jennifer Parmenter, Natalie Parnell, Sam Parry, Lp Parsons, Freya Parsons, Deirdre Pascall, Darshna Patel, Meshali Patel, Mitesh Patel, Reshma Patel, Sanoobar Patel, Charisse Patton, John Paulsen, Anna-Joi Payawal, Steve Payne, Hannah Pearce, Emily Pearse, Victoria Peck, Lu Peng, Xavier Perez, Rachel Periam, Louise Perrin, Ambi Nick Name Phgura, Lee Phillips, Sarah Phillips, David Phillips-Peters, Balwant Phlora, Abigail Pickard Price, Persephone Pickering, Katie Pickford, Jennifer Pidgeon, Louise Piper, Charles Pitt, Delvene Pitt, Sasha Plache, Merriel Plummer, Karelle Plummer-Walrond, Henry Poh, Lindsey Pollard, Rose Pook, Kate Popham, Sarah Portou, Caroline Portsmouth, Charlie Pottle, Dillon Powlett, Verity Pownall, Charlotte Preko, Ben Preston, Jolyon Price, Natalie Prosser, Bright Pryde, Despo Pseftodiakou, Amber Pyott, Adriano Quieti, Kelly Quintyne, Sam Quy, Rebecca Radford, Mariam Rahman, Jai Raichura, Nahema Rajabali, Ziyana Rajabali, Iniya Rajendran, Sara Ranthe, Laura Rapley, Alison Ray, Charlotte Rebecca Read, Al Reburiano, Emma Reeder, Helen Reeve, Karen Registe, Magnus Reinvik, James Rene, Jo Restall, Christopher Reynolds, Nicky Reynolds, Charlie Richards, Nicholas Richards, Christi Richardson, Freya Richardson, Naomi Richardson, Hannah Richbell, Carissa Rickeard, Fran Ridge, Kelly-Marie Ridgers, Mel Ridley, Christopher Ridley, Jennifer Riley, Shaun Riley, James Roberts, Bola Roberts, T'Rell Robinson, Gemma Robinson, Victoria Robinson, Kate Roche, Catherine Rock, Francy Milena Rodriguez, William Javier Rodriguez Laverde, Francisco Rodriguez Weil, Consuela Rolle, Sara Roman De La Pena, Aaron Romano, Chloe Rooney, Nathalie Rosamont, Katie Roscoe, Alexis Rose, James Rose, Ella Ross, Claire Rowley, Zheng Ruan, Karen Ruddock, Dhruv Rupapara, Nicole Rush, Ruwodo Ruwodo, Hayley Ryan, Tamsin Ryder, Sarah Saba, Sejal Sachdev, Yvette Sackey-Addo, Noita Sadler, Chantal Sainsbury, Amanda Sallis, Nicole Sallis, Anna Salmon, Troy Salmon, Natalie Salmons, Chanel Sam, Aran Samaroo, Sami Samid, Jessica Samuels, Eleanor Sandars, Amar Sandhu, Harleen Sandhu, Ashley Sandsmith, Amber Sansom-English, Ben Sansum, Sara Sazan, Akosua Scantlebury, Shelley-Anne Scarff, Briony Scarlett, Marit Schep, Phillip Schone, Nichola Schwarz, Sandra Sciutto-Cook, Lauren Scott-Berry, Robert Searle, Carli Searson, Charlotte Selwyn, Stephanie Sen, Charlotte Series, Zarah Serrano, Sarah Serunjogi, Rebecca Sewell, Mahvish Shafi, Rakhee Shah, Kirstie Shand, Kapilan Shanmuganathan, Katie Shapiro, Sarah Sharkah, Ankur Sharma, Ruchit Sharma, Ellie Sharp, Rachel Sheahan, Natalie Shelton, Lucie Sheppard, Stella Shepherd, Kelsie Shingler, Faith Shires, Kirstin Shirling, Mark Short, Dominik Siedlecki, Adilson Silva Santos, Wilza Silva-Mendes, Rachel Silveria, Joseph Simmons, Paige Simmons, Claudia Simos-Dziewonska, Monique Simpson, Elaine Simpson, Rebecca Simpson, Sherene Skinner, Robert Skinner, Katy Slade, Sarah Smallbone, Susannah Smallman, Jack Smart, Adele Smith, Faye Smith, Gemma Smith, James Smith, Joanne Smith, Katherine Smith, Kirstie Smith, Lauren Smith, Mark Smith, Natalie Louise Smith, Russell Smith, Sophie Smith, Victoria Smith, Zenna Smith-Allen, Bailey Smith-Bailey, Nicola Smithers, Katrina Smith-Jackson, Cienna Smyth, Pritpal Sodhi, Sakhdeep Sohi, Matthew Solomon, Stephanie Sorum, Emma Soulby, Kate Sparling, Louise Spearing, Lizzy Spencer, Liz Spratt, Rochelle Squires, Bethan Stacey, Catherine Stambouzou, Lukas Stanczuk, Amy Standing, Lizi Stansfield, Nicole Starling, Catriona Statham, Laura Steedman, Gemma Steel, Grant Sterry, Jordon Stevens, Peter Stevens, Guy Stewart, Vicky Stickland, Susan Stickley, Bobbie Stone, Peter Stonnell, Jonathan Stringer, Lucy Strudwick, Jakiya Sultana, Xiangchen Sun, Mengdi Sun, Adithya Sureshkumar, Laya Suseelan, Amy Swalwell, Sophie Sweeney, Ben Sykes, Sandra Szadkowska, Eszter Szalma, Cat Szygula, Bhavin Tailor, Karinlolita Takacs, Emma Tallamy, Josaia Tamani, Johnny Tan, Ricky Tanna, Liliana Tavares, Caroline Taylor, David Taylor, Jaclyn Taylor, Stephanie Taylor, Theresa Taylor, Valeria Tello Giusti, Harriet Rose Temple, Gary Thatcher, Sarah Thayre, Asha Thomas, Geoffrey Thomas, Hannah Thomas, Louise Thomas, Mica Janet Thomas, Raewyn Thomas, Simon Thomas, Sita Thomas, Andy Thompson, Cherie Thompson, Eleanor Thompson, Felicity Thompson, Lisa Thomson, Eleanor Thurlow, Robin Thurlow, David Tihanyi, Damola Timeyin, Patricia Tobin, Steph Tollan, Blair Tookey, Husna Torabally, Naomi Trimble, Vanessa Trotter, Rebecca Trumble, Hoang Truong, Heloise Tsang, Aiston Tucker, Emma Tugman, Guzen Tuna, Hana Turkova, Andrea Turner, Beatrix Turny, Angela Turvey, Petia Tzanova, Matthew Ubogagu, Kenya Uchida, Marta Ucinska, Zafar Uddin, Francesca Florence Leatrice Ugwuegbulam-

Condor, Mehreen Umar, Julie Unwin, Devanshi Upreti, Toby Urie, Ruth Uwadiale, Maudette Uzoh, Rachel Vallance, Daniella Varadi, Gabor Varga, Ben Vasey, Hannah Vaudin, Reanna Venn, Navadini , Emma-Louise Vincent, Hannah Vincent, Natasha Wade, Louise Wainwright, Sophie Wakefield, Clare Wakeling, David Waker, James Walker, Kay Walker, Kyle Walker, Shána Walker, Stuart Walker, Leah Jean Walker Murrain, Eliza Walkling, Rachel Wall, Carla Wallace, Jacqui Wallace, Abbie Waller, Nicole Walton, Wai-Mei Wan, Danlin Wang, Siwei Wang, Ivy Warari, Frankie Ward, Judith Ward, Julie Ward Ward, Kayleigh Ward, Rebecca Ward, Morgane Ware, Jess Warin, Laura Waringer, Michael Warrick-Gooding, Liz Waters, Daisy Watford, Sherryn Watkin, Watson Watson, Melanie Weatherhead, Katy Weaver, Lucie Weaver, Annalise Webb, Larissa Anna Webb, Amy Webster, Joseph Webster, Olivia Weeks, Basia Węorzewska, Holly Welham, Sophie Wells, Tony Weston, Kate Whalesby, Georgie Wharton, Milly Wheal, Peter Wheeler, Sharmaine Whilby-Brown, Alice White, Alyssia Symone White, Bria White, Hana White, Ian White, Jane White, Mary-Liz White, Natasha White, Samantha White, Denwin Whitebooi, Martin Whitehair, Katie Wignall, Rachel Wilcock, Laura Wilkes, Alison Wilkin, Jocelyn Wilkinson, Brooks Williams, Cheryl Williams, Dalanda Williams, Janette Williams, Jody Williams, Lisa-Ann Williams, Michell Williamson, Emily Willis, Maisie Wilson, Max Wilson, Sebastian Wilson, Bo Marcus Win, Becky Wingham, Susanne Winkler, Laura Winnan, Rochelle Wisdom, Paige Wise, Avital Wittenberg, Thais Wizenberg, Adam Wojcik, Max Wolf, Russell Woo, Clare Wood, Jemma Wood, Jamie Woods, Mark Worthington, Carina Wrapson, Katherine Wrench, Ayesha Wright, Keeley Wright, Lucy Wright, Nikki Wright, Victoria Wright, Thomas Wynn, Alicia Wynton, Bethan Wynton, Shannen Xenofontos, Rui Xi, Yaz Yahya Alahdal, Mu Yang, Tiffany Yarde, Kimberley Yarde, Selina Yasmine, Emily Yau, Gabriel Yau, Mona Yeganegi, Juliet York, Shereen Young, Grace Yusuf, Mohsin Zaidi, Omer Zakaria, Ao Zhang, Louisa Ziane, Sylvia Zsigmond **Welcome** Salim Abdulwasie, Yewande Abiodun, Adejoke Abudu, Nell Adams, Elizabeth Adediran, Oluwafoyinsayo Adekusibe, Naseem Adeniran, Elizabeth Adlington, Cintea Ahamefule, Saber Ahmed, Shuel Ahmed, Tanyel Ahmet, Oluwatosin Ajibade, Nazia Aktar, Kalsuma Akthar, Blessing Aladetoun, Camille Alleyne, Samantha Alleyne, Sayequl Ambia, Lisa Anderson, Emily Anderson, Marija Andrulyte, Shannon Antoine, Amy Anzel, Danielle Apakoh, Charlotte Appleby, Eylul Arif, Natasha Armitage, Ismael Arratte, Mandy Ashmore, Sonny Athey, Lola Atkins-Omojola, Niha Bajpai, Perter Bakarr, Nichola Baker, Tinashe Balayi, Chantelle Ball, Olivia Ball, Dumitru Bandol, Eva Banik, Laura Baranik, Laquisha Barden-Simpson, Guna Bareika, Brooke Barker, Alana Barnard, Natalie Barrett, Samsrithaa Baskaran, Mikaela Bates, Rayyan Bawazir, Pamela Beattie, Khiltee Beeharry, Amita Begum, Poppy Begum, Rima Begum, Cathryn Bell, Imogen Bell, Ugne Bendikaite, Lauryn Bennett, Conrad Bernard, Alice Bird, Briony Black, Harry Blake-Herbert, Christine Blayney, Mary Boateng, Fatima Boudafcha, Charlotte Boundy, Adriana Braz, Callum Brierley, Hollie Brill, Katherine Brown, Eimear Browne, Larissa Bulla, Alice Bullard, Fiona Bullard, Adam Burman, Gypsy Bushaway, Kellie Butcher, Marie Calvert, Megan Campbell, Huy Cao, Jhean Capitan, Sara Carter, Rebecca Carver, Darryl Causon, Lun Chai, Miguel Chamorro Correa, Joey Chapman, Peter Chong-Yen Gebrian, Afser Choudhury, Eshaan Choudhury, Jamal Choudhury, Maria Choudhury, Lennox Christie, Caroline Cobby, Siobhan Cockfield, Mariatu Cole, Lucas Coleman, Courtney Connolly, Roseanna Connolly, Samuel Connolly, Emily Cornuaud, Jamie Cornuaud, Amy Jane Cotter, Nerys Coventry, Rebecca Coxon, Julia Crawley-Boevey, Rhona Crewe, Ashleigh Crowhurst, Emma Curzon, Wendy Dang, Irina Danilova, Klesha Darroux, Zaynab Daudo, Catherine Davies, Tilly-Rose Day, Clare De Jode, Ellis De Stefano, Thomas Dear, Elizabeth Demetriou, Danielle Deveney, Parveen Dhanda, Kristen Dintino, Hannah Diribe, Isobel Dobson, Nazeem Doherty, Xianhui Dong, Liza Dos Santos, Rayner Dougan, Meilan Duong, Maria Emilia Dutto, Nicola Dykes, Emeke Ejimadu, Leila Elbahy, Ayorinde Elegbe, Molly Eley, Selina Elliott, Blessing Emenike, Erica Emm, Crystal Emmanuel, Gokay Emre, Ellyse Essel, Simone Etienne, Katie Evans, Lewis Evans, Chidnma Ezeabasili, Melanie Farquharson, Adele Fash, Martine Faulkner, Rocio Fernandez Fresquet, Ellen Fife, Syra Flaxman-Ali, Morgan Forlan, Morgan Forrester, Georgie Foster, Jennifer Franich, Shea French-Gibbens, Sophie Fuller, Kristina Gadalin, Fei Gao, Patrisha Garlang, Clooniy Gaspar, Marissa Geldenhuys, Monique Geraghty, Joy Grace Gilbert, Alice Gilkes, Jennifer Gilkes, Nathan Giraudel, Cherelle Gogar, Charlotte Goodhew, Olivia Gooding, Joanie Goss, Aimee Goyette, Amber Grange, Natalie Gray, Sophie Greaves, Charlotte Green, Jordan Green, Jack Grimwood, Kacper Grochocki, Hiruni Gunasekara, Lisa Ha, Millie Hagland, Nicola Haji-Antonis, Clare Halifax, Maria Hamalainen, Christopher Hancock, Paul Hansen, Ornella Hardie, Mersyl Harding, Yonis Hashi, Amina Hassam, Aoife Hawe,

169

Victoria Hawkes, Amanda Hawthorne, Caryn Haynes, Nathan Haynes, Nathan Hayward, Patsy Hayward, Leticia Alejandra Herrera Perez, Ryan Heselden, Ailsa Hewitt, Sara Hill, Elias Hmaimou, Wendy Ho, Emma Hobbs, Juliet Hogarth, Alice Holt, Christine Hopson, Wan-Ting Hsieh, Carrie Hua, Huarui Huang, Albert Hughes, Polly Hunt, Jakeya Hussain, Rahinoor Hussain, Lufton Hyseni, Arbaaz Ifzal, Inemesit Imoh, Victoria Irving, Sayka Islam, Claire Jackson, Felicity Jackson, Tiffany Jackson, Ramazan Jakupi, Mahroof Jalil, Joely Johnson, Sheree Johnson, Jessica Johns-Parsons, Georgia Johnston, Bradley Jones, Ezgi Kahraman, Adelina Kalanyos, Phoebe Kane, Miriam Karanja, Millie Karn, Viktoria Kasetaite, Balwinder Kaur, Paul Keating, Hana Kelblova, Kase Keogh, Frances Keyton, Hakim Khan, Fateha Khanam, Shorifa Khanam, Thameda Khanam, Liudmila Khvan, Ahsan Kibria, Lyndsey Kilkenny, Ceara King, Ellie King, Eboni Kirton, Harry Kitchener-Trevillion, Thomas Knight, Yvonne Kumi, Ergys Kurtulaj, Selda Kurtuldu, Margaret Labongo, George Lagalle, Clare Lane, Constance Lawton, Bethan Lee, Danyang Lei, Viktoria Lengyel, Kristina Lewis, Tia Lewis, Zhen Lim, Hannah Lloyd-Jones, Sophia Loi Shaw, Diane Longmuir, Musa-Eiggie Luba, Emmanuelson Luizi, Flo Lunt, Xiaomin Luo, Michaela Lupton, Morgan Lyons, Leon Mabiala, Robert Macdonald, Magdalena Maciejewska, Nida Mahmud, Corinne Maillet, Danilson Malungu, Benedicty Mambi, Zachary Manamella-Chwalek, Mary Ann Mangano, Kayleigh Mann, Cheryl Manning, Jessica Manuel, Japera Marshall-Mcdavid, Cristina Mascia, Daisy Mayhew, Ana-Paula Mazarini, Aiden Mccarney, April Mccarthy, Natalie Mcgrath, Megan Mckenna, James Meikle, Tanya Melia, Caesar Mendee, Forhad Miah, Zoe Middleton, Anna Miles, Caroline Mistry, Aye Moe, Angela Moran, Rebecca Morgan, Sonia Morjaria, Michael Morris, Reanne Morris, Rachel Morton, Sarah Mujinya-Motima, Shirley Mukisa, Luke Munro, Liam Murphy, Lis Mustafa, Christina Myers, Nila Natkunan, Beverley Nderu, Caroline Nembharde, Wein Ng, Annine Ngesang, Sabine Nguini, Susan Nguyen, John Nguyen, Charlotte Nice, Danica Noh, Adil Noor, Holly Norman, Thea North, Tabassum Nusiba, Alexander Nutt, Owen Nwanebu, Kariba Nwodo, Cindy Obasa, Mirian Obiozo, Mary Obrien, Olivia O'Callaghan, Caroline Odogwu Odogwu, Fajila Oguz, Michael Okosie, Anike Okusanya, Suliet Oladokun, Olamide Olaiya, Diana Olloova, Samson Oludemi, Charlton Omo-Edoh, Rugile Oraite, Elsie O'Rourke, Jonathan Ortavikiabakufi, Karl Osei Kwateng, Mercy Osinlaru, Kima Otung, Willaim Palaganas, Caitlin Parr, Rupal Patel, Ibrahim Patel, Nimish Patel, Daniel Pearson, Sam Pellicci, Hanna Peltonen, My-Linh Phan, Sunanta Phattanavibul, Kye Plakhtienko, Monblanc Pondani, Tabitha Porter, Hannah Powell, Janette Powell, Rasheed Powell, Spencer Prichard, Katie Proctor, Michele Puliti, George-Martin Purssord, Jacob Radford, Izzie Radley, Peter Rafferty, Mahjabin Rahman, Tahmidur Rahman, Firdausi Rahman, Vanessa Ralte, Sinead Rampat, Preeti Rana, Anya Reevell, Jo Regis, Charlotte Reilly, Charlotte Riche, Veronica Ripo, Marisa Robinson, Natasha Robinson, Stephen Robinson, Ilaria Rovera, Agnieszka Rudnik, Shannon Rule, Karim Saber, Hardeep Sahota, Arafat Said, Fahad Said, Jacob Said, Esat Saiti, Danielle Sampson, Dominique Sapsin, Berry Saunders, Lucy Scotchmer, Charlotte Scott, Kathrin Selbmann, Dilara Sert, Rita Sexious, Nishtah Sian, Leah Simmons, Rachel Simmons, Isobel Slater, Hayley Smith, Janesia Smith, Pippa Smith, Hilary Smith, Daria Solovyeva, Deidre Sorensen, Vaishnavee Sreeharan, Kimani St. Hill, Amanda Stewart, Ellie Stringer, Lilith Sumesar-Rai, Hayley Syme, Kerry Tabb, Elba Tapia Montes, Olivia Taviani, Archie Taylor, Morgan Taylor, Julie Taylor, Liam Taylor, George Thompson, Soriah Thompson-Dunkley, Cat Thrower, Eleanor Thrower, Justine Thrower, Anthony To, Hannah Tobin, Anna Tomlinson, Monique Toussaint, Frances Tresadern, Isabella Tresadern, Yulia Tskhay, Yvana Tuladhar Lorenzo, Aisha Tunio, Bonny Turner, Lorna Turner, Michael Tyler, Oliver Tyzack, Adam Uddin, Amirul Uddin, Chantelle Ullah, Ilayda Uludag, Sarah Usuanlele, Amanda Vacianna, Laura Viander, Vivien Vinning, Katie Vorontsova, Scott Wallis, Joshua Walsh, Wenjing Wang, Emily Ward, Jodie Watson, Susannah Wells, Ryan West, Sarah Westergaard, Aimee White, Nyome Whitfield, Gemma Whyley, Amy Wicks, Jennifer Wilkins, Bethan Williams, Samantha Jane C Williams, Tahirah Williams Espinosa, Tommy Wills, Avenell Winston, Katey Wood, Thomas Wray, Josh Wright, Louise Wright, Aliki Zachariadi, Aliza Zafar, Oscar Zebala, Violeta Zepinic, Linda Zeqja, Chen Zhang, Jia Zhao **Bike a.m.** Maryam Amatullah, Benjamin Askin, Ian Barrow, Scott Baxter, Martina Ben-Shaul, Paul Bird, Peter Bowers, Joanne Bradley, James Brooke Turner, Andrew Caldwell, Damian Cannon, Adam Capes, Zoe Capstick, Christopher Carter, Geoffrey Castello, Michael Coles, Anthony Collier, Wayne Crombie, Orlando Cubitt, Ian Curran, Jacob Dean, Andrew Dowden, Tracy Farrell, Wendy Flicker, Barry Garnham, Darius Garnham, Paul Gathercole, Peter Gottlieb, Martha Grekos, Matt Griffin, Adrian Harrison, Peter Harvey, Tony Harvey, Jeff Hathaway, Richard Herbert, Rory Huston, Gareth Jones, Joseph Kamau, Dean Keable, Fraser Kennedy,

Richard Kerslake, Sandra Levet, William Mcavock, Julian Mccarthy, Alex Milne, Vincent Mullen, Stuart Newman, Geoff Nutter, Simon Oxley, Rob Parry, Debbie Patel, Leo Perez, Anthony Price, Mark Reader, Adrian Robinson, James Robinson, Steph Robinson, Victor Romsom, Louis Sargent, Matthew Shaw, James Shore, David Taylor, David Tiplady, Peter Tyler, Arlen Vartazarian, Charles Whelan, Tony White, Alex Whiting, Joe Willis, Tim Worboys **There is a Light That Never Goes Out** Alex Adams, Joseph Adams, Andrew Ainscough, Patrick Aiyeola, Paloma Algarra, Niall Allen, Anthony Anderson, David Ansell, Julian Ansell, Paul Ansell, Megan Ashfield, Sabah Ashiq, Simon Atherton, Cecilia Bagenholm, Anna Baker, Gareth Baker, Steven Baldry, Lesley Barratt, Roger Barratt, Rastislav Bartek, Alexander Beck, Daniel Beck, Robert Bedford, Stephen Berry, Zak Bickerstaffe, David Birchall, Matthew Birchall, Anthony Birkbeck, Tony Blackmore, Gary Blakemore, Mark Blunnie, Catherine Bocken, Simon Borg, Julie Bowerman, Mark Bragg, Richard Breslin, David Brewer, Owen Brewster, Emma Bridges, Nicholas Bristow, Julian Britnell, Keith Brown, Kelly Brown, Stephen Brown, Stephen Burley, Andrew Burns, Cheryl Burpitt, Gillian Butcher, Royston Butcher, Roger Button, Sean Byrne, Colin Caddy, John Calland, Jason Calvert, Juan Canada, Nichola Chambers, Karl Chaplow, Mustapha Charki, Sarah Chimes, Suzanne Clark, Samuel Cocker, Dafydd Coe, David Coffey, Andrew Collins, Edward Collis, Catherine Colman, Charles Cooke, Colin Cooper, Zac Cornish, Charlotte Cox, Kevin Crean, Christine Crosby, Ian Crosby, Oonagh Crotty, Robert Crouch, Tomothy Culverhouse, Stephen Daly, Scott Dark, Colin Davies, Kevin Davies, Malcolm Davies, Richard Davies, Wyn Davies, Andrew Davison, Jeffrey Denehan, John Dennis, Ryan Derbyshire, Mykola Derevinskyy, Dexter Dest, Daniel Devonport, Brian Ditchburn, Craig Ditchfield, Adam Doak, Phillip Dodd, Neil Doherty, Andrew Downes, Dr. Florian Block, David Dropkin, Robert Druce, Michael Duncan, Martin Eastham, Stuart Eastmead, Matthew Eastwood, Victoria Eddins, Christine Edwards, Derek Egan, Roy Elliott, Scott Ellis, John Ellision, Soraya Elwin, Lucas Epp, David Evans, John Evans, Nicholas Evans, Timothy Evans, Keith Farthing, Michael Fee, Adam Feeney, Neil Fernee, Warren Few, Christine Fielding, Lauren Finch, John Fisher, Stephen Fogg, Timothy Forbes, Billy Ford-Langan, David Fortey, Paul Foskett, Gary Francis, Robert Frost, Kevin Fryer, Siegmar Gabler, Constantin Gainat, David Galavan, Joe Gallagher, Elsa Garcia Lopez, Paul Gare, Robert Garland, Patrick Gavin, Arthur Gelling, Samuel Gilston, Marcus Ginns, Kandiah Gnaneswaran, Belinda Goh, Alv Gomez, Javier Gonzalez Hernandez, Robert Goodall, Clifford Gordon, Peter Gordon, John Gradwell, John Graham, Michael Green, Paul Green, Andrew Grice, Malcolm Gulvin, Lotay Gurmeet, Stephen Hackney, Christopher Hall, Edwin Hamilton, Stephen Hamnett, David Harley, Jeremy Harmsworth, Graham Harvey, Jonathan Hawes, Jamie Hay, Andrew Hayward, Lisa Hearse, Juergen Helmer, Darren Henderson, Joby Henderson, Michael Hewlett, Gaynor Hill, Clive Hills, Mark Hindle, David Hines, Gerald Hogben, Craig Hooper, Kevin Houlihan, Shaun Hoyle, Daniel Hudson, Jarrod Hulme, Akbar Hussain, Naveed Hussain, Joanna Hyland, John Hyland, Patrick Hyland, Susan Hyland, Francesca Ibrahim, Eloise Irving, Soaad Islam, Heiko Jaap, Antony Jackson, Stephanie Jackson, Colin Jacob, Anthony Jameson, Daniel Jarvis, Paul Jearum, Kingsley Jenkins, Richard Jenkins, Dale Jennins, Gwenael Jerrett, Martin Johnson, Philip Johnson, Antony Jones, Huw Jones, Matthew Jordan, Darren Joyce, Stanislav Kamburov, Andreas Karaiskos, Benet Kaser, David Kay, Tony Keane, Keith Kearton, Christopher Keenan, Andrew Kelly, Manus Kelly, John Kennedy, Alena Kereshun, Michael Keverne, Eamon Kilgannon, Freddy Kinavuidi, David King, Nicola King, David Kirkland, Barry Knight, Joanna Kuzelewska, David Langley, Damon Lavelle, Susan Leach, Mark Leeming, Darren Lever, Scott Lewis, Michael Line, Paul Lloyd, Samuel Longley, Adam Lucas, Daniel Lucas, Katie Lucas, Annette Macauley, Roderick Macauley, Thomas Maccarron, Anil Mahey, David Mahoney, Tim Mak, Thomas Mann, Elvet Mantle, Richard Marsh, Clifford Martin, Mark Maynard, Neil Mccallum, Hugh Mccann, John Mcclafferty, Fergus Mccormick, Donald Mcdade, Daniel Mcdermott, Michael Mcdonald, Martin Mcevoy, Sean Mcgranaghan, Paul Mcgrath, Martin Mcguire, Patrick Mcmanus, Paul Mcsloy, Ray Mcspadden, Paul Mead, Mark Melnick, Laura Menzies, Henry Miller, Caroline Mills, Victoria Milnes, Paul Mitchell, Rhett Monahan, Brian Moone, Carly Moore, Brodie Moran, Virginia Morris, Kenneth Mulholland, Andrew Mulligan, Declan Murphy, Hensley Murray, Laurence Murray, Sean Neary, James Neill, Bruce Nixon, Brian O Brien, James O'Dwyer, Joshua O'Hagan, Denis O'Leary, Mark O'Neill, Kendal O'Reilly, Dean Orr, James Owens, Gordon Park, Abdul Kadir Parkar, Robyn Parton, Bhogilal Patel, Pirathapan Perayeravar, Saverimuthu Phillips, Daniel Phillips, Daniel Pilling, David Pitchford, Henning Plschke, Claudia Poller, Stuart Potts, Matthew Preston, Philip Quedou, Michael Quinn, Jacqueline Radford, Christopher Randall, Somkiat Rangkla, Stephen Raw, Philip Rayment, Matthew Razzell, Garry Reeves, Gary Reeves,

Lindsay Reid, John Rhodes, Ceri Richards, Alan Richardson, Robin Rix, Jacqueline Roberts, Sophie Roberts, Jack Robinson, Bryn Rodgers, Anke Rollenhagen, Phillip Rosby, Scott Roscoe, Paul Rothwell, James Rowe, Charlotte Rowell, Christopher Rowell, Jean-Baptiste Ruat, Roshantha Rupesinghe, Andrew Russell, Mark Russell, David Ryan, Gurminder Saron, James Saunders, Judith Schulz, Russell Scrase, Alfie Scully, Megan Seal, Michael Searle, Sophie Severs, Prabjit Shehri, Kieron Shepherd, Michael Simmons, Russel Simmons, Dave Simpson, Janine Sjoblom, Stig Sjoblom, Christopher Slater, Mark Slater, Sara Slaytor, Ben Smith, Christine Smith, Derek Smith, Howard Smith, Joanne Smith, Paul Smith, Raymond Smith, Scott Smith, Trevor Snell, Neil Snow, Kar-Paik Soon, Gary Soutan, Robert Sperring, Marc Spinner, Anthony Stanford, Elvira Stathatou, Jacob Steele, Michael Stephens, Barry Stone, Lee Stones, Hugh Strathern, Ashokkumar Subbiah, Hamish Sutherland, George Sweeney, Rafiuddin Syed, Jonathan Tague, Brian Tapp, Isobel Tapp, Derek Taylor, Gary Taylor, George Taylor, Susan Taylor, Tom Taylor, Martin Teasdale, Matthew Teasdale, Benjamin Thomas, Dean Thomas, Jeffrey Thompson, Robert Thompson, Andrew Timbers, Van Tran, John Travers, Nadia Trepkowska, Kenneth Trippick, Clare Tubman, David Tull, Keith Turnbull, Joseph Turner, Badar Uddin, Richard Unwin, Vadims Unzakovs, Maria De Jesus Villar Canovas, Akash Wadhawan, Jamie Walker, Thomas Walker, Stephen Wallace, Daniel Walls, John Walton, James Ward, Jeffrey Warner, James Warren, Joanna Waterfield, Tracy Waters, Kay Watson, Anthony Welsh, Karen Welsh, Robert Wesoly, Aisling Whelan, Joseph White, Paul White, Richard White, Lee Whiteaker, Robert Wildman, Peter Wilkinson, David Wilks, Lara Williams, Roger Willicott, Amy Wilson, Richard Wilson, Michelle Winstone, Andrew Wintle, Louisa Wood, Sharon Wood, Nicholas Woolley, Frank Worsley, Craig Yates, Scott Youlds, Michael Young, Hernando Zambrano, Yanev Zlatko, Andreas Zoch **Creative Team** Makayla Abraham, Ash Sohyun Ahn, Caroline Akselson, Jessica Albon, Tanya Alexander, Fatima Ali, Nazia Ali, Jahir Ali, Louise Allberry, Jennifer Allen, Justin Allin, Josephine Allitt, Shaimaa Alruwaished, Hana Amer, Katherine Anderson, Ashley Andrews, Maria Anning, Alicia Apaloo-Edwards, Jack Appleyard, Helene Arnesen, Isabella Asimadi, Storm Athill, Sophia Austen-Meek, Sian Ayres, Yvonne Bailey, Mathura Balanadarasan, Sophie Bann, Claire Bannister, Rebecca Barclay, Penelope Bardoni, Lyndsey Barnewell, Matej Barszcz, Tonia Bastyan, Dean Batte, Natalie Beales, Daisy Beattie, Anna Beckett, Apia Begum, Shahania Begum, Shamama Begum, Katie Bell, Eki Belo-Osagie, Carol Belston, Charlotte Bentham, Piotr Berkowicz, Agathe Bernardon, Deepti Bhalla, Sobia Bhatti, Grant Bigland, Jennifer Bigland, Gemma Bishop, Poppy Biswell, Chloe Blake, Matthew Blount, Kathleen Boland, Anna Bonomi, Natasha Bott, Charlotte Boulton, E Boussekson, Katie-May Boyd, Eve Bradshaw, Geno Brantley, Molly Bray, Eve Brayshaw, Bernadette Brennan, Eleanor Brereton, Amy Brian, Ross Britten, Charlotte Brook, Gregory Brown, Claire Bunyard, Tazmin Burr, Lily Burrows, Eleanor Butcher, Lauren Butler, Sarah-Jane Caddock, Luman Cai, Fabianne Calitri, Grace Cameron, Charlotte Campbell, Stuart Campbell, Lisa Carracedo, Rachel Carter, Danielle Casey, Bridget Cass, Amy Cassell, Ella Chadwick, Bonnie Chai, Kit Shuen Chan, Yu Hui Chan, Ying Tung Chan, Rosie Chaplin, Nadine Chapman, Jason Charles, Grace Cheetham, Szu-Jung Chen, Viviane Chen, Eponone Chen, Dong Hoon Choi, Joanna Christou, Lidia Cimule, Loren Clark, Emma Connor, Victoria Conte, Alison Convery, Adam Cookson, Eleanor Coole-Green, Anne Cooper, Shaun Corcoran, Helga Cory-Wright, Florence Court, Chloe Cowan, Zac Coyle, Alex Crawford, Alexandra Cresswell, Amy Cresswell, Emma Cresswell, Connie Croasdale, Mary Cuffe, Mary Cuffe, Danielle Cullen, Henrietta Curtis, Anna Czerniavska, David Daglish, Miriam Damanhuri, Alice Dan, Sharna David, Gabrielle Davies, Frances Davies, Holly Davies, Lucy Davis, Julia Day, Amy De Rees, Daniel Defreitas, Amy DeRees, Amanda Derrick, Joana Dias, Claire Docherty, Rebecca Doidge, Tatiana Dolmatovskaya, Blake Douglas, Harriet Dyson, Danielle Eagles, Anthony Earles, Harriette Earp, Samantha Easey, Joanna East, Carolyn Ebanks, Katie Eden, Georgina Edwards, Bryony Edwards, Maja Ehliar, Charlotte England, Gemma Evans, Constantina Evriviadou, Tobias Fairclough, Josie Falconer, Aileen Faller, Jonathan Fensom, Sophie Finch, Wendy Foggin, Charley Fone, Edwin Ford, Rebecca Forknall, Luca Formica, Jessica Fournier D'Albe, Samantha Fox, Melissa Francis, Christabel Franklin, Chloe French, Marjorie Frick, Gemma Friel, Momoko Fujiwara, Katie Garden, Ruby Gaskell, Suchen Ge, Lauren Gee, Noella Geoghegan, Eleanor Gibson, Enka Gill, Caroline Gladwin, Beata Goaszweska, Joanna Goodman, Danielle Grant, Elizabeth Grant, Jessica Green, Elaine Guillon, Tharanga Gunawardena, Karen Gurney, Sandra Gustafsson, Zlatka Halkova, Melissa Hall, Jessica Halsey, Holly Hamblin, Kim Hamilton, Meng Hao, Alissa Harger, Iyo Hasegawa, Geraldine Hawkins, Alison Haworth, Jemma Haywood, Florence Hazard, Celestine

Healy, Emma Heard, Audrey Elizabeth Hedgecock, Chloe Henderson, Holly Rose Henshaw, Clare Hepburn, Abigail Hernon, Francesca Hey, Amy Hickie, George Hims, Lysette Hodgson, Ruby Hodgson, Alix Holdaway-Salmon, Scarlett Hooper, Rachel Hopper, Sarah Hosein, Tina Hsu, Shuyi Huang, Chanel Huang, Jessica Hughes, Rosina Humphrey, Joanna Hunnisett, Toria Hunt, Jamila Hussain, Michelle Huynh, Silje Isaksen, Nur Ismail, Annan Jaggernauth, Gillian Jarvis, Rebecca Jempson, Madeleine Jenkins, Laura Jenkins, Katie Jenkinson, Laura Jenkinson, Charlotte Jepson, Amy Job, Bob Johnson, Margaret Johnson, Natasha Johnson, Georgia Jones, Lucy Jones, Rebecca Jones, Sophia Joseph, Eleanor Joyce, Holly Judd, Elizabeth Kane, Abul Kasam, Abul Kasam, Megan Keegan, Holly Keen, Tanya Keen, Muireann Kelly, Charlotte Kelly, Kristine Kenmochi, Ahhyun Kim, Joseph Kim-Suzuki, Harriet Kings, Leanne Kinnie, Osnat Koblenz, Veronika Kovacikova, Igli Kroqi, Georgina Lamb, Darren Lancett, Alexandra Langman, Sophie Langsford, Sara Laratro, Josie Lee, Tom Leggat, Demelza Leng, Caroline Lewis, Ge Ll, Yangyang Li, Ruoxuan Li, Shuang Liang, Kate Lithgow, Roberta Lockett, Narash Lohia, Sue Lowe, Antonia Lynch, Emilie Lyons, Amy Macpherson, Emma Madray, Sara Maggi, Beverley Magtibay, Saad Mahmood, Rebecca Mahoney, Maria Mantilla, Ivan Manzella, Kathryn Marooney, Joanna Marshall, Freya Martin, Sierra Martin, Anna Martin, Tasha Marvell, John May, Ann-Marie Mays, Tansy McCluskie, Pete McDonagh, Jo McDonald, Sammi McGuigan, Michelle McHale, Letitia McLaughlin, Dorothy McLennan, Amy McPherson, Laura Meichtry, Olivia Catherine Mellowes, Cheramour Meoquanne, Florence Meredith, Gabrielle Milanese, Stephanie Miles, Jennifer Millen, Darci Miller, Dan Miller, Bo-Kyung Min, Clodagh Miskelly, Jasumati Mistry, Hannah Mitchell, Connor Mitchell, Sabrina Mohamed, Abigail Moller, Paula Gonzalez Montecino, Rosey Morling, Ronan Morrow, Madalaine Mould, Jillian Murray, Yuki Nakamura, Kamal Natt, Chloe Newman, Candice Newton, Billy Yu Lok Ng, Mandy Ngo, Fern Nolan, Jo Noon, Tanya Noor, Biannca Nugent, Michael Offei, Tosin Ogunsanya, Rebecca O'Higgins, Christina Omideyi, Zanna Orage, Zeanab Oshinbolu, Rainelle Osuji, Priscilla Otema, Lucy Packham-O'Brien, Sharon Page, Georgia Paget, Samuella Palmer, Natasha Payne, Donna Pendarvis, J. Childe Pendergast, Manavi Perera, Cathy Perkins, Fong Perry, Shamaela Perwiz, Louise Phelan, Gloria Enechojo Philip, Sabina Piccini, Hannah Pick, Patrick Pintaske, Lucy Pittard, Richard Pledge, Alice Pocock, Fiona Pollard, Claire Pompili, Lucy Ponting, Lara Prentice, Natasha Prynne, Faye Pulleyn, Anna Radecka, Syd Rae, Samantha Ranaweera, Kernisha Ransome, Nadia Rasheed, Harriet Reed, Megan Reidy, Natasha Ridley, Barbora Rimkova, Reenell Roach-Williams, Mark Roberts, Pamela Roberts, Elizabeth Roberts, Emma Robinson, Katherine Rogers, Madeleine Ross-Masson, Calista Ross-Peterson, Sophie Rowatt, Megan Rowlands, Sunita Sagoo, Nassima Saidani, Rachel Salenius, Clara Samuel, Kaylee Sanford, Billie Sanger, Marcio Santarosa, Pranav Sarin, Gerda Satunaite, Anna Saunders, Kate Seckington, Wamika Sehgal, Mai Seida, Rabeeah Shah, Melissa Sharpe, Sobia Shatti, Mengqin Shen, Deric Shen, Emma Sheppard, Poonam Shukla, Monika Sievers, Yana Simakova, Rachael Simpson, Gurfateh James Singh, Charlotte Slade, Mark Smith, Charlotte Smith, Lucia Smith, Olivia Broadbent Smith, Rosanna Smith, Chris Smith, Emme Sparre-Slater, Angela Spink, Lorna Stimson, Camelia Sule, Kemi Sulola, Tamanna Sultana, Emma Sutcliffe, Philippa Sutcliffe, Hannah Sutherland, Sarah Sweet, Kazusa Takamura, Angel Tam, Nicola Tattersfield, Poppy Taylor, Matthew Taylor, Molly Taylor, Nicola Teale, Helena Tegeder, Marina Tegeder, Helen Thomas, PK Thummukgool, Kathryn Tickle, Mai Tieu, Beth Tilly, Charlie Todman, Bryony Tofton, Isabelle Tollitt, Billie Towers, Katherine Towerton, Julia Townend, Sekou Traore, Cecile Tremolieres, Louisa Trickett, Gina Trinchese, Anastasia Tsangarides, Melanie Tse, Alice Tucker, Beca Tuffnell, Jonathan Turner, Lisa Valde, Wendy Castano Vega, Sophie Venes, Ruby Vestey, Paul Vincent, Daniel Vincenze, Kalpani Vitharana, Tom Voller, Jana Vrabelova, Angela Wade, Angela Wade, Caroline Walotka, Xiaoyun Wang, Victoria Watson, Jordan Watson, Elizabeth Webb, Jamey-Leigh Weber, Lianna Weidle, Jess Wheelband, Leanne White, Gianne Williams, Naomi Williams, Anna Witcombe, Finola Woolgar, Stephanie Woolven, Ying Wu, Lixiaoxue Xia, Jing Yang, Lanxiubo Yang, Yang Yang, Farhana Yeasmien, Amanda Yuan, Jovana Zarubica, Mona Zaw, Ruth Zewge, Xinyu Zhang, Yiyi Zhao, Min Zhou **Technical Team** Tracy Abercombie, David Adkin, James Adkins, Mauricio Affonso, Ash Ahn, Christopher Amaning, Keren Amroussi, Eleanor Andrews, Nick Ashby, Theo Athanasopoulos, Miles Baldwin, Charlotte Banner, Jonathan Barlow, Andrea Bennett, Paul Bond, Nikki Boone, Bekki Boot, Alastair Borland, Matt Boswood, Rachel Bottomley, Charlotte Boulton, Heather Bourne, Alex Braithwaite, Alex Bratza, Natalie Braune, Simon Brockwell, Chris Brown, Claudia Bryan-Joyce, Jess Buckley, Jarrett Bulat, Mike Burke, Rowan Burton, Elliot Carmichael, Becky Carolan, Kriss Carr, Laura Carus, Pamela

Casasa, Danielle Casey, Claire Charlesworth, Tania Clarke, Peter Clerkin, Matthew Compton, Matt Compton, Itziar Coteron, Megan Courage, Lesley Covington, Roz Creusson, Reece Crisp, Moira Cross, Holly Curtis, Anna Czerniawska, Adam Dallman, Merlin Dass, Lee Davies, Christian Davies, Tom Davis, Amanda Derrick, Hannah Dimelow, Stuart Dingley, Ian Dixon-Wilkinson, Ben Donoghue, Grace Douetil, Myfanwy Dowding, Katie Ducarreaux, Alex Durrell, Sasja Ekenberg, Sandra Elsom, Susan Entwistle, Ilse Euser, Gabriella Fewster, Holly Fitch, Nathalie Fitzgerald, Luke Flint, Hazel Frame, Gemma French, Juno Frewing, Laizan Fung, Sean Gallacher, Jimmy Garner-Currie, Jayne Gibson, Sam Gilham, Abi Gill, Lesley Gill, Caroline Gladwin, Phil Gomme, Linda Gray, Adam Gray, Erin Green, Simeon Green, Jamie Grossman, Charlie Hain, Laura Hammond, Kate Harries, Rachel Harris, Iain Harvey, Iyo Hasegawa, Joyce Hastings, Ceri Hazelden, Anthony Holme, Abby Holmes, Chris Howard, Emily Howie, Emma Hughes, Rebecca Humphreys, Hilary Hunt, Amy Insole, Sarah Jackson, Piran Jeffcock, Charlie Johnson, Lisa Juergensen, Maria Kalamara, Helena Kanoute, Jessica Kelley, Francesca Kelly, Marie Kristine Kenmochi, Reese Kirsh, Olivia Alice Knight, Eleftherios Kotsis, Katie Kozlowska, Kemey Lafond, Jennie Leach, Nigel Letheren, Charlotte Levy, Qiming Liu, Tink Lloyd, Chris Lloyd, Edward Locke, Daisy Long, Sam Mannis, Theodora Marlas, Elisabetta Massimi, Hannah McArdle, Jo McDonald, Danielle McNiven, Marta Micallef, Hannah Moore, Josh Moore, Joe Morgan, Rikhil Morjaria, Luke Morton, Luisa Mota, Valerie Munday, Sophie Naisbitt, William Newman, Anna Newton, Anh Hoang Nguyen, James Nicholson, Katy Nixon, Sam Ohlsson, Connaire Packeer, Christina Palaiologou, Amelia Palmer-Johnston, Hannah Pardon, Joe Park, Heather Passmore, Ryan Penny, Alex Peters, Philip Peters, Theresa Pine, Patrick Pintaske, Ellie Pitt, Gareth Prentice, Beth Price Williams, Alison Prior, Will Purton, David Putman, Alex Randall, Joe Ratcliffe, Sonia Razi, Caroline Rechter, Greg Reekie, Yuan Ren, Daisy Rigley, Daniel Roach-Williams, Jonathan Roberts, Thomas Robinson, Tom Robson, Seth Rook Williams, Jack Ryan, Alison Rycroft, Alison Rycroft, Venetia Samuel, Priti Shah, Caroline Sheard, Kathryn Shooter, Jeremy Silverstone, Elliot Sinclair, Sophie Skelton, George Smith, Ollie Smith, Damien Stanton, Hannah Stewart, Sharna Stockdale, Sam Stuart, David Tague, Sabina Tajbhai, Karl Taylor, Ann Taylor, Richard Thurlow, Charlie Todman, George Townsend, Dave Train, Michael Trasmundi, Lucy Vann, James Wakerell, Luke Wallace, Paul Walmsley, Caroline Walotka, Becca Walters, George Walters, Louisa Ward, Shirley Ann Waterhouse, Gina Watson, Amy Watts, Ben Watts, Jenny Webster, Tara Wells, Laura Whitley, Amy Whittle, Paul Williams, Anthony Willis-Osborne, Liz Wimms, Jon Wing, Jonathan Wright, Ben Yager, Noemi Zajzon Operations Team Temitope Adetunji, Tryvell Allen-Charles, James Angel, Nabeel Arshad, Becki Austin, Dandan Bai, Loudmar Bento Portilho, Chris Blackledge, Cormac Bonar, Reece Bourne, Mary Boyes, Jenna Brailey, Doyin Brown, Delphie Callender-Foster, Laura Cantegreil, Jody Chappell, Meng Chen, Tianran Chen, Cheng Cheng, Amy Christie, Lea Clark, Sue Clarke, Christal Clashing O'Reilly, Alexandra Clipa, Nicholas Columbo, Joshua Connolly, Scott Crowhurst, Andrew Davidson, Gemma Davis, Li Ding, Andrea Donigan, Efi Doron, Farid Dudha, Laurene Duret, Katy Earth, Rowanne Eeles, Toby Erskine Crum, Rhea Foy, Mary Furlong, Vanda Galazka, Rosie Gamble, Gus Garcia Lopez, Charmaine Nicole Griffith-McCann, Emma Gyasi, Julie Haggar, Hannah Hand, Emma Hannibal, Coretta Hart, Suchita Hathiramani, Philomena Hayward, Jay Heard, Sophie Heath, Sze Lok Ho, Barbara Hochrath, Danielle Holland, Shan Howes, Minghan Hu, Chen Huang, Jessica Ibeh, Susan Johansson, Akshata Kamath, Tijana Kasic, Ambrosia KejingZhu, Michelle Lacey, Holly Laws, MartinaLee, William Leung, Yee Row Liew, Mei Chern Lim, Henry Lin, Sasha-Louise Lopez, Richard Lorde, Mark Luggar, Laura Macrae, Rob Madeley, Tanisha Malkki, Peter Marley, Shayesteh Mazloumian, Rachel McDermott, Sharon McElhinney, Ambre McGee, Peter McGuinness, Alexander McKinven, Danni Mehta, King Mensah, Saira Mirza, Kirsty Moss, Hollie Munford, Carol Nascimento, Laura Nastase, Selena Ng, Sian Nicholas, Laura Oakley, Sarah-Jane O'Brien, Dawn O'Brien, Sevda Onder, Luis Ortega Contreras, Hilary Osei-Asibey, Julia Ouzia, Jonny Paim, Viktorija Panfilova, Wai Yee Pang, Louise A Panteli, Franklin Pate, Vaneshaben Patel, Kathy Peacock, Amanda Peck, Zoe Pickburn, Olivia Pole-Evans, Elizabeth Redpath, Alexandra Redpath, Tammy Rennie, Tim Reynolds, Olivia Roach, Niel Robbins, Joanna Rockliff, Sue Rowland, Jack Rule, Lena Ruprai, Nathan Ryan, Kimberley Sayers, Shreeya Shah, Mark Shannon, Bing Sheahan, Matilde Silva, Bhupinder Jit Singh, Aga Spiewak, James Stock, Yuka Tanaka, Kath Tatlock, Jack Tattersall, Alex Taylor, Carol-Ann Tennant, Ruth Tesfai, Emma Thompstone, Vuong Tong, Jeff Tong, Kate Tucker, Edson Sydney Tucker, Andrew van Blommestein, Nancy Vigrass, Benjamin Walker, Gavin Walsh, Charlie Welch, Toni Wong, Jing Zhao, Ji Zhu **The following groups appeared in the Ceremony.**

The BRIT School, Grimethorpe Colliery Band, Howard Goodall Choir, The London Pearly Kings & Queens Society, Mahogany Carnival, Nostalgia Steel Band, Only Men Aloud, The Original Pearly Kings and Queens Association, staff and In-Pensioners of the Royal Hospital Chelsea. **East London Host Borough schools whose pupils appeared in the Ceremony**. All Saints Catholic School, Barking and Dagenham College, Brook Community Primary School, Colegrave School, Crown Woods College, Cumberland Secondary School, Essex Primary School, Gainsborough Primary School, Grafton Junior School, Hackney Community College, Hallsville Primary School, Heathcote School, Henry Maynard Junior School, Heronsgate Primary School, Hunters Hall Primary School, Jenny Hammond Primary School, Langdon Park School, Leyton Sixth Form College, Lister Community School, Manorfield Primary School, Marian Richardson Primary School, Marner Primary School, Newham College of Further Education, Newham Sixth Form College, Nightingale Primary School, Sherington Primary School, Sir Thomas Abney Primary School, Skinners' Academy, St Angela's and St Bonaventure's Sixth Form, St Josephs RC Junior School, Waltham Forest College, Warren Junior School. **All the Games-time role volunteers who contributed to the delivery of the Ceremony. All the drama, dance, music and sports groups, societies, centres, organisations and clubs throughout the UK for all their help and support and for publicising the call for volunteers.**